International Education *and* Cultural-Linguistic Experiences *of* International Students in Australia

Edited by Abe Ata & Alex Kostogriz

First published 2015
Australian Academic Press Group Pty. Ltd.
18 Victor Russell Drive
Samford Valley QLD 4520
Australia
www.australianacademicpress.com.au

Copyright © 2015 rests with the identified authors of all contributions to this book.

Copying for educational purposes
The *Australian Copyright Act 1968* (Cwlth) allows a maximum of one chapter or 10% of this book, whichever is the greater, to be reproduced and/or communicated by any educational institution for its educational purposes provided that the educational institution (or the body that administers it) has given a remuneration notice to Copyright Agency Limited (CAL) under the Act.
For details of the CAL licence for educational institutions contact:
Copyright Agency Limited, 19/157 Liverpool Street, Sydney, NSW 2000.
E-mail info@copyright.com.au

Production and communication for other purposes
Except as permitted under the Act, for example a fair dealing for the purposes of study, research, criticism or review, no part of this book may be reproduced, stored in a retrieval system, or transmitted in any form or by any means electronic, mechanical, photocopying, recording or otherwise without prior written permission of the copyright holder.

National Library of Australia Cataloguing-in-Publication entry

Title: International education and cultural-linguistic experiences
 of international students in Australia
 / Abe Ata, Alex Kostogriz.

ISBN   9781922117465 (paperback)
ISBN   9781922117472 (ebook)

Subjects: Education, Higher--Australia.
 Education and globalization.
 Students, Foreign--Australia--Social conditions.
 International education--Australia.

Other Creators/Contributors:
Ata, Abe, editor.
Kostogriz, Alexander, editor.

Dewey Number: 378.94

Publisher: Stephen May

Copy Editor: Rhonda McPherson

Cover Designer: Maria Biaggini, The Letter Tree

Typesetting: Australian Academic Press

Printing: Lightning Source

Cover image: iStock 45115574 © nevarpp

Contents

Acknowledgments v

Contributors vi

Introduction 1
    Alex Kostogriz & Abe Ata

Chapter 1
    An Everyday Life Perspective on the Institutional and
    Cultural Identities of Chinese Students in Australia 13
    Ai Bin and Alex Kostogriz

Chapter 2
    Cultural Translations: The Art of Cosmopolitan Learning
    as an International Student 29
    Carol Reid, Hussain Alsaiari and Ila Rosmilawati

Chapter 3
    How International Students' Attitudes and Orientations
    Towards Cultural Differences and Multiculturalism Affect
    Their Engagement With Learning 43
    Edilson Arenas

Chapter 4
    International Graduates' Endeavours for Work in Australia:
    The Experience of International Graduates of Accounting
    Transitioning Into the Australian Labour Market 59
    Ruth Arber and Mark Rahimi

Chapter 5
    The 'English Language Question' in Higher Education:
    Some Reflections on Issues and Strategy 77
    Neil Murray

Chapter 6
    International Students and the "English Problem"
    In Australian Universities: A Discursive Perspective 91
    Michael Haugh

Chapter 7

Towards a Pedagogy of Experiential Thirding in Language Education 105
Alistair Welsh and Alex Kostogriz

Chapter 8

Arabic Language Interferences in ESL Amongst International Students in Australian Language Centers 121
Abe Ata

Chapter 9

Reconceptualising the Academic Writing Difficulties of International Students 133
Linda Y. Li & Yanyin Zhang

Chapter 10

Exploring the Consequences of IELTS Through International Students' Personal and Academic Experiences: A Qualitative Analysis 149
Catherine Montes and Megan Yucel

Chapter 11

Steps to Assuring EAL International Students' ELP at Exit: It's Not Rocket Science 167
Sopie Arkoudis and Lachlan Doughney

Chapter 12

"But isn't IELTS the most trustworthy?": English Language Assessment for Entry Into Higher Education 181
Kieran O'Loughlin

Chapter 13

An Investigation Into the Knowledge, Education and Attitudes of Chinese, Arab (Gulf Region) and Indian Candidates to IELTS: The Case of Australia 195
Abe Ata

Chapter 14

The Influence of Race, Ethnicity and Gender on Education Policy Reforms 215
Joseph Zajda

Index 233

Acknowledgments

Many individuals, including the contributors, have provided various levels of support, comments and valuable feedback that led to the production of this book. Professors Chris Hickey and Brenda Cherednichenko at Deakin University were foremost in ensuring its success.

Likewise, the ongoing support from the William Angliss Charitable Foundation through Joy Tannock, and Hass Dellal of the Australian Multicultural Foundation, is much appreciated.

The contributors are Nigel Rockliffe, Wendy Pump, Michael Grimley, Laurie Chapin, Barbara Yazbeck, Debra Houghton, Nadine, Simon and Samer Ata; and a most trusted colleague, Alex Kostogriz, who made several other collaborative pieces of work both achievable, and of the highest standard.

AA

Contributors

Abe W. Ata was born in Bethlehem. He graduated in social psychology at the American University of Beirut and was soon nominated as a delegate to the United Nations' World Youth Assembly in New York. He gained his doctorate at the University of Melbourne in 1980 and has since been teaching and researching at several Australian, American, Jordanian, West Bank (Al-Quds) and Danish universities. Abe's publications span 114 journal articles and 16 books including *Education Integration Challenges: The case of Australian Muslims* (2013); *Us and Them* (Australian Academic Press), nominated for the Prime Minister Book Awards in 2009; and *Christian-Muslim Intermarriage in Australia* (2003). Dr Ata contributed several articles to the *Encyclopaedia of Australian Religions* (2009); *Encyclopaedia of the Australian People* (2001) and *The Encyclopaedia of Melbourne* (2005). He was nominated as Australian of the Year in 2011 and in 2015. Dr Ata is currently an Honorary Fellow at Deakin University.

Alex Kostogriz is Professor of Education and Head of Education Victoria at Australian Catholic University. His research and publications focus on teacher education and professional ethics. Alex has been chief investigator on a number of projects funded by the Australian Research Council and other national and state-based funding schemes. These projects have explored the effectiveness of initial teacher education, mandated literacy assessment and reorganisation of teachers' work, professional practice and ethics of language teachers, and literacy practices in diasporic communities.

Alistair Welsh is a lecturer in Indonesian language at Deakin University. He teaches Indonesian language units across all levels and coordinates Deakin's in-country Indonesian language program, held biennially in Malang, East Java. With a background predominantly in language teaching, but also having worked as an interpreter in the Cocos (Keeling) Islands, Alistair has enjoyed living and working in different Malay/Indonesian cultural environments. His experience in language education includes the teaching of English in Indonesia, where he worked as a teacher trainer in 2005 to 2006 on an AusAID-funded project. Alistair's doctoral research focused on cultural perceptions and intercultural experiences of Australian university students as language learners. He is interested in pursuing further research to explore what it means to act and interact inter-culturally, and the implications for language learners and educators.

Bin Ai is an English lecturer at the Faculty of Foreign Languages, Zhongnan University of Economics and Law, Wuhan, China. Dr Bin Ai has worked as an English lecturer for more than ten years at several universities in Mainland China. He completed his doctoral degree at the School of Education, Deakin University, Australia in 2014. His main research interests include identity, TESOL, intercultural communication, and internationalised higher education.

Cate Montes is currently in the final stages of her PhD at the University of Queensland, in the School of Education. Her project is titled 'Navigating the waters of academic writing language shock: A case study of undergraduate Chinese students in Australia'. She has undergraduate degrees in Business Management and Languages and Applied Linguistics, as well as an MA in Applied Linguistics (TESOL). Cate has worked as an English language teacher in Japan, Spain, and Australia.

Carol Reid is an Associate Professor in the Centre for Educational Research, University of Western Sydney. Carol is a sociologist of education researching processes of globalisation on youth, ethnicity and race and the intersections of these social identities with the changing nature of teacher's work. Her most recent work uses cosmopolitan theory to analyse educational mobilities and to open up north–south and south–south dialogue. She is the International Sociological Association's Vice President for Oceania (2014–2018) and editor of a new series for Palgrave Macmillan titled *Education Dialogues with/in the Global South*.

Edilson Arenas has an extensive industry experience in the areas of Software Development, Internet Systems and Educational Technologies. From 1992 to February 2002, Edilson worked for Melbourne University, initially as a Multimedia Systems Specialist and then as an Educational Designer. Before Melbourne University, Edilson was the Head of the Division of Engineering of Discos Fuentes, South America. There, Edilson was in charge of the evaluation, research and development of engineering projects. In 2002, Edilson joined Central Queensland University, Australia, where he is currently the Discipline Leader of Networks and Information Security in the School of Engineering and Technology. Edilson holds a Bachelor of Electronics Engineering from the University of Antioquia and a Masters of Engineering in Information Technology from RMIT, Melbourne, Australia. Edilson also holds a PhD in Education from Deakin University, Australia.

Hussain Alsaiari is a PhD candidate, University of Western Sydney, School of Education, Bankstown Campus. His doctoral thesis is titled: 'The use of technology in teaching Arabic through communicative language approach informed by new understandings of literacy in primary schools in Tabuk, Saudi Arabia'. He holds a Bachelor in Primary Education, 2004 (Tabuk Teachers' College, Saudi Arabia) and a Masters in Education, 2009 (Griffith

University, Australia). He has been teaching as a lecturer at Aljouf University, Saudi Arabia since 2004 in the School of Education (Curriculum and Instruction Department) and extensive experience working at Aljouf University in the teaching, course delivery and assessment of student teachers in Saudi Arabia for more than three years. He was a voluntary advisor for new Saudi students in the Saudi association in the Gold Coast from July 2007 to December 2008.

Ila Rosmilawati is a PhD candidate in the Centre for Educational Research at the University of Western Sydney. Her doctoral work investigates Indonesian young people's re-engagement with alternative schooling. Her research is financially supported by the Directorate General of Higher Education (DGHE), Ministry of National Education of Indonesia. Ms Rosmilawati has been a lecturer at Sultan Ageng Tirtayasa University since 2004 in the Faculty of Teacher Training and Education Science (Non-formal Education Department).

Joseph Zajda, BA (Hons), MA, MEd, Ph.D, FACE, is Associate Professor in the Faculty of Education and Arts at the Australian Catholic University (Melbourne Campus). He specialises in globalisation and education policy reforms, social justice, history education, and values education. He has written and edited 24 books and over 200 book chapters, and articles. Recent publications include *The Second International Handbook of Globalisation and Education Policy Research; Nation-Building and History Education in a Global Culture*; 'Globalisation and Neo-liberalism as Educational Policy in Australia' in H. Yolcu and D. Turner (Eds.), *Neoliberal Education Reforms: A Global Analysis*; 'The Russian Revolution' in G. Ritzer and J. M. Ryan (Eds.), *The Wiley-Blackwell Encyclopedia of Globalization Online*; 'Values Education' in D. Phillips (Ed.), *Encyclopedia of Educational Theory and Philosophy*. His works are held in over 7,400 university libraries around the world.

Kieran O'Loughlin is an Honorary Senior Fellow in the Melbourne Graduate School of Education at the University of Melbourne. He has worked as a teacher, manager, lecturer and researcher in international education for more than thirty years. His research has focused mainly on the assessment of English as an additional language for both higher education and immigration purposes. He has published widely in this area with a particular focus on the valid and ethical uses of standardised language proficiency testing in such high stakes contexts.

Lachlan Doughney is a Research Fellow in Higher Education at the Centre for the Study of Higher Education, The University of Melbourne. His research interests include English language proficiency (ELP), the development of employability skills in the curriculum, international students, and doctoral program design and development. He has been a contributor to a range of government-funded projects in these areas, and has co-authored several journal articles and research reports concerning these topics.

Linda Li has a PhD in Second Language Acquisition and Teaching from the University of Arizona. She is an Adjunct Associate Professor in the Faculty of Arts and Design at the University of Canberra, Australia. She has published extensively on academic writing in English as a second language. Her recent research has focused on academic language and skills development for international students and writing support for international research students. Her publications have appeared in journals such as *International Journal of Pedagogy and Learning, Innovations in Education and Teaching International, Active Learning in Higher Education, Journal of University Teaching and Learning Practice*, and *Journal of Academic Language and Learning*.

Mark Rahimi a Research Fellow of international education at the Centre for Research in Educational Futures and Innovation at Deakin University in Melbourne, Australia. His past work has examined different practices in Australian transnational vocational education and training. He also has research interest and experience in international higher education and international graduates' employability in Australia. His current focus is on international secondary education and inter-culturality. Mark has extensive experience in quantitative and qualitative research in education.

Megan Yucel teaches at the Institute of Continuing and TESOL Education, The University of Queensland (ICTE-UQ). She has worked as a teacher, examiner and item writer in Turkey, the United Kingdom, and Australia. She has the Cambridge DELTA and an MA in Applied Linguistics (TESOL). Megan is currently doing a PhD at The University of Queensland, in the School of Languages and Comparative Cultural Studies. The project, which is in the area of English language assessment, is titled 'Living with IELTS: A Narrative Inquiry into the Lived Experiences of IELTS Candidates'.

Michael Haugh is an Associate professor in Linguistics and International English in the School of Languages and Linguistics at Griffith University, Brisbane, Australia. His areas of research interest include pragmatics, conversation analysis and sociolinguistics. He is the author of a number of books, including *Understanding Politeness* (2013, Cambridge University Press, with Dániel Z. Kádár), *Pragmatics and the English Language* (2014, Palgrave Macmillan, with Jonathan Culpeper), and *Im/politeness Implicatures* (2014, Mouton de Gruyter).

Neil Murray is Associate Professor of Applied Linguistics (Reader) in the Centre for Applied Linguistics at the University of Warwick, United

Kingdom, and adjunct member of the Research Centre for Languages & Cultures at the University of South Australia, where he was previously Head of Language and Literacy. He has over 30 years experience directing and lecturing on English language education and applied linguistics programmes in Italy, Japan, the United Kingdom and Australia. He has published widely on language assessment, academic literacy, pragmatics and widening participation. His current research interests include English language policy and regulation in higher education and English as a lingua franca. His recently published *Writing Essays in English Language and Linguistics* (Cambridge University Press) and is currently completing a book on *Standards of English in Higher Education* (Cambridge University Press).

Ruth Arber is Senior Lecturer at Deakin University, Melbourne, Australia, Co-Director of the Centre for Teaching and Learning Languages (CTaLL) and Director of Masters of Education (TESOL). Her research explores the theories and methodologies which frame identity and difference, particularly the study of race and ethnicity in education; the implications of this research for programs for language, mobility and cosmopolitanism; and the consequences of this thinking for critical and inclusive education. Arber's publications include *Race, Ethnicity and Education in Globalised Times*, (2008; Sole) and *Mobile Teachers, Teaching and International Schooling* (2014; co-editor), book chapters, journal articles and funded projects which investigate the manifestation of intercultural education, student and teacher mobility and language programs within and outside of Australia. Arber is co-editor for *TESOL in Context*.

Sophie Arkoudis is Deputy Director of the Melbourne Centre for the Study of Higher Education at the University of Melbourne, Australia, and an Associate Professor in Higher Education. Sophie has published widely in the area of English language education. Sophie has led major national studies in recent years. In 2014, she led a project commissioned by federal Government Australian Education International on English language proficiency and international students' employability. Sophie recently completed an Office for Teaching and Learning National Senior Teaching Fellowship on integrating English language learning outcomes in higher education curricula. She directed a national project funded by the Australian Learning and Teaching Council on enhancing interaction between international and local students, which was awarded the International Education Association of Australia Award for Best Practice/Innovation in International Education in 2011.

Yanyin Zhang holds a PhD in Linguistics from the Australian National University (ANU). She is Senior Lecturer in the Department of East Asian Studies, College of Asia and the Pacific, ANU. Specialising in Applied

Linguistics, she has taught English, Chinese and TESOL at tertiary institutions in China, the United States, Vietnam, and Australia. Her research interests cover Second Language Acquisition (Chinese and English), second language pedagogy, cross-cultural pragmatics, and international education. Her recent research focuses on the second language development of Chinese syntax through the process ability approach.

Introduction

International Education and Cultural-Linguistic Experiences of International Students in Australia

Alex Kostogriz and Abe Ata

The original idea of a university has been rooted in a translocal understanding of education from the outset. The oldest universities in Europe, North Africa, Middle East and Asia were genuinely universal in their openness to people from proximal and distant places and provided a forum for scholars representing different cultures and religions to study and exchange knowledge and ideas. Indeed, as some historians of higher education argue, the student population of ancient and mediaeval universities was more culturally and socially diverse than they are today (Guruz, 2011). It is only with the rise of nation-states and their industrialisation that the universities acquired more nationally oriented characteristics, addressing occupational and professional demands in developing a workforce that would service various sectors of increasingly complex national economies. Yet, liberal university education presupposed that knowledge and learning permeated national boundaries. The ideal of university education, according to Nolan (2012), at that time was informed by the idea of learned or educated communities 'where inquiry is pushed forward, and discoveries verified and perfected, and rashness rendered innocuous, and error exposed, by collision of mind with mind and knowledge with knowledge' (Newman, 1856, as cited in Nolan, 2012, p. 109). The university was re-imagined as 'a place of concourse, whither students come from every quarter for every kind of knowledge' (Newman, 1856, as cited in Nolan, 2012, p. 109).

The international component of higher education in the 20th century was further strengthened due to an unprecedented expansion of transport and communication networks and the scope of international scholarly activities. Particularly in the post-war years, the economic boom triggered a massive flow of people due to workforce demands in particular countries. In this context, geographically remote countries, such as Australia, became more attractive and accessible to migrants from Europe. Internationalisation of higher education in Australia emerged as a priority in the 1950s due to the unprecedented waves of immigration and rapidly changing global and national circumstances. According to the analysis provided by Cleverly and Jones (1976), an early stage of internationalisation was a distinctive feature of shifting the system of higher education away from a British Anglo-Saxon foundation to a new, distinctively Australian foundation based on multiculturalism.

With the rise of Australia as a regional power during the post-war economic boom, the early internationalisation process was supported by a political-economic rationale of providing aid or assistance to developing countries in the Asia–Pacific region. The 1951 Colombo Plan was introduced precisely as a framework to boost the economic and social development of the region through the transfer of technology and capital, as well as through the development of human capabilities. Adhering to the concept of capacity building, Australia sponsored thousands of international students to receive education in Australian universities so that they could contribute to the development and management of economic infrastructure in the developing countries. The socio-political rationale of the Colombo Plan continued influencing the internationalisation of higher education in Australian universities until the introduction of the market-based Overseas Student Policy in the mid-1980s. Since that time, higher education has become a strategic export commodity and Australia has positioned itself as a key provider of international education in the world.

Today, international education in Australia is under enormous pressure to reinvent itself. Australian universities operate in what Ulrich Beck (1992) once defined as a 'risk society' — a society that is characterised by increasing uncertainties and, related to these, economic and political anxieties. Indeed, the processes of late modernisation and globalisation have produced a number of social, economic and political side effects, such as changes in work and its organisation, transformation of lifestyles and social relations, changes in political life and forms of participation and in views of reality, norms of knowledge and ways of knowing. Most of the universities in Australia, to a varying degree, have become global universities and, as such, their activities are no longer oriented exclusively towards the nation-state. The universities are encouraged to think and act globally. If previously they were positioned in a relatively predictable and controllable space between the state and the workforce, now they find themselves located in an uncertain space of various transnational flows and trends. Global knowledge markets have become the drivers of higher education, influencing what knowledge(s) should be produced and taught and what competencies have values in the knowledge-based economy. Universities are obliged to respond to the rapidly changing market conditions in order to be competitive and continue attracting human capital and 'customers' from proximal and faraway places.

In the context of multiple and extensive mobilities (e.g., epistemological, cultural, semiotic, human, financial), globalised higher education also triggers quite a number of 'side effect'. As the university becomes a nodal point of global flows, higher education opens up to market forces and gets perceived as a 'private good' to be paid for by students. With this comes an increasing pressure to attract 'customers' and external funding and to raise efficiency and quality. Hence, the current model of neo-liberal governmentality in higher education incorporates some major characteristics of hyper-capitalism, particularly the preponderance of private interests and pursuits over the public sphere, the replacement of social agency and responsibility by market forces and social Darwinist competition (cf. Apple, 2006). As a result the university gets entangled into a process of so called 'reflexive modernisation' — that is, the re-visioning of its activities at the institutional and individual levels through various accountability and performativity measures (cf. Beck, Giddens & Lash, 1994). In part these processes come to regulate a risky territory of 'academic capitalism' where the universities are squeezed between a highly completive international market and declining government funding (Rizvi & Lingard, 2010). This has significant implications for how international education is (re)framed.

One of these implications for international education is a contradictory experience of students and university educators. On the one hand, internationalisation of education continues to be framed in liberal terms as something that reinforces intercultural graduate attributes needed for students to operate in globalised and multicultural learning environments and, subsequently, workplaces. In this regard, the internationalised curricula claim to provide an opportunity for students to see the world from multiple perspectives and be responsive to differences. On the other hand, accountability and performativity measures are in part responses to the heightened risk consciousness that educators in a globalised university should be controlled to ensure nation-building objectives and skill-sets needed for the national workforce. Professional education, in particular, is nationally regulated and thus resistant to internationalisation in practice. This provides little opportunity for local and international students to interact about and critique professional practices and knowledge. Social, cultural and linguistic barriers to the intercultural discourse and learning add significantly to the professional ones (Knight, 2004). As a result, the neo-liberal discourses and practices of higher education tend to be in contradiction with the cosmopolitan idea of international education as a way of developing both the intellectual and intercultural capabilities of graduates for them to operate effectively in globalised contexts of work and life.

It is not then surprising that studies into international students' experience tend to focus on the quality of service provision and student satisfaction. Thus, large-scale research into the experiences of international students has been informed by such determinants of students' success as their performance, retention, attrition and satisfaction and less focus is given to their wellbeing and the quality of their life. For example, Olsen's (2008) study provided a comparative analysis of local and international students in Australia to represent the experiences of international students. The data demonstrated that international students perform academically just as well as Australian students; 92% of students in both cohorts passed their units. International students were more likely to continue with and/or complete their degrees than domestic students. Their attrition rates constituted 10.5%. The overwhelming majority of students were satisfied with their studies in Australian universities and would recommend their programs to others (Australia Education International [AEI], 2008). Safety and appropriate accommodation were identified as factors contributing to students' satisfaction with their study experiences. However, high living costs, lack of part-time employment opportunities, social integration, intercultural relationships and communication opportunities with local students and others were identified as the major factors that needed to be improved (AEI, 2008).

There is little information on the experience, knowledge and perceptions of international students in Australia. Research into the difficulty of understanding colloquial language, feelings of isolation, culture shock and social conflict, mental health and wellbeing, experiences of rejection and homophobia, identity problems, students' academic literacy and critical thinking skills and their attitudes and perceptions of language testing and the like are preliminary, inconclusive and not plentiful. For example, some international researchers have identified key factors that influence the experiences of international students from the point of view of affects that new cultures produce in students' lives (Lustig & Koester, 2010; Ting-Toomey & Chung, 2005), leading to their sense of loss and feelings of helplessness, isolation and often rejection and anger. Among cultural experience, communication in English language has been identified as a key to students' success in learning and to their wellbeing, more broadly (Kim, 2001). However, cultural adaptation and acculturation (Hofstede & Hofstede, 2005) have been often perceived as the only response to counter the negative experiences of culture shock, poor intercultural communication and uncertainty about one's identity.

Stereotypical representations of learning styles, particularly of international students from Asia, continue to dominate discussions about challenges in higher education. The common stereotypes of othering the students as 'obedient listeners' and non-critical rote learners who tend to plagiarise other people's works (Littlewood, 2000) are not helpful in thinking about internationalisation agenda and its potential to dislodge these representations and challenge the western-centred curricula design. Equally, the pervasive nature of stereotypes is detrimental to the provision of language and learning support services in higher education institutions. Higgins(2003), for example, has found that Asian students try to overcome the poor language proficiency stigma by seeking help from their social networks, including friends and family, rather than from the professional support structures available in their host universities.

In this regard, the authors of this publication, who come from diverse backgrounds and regions, offer insights into significant developments in international education as they address crucial questions faced by educators in Australia and compare them with North America and Europe in a comprehensive and critical ways. This includes shifts in methodological approaches in education and policy research, as well as other issues arising from comparative research, such as improving educational quality and responsiveness of education to the needs of international students. Several articles address more specific problems of providing equality, access, and equity for all students, narrowing the achievement gap, and the ways of offering education that is free from prejudice and discrimination on the grounds of race, ethnicity, gender, social class and religion. Language testing issues have been addressed in several chapters because of the absence of systematic data to evaluate the appropriateness of and overemphasis on language test scores as the basis for selection decisions without reference to other relevant factors which might have a bearing on students' academic success. Another set of concerns refers to the validity of a premise that specifies International English Language Testing System (IELTS) scores and English proficiency as sufficient to successfully complete rather than commence their courses.

Structure of the book

The book offers a collection of chapters that cover various dimensions of international education in Australia. The issues covered in this book span from political and student identity concerns to the pedagogical and curriculum dimensions of international education and to the areas of language acquisition and language assessment. Each chapter formulates implications for the education of international students as Australia enters a new phase of hyperglobalism and competition with the rise of global cities and educational hubs that they provide beyond the traditional Western providers of higher education.

Chapter 1, written by Bin Ai and Alex Kostogriz, opens up the discussion of these issues by focusing on the everyday life of Chinese international students in Australia. This chapter argues that research into international education has not yet addressed in a focused way the experiences and standpoints of these students to explore their perceptions of how institutional, cultural and language practices affect their identity work. The authors of this chapter attempt to fill in this gap by exploring how Chinese students' identities emerge in their everyday communication practices. The chapter examines how Chinese students represent themselves and how they and those others perceive their institutional and cultural identities both inside and outside the university boundaries. This chapter also connects the cultural identity work of Chinese students with their lived experiences of cultural events. By presenting the ethnographic research data, this chapter aims to inform and assist the providers of international higher education in Australia in developing an internationalised higher education that is more responsive to socio-cultural differences.

Developing the identity issues of international students further, Carol Reid, Hussain Alsaiari and Ila Rosmilawati focus on the dialectics of knowledge exchange as conditions for cosmopolitan learning. As the authors of Chapter 2 argue, these conditions are grounded in the notion of countries investment in educational capital in the developing countries to enable students to study in the developed countries. In this chapter, cosmopolitan learning is explored through the notion of 'cultural translation'. Connecting, comprehending and evaluating are key processes in cultural translation, the authors argue. The chapter first outlines the key concepts of cosmopolitan learning and cultural translation. It then draws on the experiences of two international students — one from Saudi Arabia and another from Indonesia — to reveal the comparisons and expressive acts that are part of the process of cultural translation. The chapter concludes with a discussion of the ways in which these translations and transformations constitute cosmopolitan learning.

In chapter 3, Edilson Arenas focuses on the attitudes and orientations of international students to multicultural and cultural differences and how they affect their engagement with learning. There is a cluster of research in international education suggesting that the resulting quality of learning and engagement of international students is closely linked to their attitudes and orientations towards cultural differences and multiculturalism. In this chapter, Arenas provides further empirical evidence on this specific issue, particularly in the way it affects students' learning outcomes. A culturally diverse sample comprising 18 students from nine countries of origin were interviewed and their learning behaviours observed during a semester term at two qualitatively different Australian universities. The findings show fresh arguments about social and cultural issues that currently affect international students' learning journey and what it implies in terms of the type and complexity of support that they might need.

Chapter 4, written by Ruth Arber and Mark Rahimi, shifts readers' attention from the learning experiences of international students to their transition into labour market. The focus of this chapter is on the ways in which international accounting graduates of Australian universities negotiate their professional and socio-cultural identities during their study and post-study stay in Australia. Drawing on 36 in-depth interviews over a three-year period with 12 international students and graduates, and using two case studies, the authors examine the transition of international graduates from university to workplace. A number of structural and non-structural challenges mediate the ways students seek to reach their goals before and after completing their university qualifications. Using socio-cultural theory, the chapter explores how international students endeavour to overcome these challenges. International graduates' success in finding work and staying in Australia varied widely, depending on their communication skills, involvement in extracurricular activities at university, and the extent they were able to fulfil the criteria for a permanent resident visa. They argue that these personal and structural components were impacted on by systemic terms and conditions that frame cultured discourse.

The next couple of chapters discuss the role of language in shaping perceptions about students as well as their own perceptions. Neil Murray, in chapter 5, draws our attention to the 'English language question' in higher education. He argues that higher education today is a global enterprise, and this, along with the economic development and opening up of countries such as India and China, has led to unprecedented numbers of students seeking degrees from English-medium universities in inner-circle countries in particular, and with it a notable change to the student demographic. Obtaining such a degree gives many students the kind of prestige and well-developed language skills that can result in increased job prospects in their home countries and thereby help them realise their aspirations to a better lifestyle. While for the universities concerned, this increase in international student numbers represents security and opportunity, it also presents significant challenges. This chapter considers some of those challenges and the initiatives that have been taken — and might be taken — to address them, and highlights some of the leading work undertaken by Australian universities in this space.

Michael Haugh, in chapter 6, discusses a discursive construction of international students as the 'English problem.' International students, according to Haugh, have continued to be the focus of simplistic stereotyping in media discourse where they are frequently identified as one of the forces behind declining academic standards or as 'cash cows' for cash-strapped universities in an increasingly competitive international education market. Their alleged lack of sufficient English language skills, in particular, has continued to be the focus of debate both in the mainstream media and in the arena of higher education policy. It is argued in this chapter, however, that such debates do not sufficiently acknowledge the complexity of the so-called 'English problem' among international students in Australian universities. Drawing from work in discursive psychology, Haugh argues that the alleged 'English problem' is multi-layered and complex, involving differences in perceptions across interactions in the classroom, the university and the wider community. A disconnect between the complexity of these discursive representations and the stereotypes invoked in media discourse and public policy thus becomes apparent through the data discussed in this chapter.

Chapter 7, written by Alistair Welsh and Alex Kostogriz, discusses the role of language and culture in shaping international and intercultural experiences of Australian students during their in-country studies in Indonesia. While exploring the outbound mobility of Australian students as a way of building Asia literacy, the authors of the chapter focus in particular on the transformation of their perceptions of self and the other. The chapter argues that the building of the Asia literate society requires a shift from a project that seeks to understand Asia as the object of Australia's economic desires to a project that enables students to engage in a dialogue with the Other. Asia literacy, beyond knowing about Asia, demands a redressing of the relational balance between the self and the other; it demands openness to the other beyond the same and a more ethical way of recognising and engaging with difference. The authors propose a pedagogy of thirding — one that seeks to enable practices of dialogic intercultural encounters in language education. The chapter attempts to articulate a framework for language education of university students which transcends the economic rationalism of current approaches to building Asia literacy through languages education.

Chapter 8 by Abe Ata discusses English language learning of international students from the point of view of their interlanguage — an experience that captures a relational nature of students' first and second languages. This chapter is largely an exposition of the influence of Arabic language on the language acquisition of Arabic speakers of English. Ata discusses different levels of relational interference, from phonemic to syntactic levels. Differences between English and Arabic are examined to assist the English as a Second Language (ESL) educators who prepare international students from the Middle Eastern region for their tertiary education courses in Australia. Primarily, the sound systems of English and Arabic, such as intonation, stress, and rhythm, are contrasted, along with selected grammatical features. Attention is directed to contrastive features that not only cause semantic confusion, but also those that may trigger a response not intended or realised by the Arabic speaker of English. Contrastive data and examples of errors are presented, based on work with Arabic speaking adult students in 3 to 5 EAP intermediate to lower advanced classes on site at a University Language Centre in Australia.

Linda Li and Yanyin Zhang, in chapter 9, focus their analysis on the academic writing of international students. In particular, they argue that most international students experience tenacious difficulties in academic writing even though their confidence in other academic language skills such as listening, speaking and reading has improved after some years of study. Drawing on second language writing theories and relevant research on international students, this chapter explores key factors contributing to academic writing difficulties for international students. The authors examine the complexity of academic writing in a second language in light of the linguistic, rhetorical, cultural and educational differences that may impact on the academic writing processes of international students. They argue that academic writing difficulties go beyond language-related problems and propose that the bilingual/multilingual, educational and cultural resources of international students should be drawn on to turn the sources of difficulty into resources useful for developing academic writing skills in a new language.

The next three chapters discuss issues related to language testing and academic standards. Catherine Montes and Megan Yucel, in chapter 10, explore the relationship between IELTS and the academic literacy experiences of international students. The chapter is timely and significant, due to the large number of students attracted to Australian universities and IELTS' growing status as primary gatekeeper when deciding who is able to gain access and who is not. From an equity perspective, such a high-stakes test requires ongoing investigation and scrutiny. Stakeholders are assured through online marketing materials that the test offers a reliable and rigorous measure of a candidate's proficiency in English, through tests of reading, listening, writing, and speaking. But once they have met the language requirements, how well-equipped are those students for university study? And what of the students who struggle to attain the required IELTS score? What are their perceptions of the university admissions process? The authors draw on interview data collected from international students studying at one of the universities in Australia to explore these questions. This chapter provides valuable insights into the linguistic and academic challenges facing international students as they interact with standards and assessment.

Chapter 11, written by Sophie Arkoudis and Lachlan Doughney, discusses minimum English language entry pathways. For many years Australian universities have used a plethora of English language entry pathways, such as the IELTS, to ensure that international students have the required English language proficiency (ELP) to commence study. The lack of comparability in the preparedness for study provided by these pathways underwrites issues that have emerged as Australia shifts the focus on quality assurance to the English language learning outcomes of students upon graduation. In sum, there is little evidence to suggest which of these pathways can better assure that students will achieve the English language graduate outcomes that are being demanded of universities. This chapter analyses the key issues and identify strategies that universities can use to assess the English language preparedness of international students for university study.

Kieran O'Loughlin, in chapter 12, continues the topic of English language entry requirements. This chapter briefly introduces the five main types of evidence of international students' English language competence currently accepted for entry into Australian universities. Next, it discusses a distinction between proficiency and achievement assessments of English and then compares the trustworthiness of the information provided by IELTS scores and by the assessments made on English pathway programs in determining international students' readiness for English-medium higher education. This comparison suggests that English preparation, enabling a successful transition to higher education, may be more important than simply demonstrating adequate scores on a standardised proficiency test such as IELTS. However, it is argued that the benefits of English pathway programs still need to be better articulated and researched than they have to date if they are to gain greater acceptance by higher education institutions and the public more broadly. O'Loughlin argues for the broad preparatory benefits of language pathway programs for the newly arrived international students, even if they have already satisfied one or more of the institution's other minimum English requirements.

Chapter 13, written by Abe Ata, explores the attitudes of Chinese, Indian and Arab speaking students in Australia towards the IELTS test. A questionnaire was administered to 200 students at six university language centres to investigate their overall attitude and knowledge towards IELTS, and their attitudes towards the four components of the IELTS test (i.e., listening, reading, writing, and speaking). It was hypothesised that having positive or negative attitudes towards a certain language can exert considerable effect on the learners' performance on a language test. Factors such as testing environment, test rubric, candidates' age, sex, and educational background and their relationship with candidates' attitude between these groups were investigated. Significant differences were found about students' misconceptions about language learning and the degree to which this may hinder their progress or persistence in language study. The reality that these students initiated their language learning, while they had negative attitudes towards the target language and interfering variables during the test, varies based on cultural background, beliefs about learning and motivation.

Chapter 14, by Joseph Zajda, concludes the book by identifying key challenges for international education in times of globalisation. This chapter examines the nexus between globalisation, race, ethnicity and gender in education policy reforms. It is argued that social stratification, along with the dimensions of race, ethnicity and gender, continues to act as a profound barrier to quality education for all, including equity, access and academic achievement globally. Despite some advances that have been made during the last two decades to eliminate discrimination on the grounds of race, ethnicity and gender, inequality still persists in numerous countries. Discriminatory practices continue to act as barriers to equality, access to quality education and achievement of educational success.

References

Apple, M. (2006). Understanding and interrupting neoliberalism and neoconservatism in education. *Pedagogies: An International Journal, 1*(1), 21–26.

Australia Education International (AEI). (2008). A user guide to international student data. Canberra, Australia: Author.

Beck, U. (1992). *Risk society: Towards a new modernity.* London, UK: Sage.

Beck.U., Giddens, A. & Lash, S. (1994). *Reflexive modernization.* Cambridge, UK: Polity Press.

Cleverly, J. & jones, P. (1976). *Australia and international education: Some critical issues.* Hawthorn, Victoria, Australia: ACER.

Guruz, K. (2011). *Higher education and international student mobility in the global knowledge economy* (2nd ed.). Albany, NY: SUNY Press.

Higgins, C. (2003). 'Ownership' of English in the outer circle: An alternative to the NS-NNS dichotomy. *TESOL Quarterly, 37*(4), 615–644.

Hofstede, G. & Hofstede, G. J. (2005). *Cultures and organizations: Software of the mind* (2nd ed.). New York, NY: McGraw-Hill.

Kim, Young Yun. (2001). *Becoming intercultural: An integrative theory of communication and cross-cultural adaptation.* Thousand Oaks, CA: Sage.

Knight, J. (2004). Internationalization remodeled: Definition, approaches, rationales. *Journal of Studies in International Education, 8*(1), 5–31.

Littlewood, D. (2000). Do Asian students really want to listen and obey? *ELT Journal, 54*(1), 31–35.

Lustig, M. & Koester, J. (2010). *Intercultural competence: Interpersonal communication across cultures.* Boston, MA: Allyn & Bacon.

Nolan, P. (2012). Internationalization and the idea of a University: The meaning of liberal education in the era of globalization. In C. Ennew & D. Greenway (eds.). *The globalization of higher education,* (pp. 105–116). Basingstoke, UK: Palgrave Macmillan.

Olsen, A. (2008). International mobility of Australian University students: 2005. *Journal of Studies in International Education, 12,* 364–374.

Ting-Toomey, S. & Chung, L. (2005). *Understanding intercultural communication.* Los Angeles: Roxbury Publishing.

Rizvi, F. & Lingard, B. (2010). *Globalizing education policy.* London, UK: Routledge.

Chapter 1

An Everyday Life Perspective on the Institutional and Cultural Identities of Chinese Students in Australia

Bin Ai and Alex Kostogriz

Introduction

Internationalisation of higher education in Australia, in the last five decades or so, has been viewed strategically by successive governments. Various reasons for and approaches to international education have been linked to shifting national policies and global trends. Although political and cultural reasons for becoming a key provider of international education continue to be central to the geopolitical re-positioning of Australia in the Asia–Pacific region, it is an economic rationale that has been driving strategic directions in tertiary education at the current stage of neoliberal reforms. Australian universities now constitute a highly profitable sector of the national economy, as well as making an essential contribution to the global education as the world's most significant destination for international students. They have become 'internationally recognised for their high quality teaching and research, and have a distinctly international character in both their student profile and outlook' (Universities Australia, 2013, p. 1). While the internationalisation of higher education generates significant income, it also calls for an increased accountability for quality education and responsiveness to international students and their needs. The economic rationale of internationalisation should be supplemented by other dimensions, such as social responsibility and development of intercultural understanding (Meiras, 2004).

This chapter discusses everyday experiences of Chinese students as a way of raising social responsibility and responsivity to their cultural and linguistic needs and, in particular, to their cultural identity work that is, arguably, linked to their study experiences. Chinese students currently represent the largest cohort of international students in Australia. Their numbers have steadily increased in the past decade, contributing significantly to the financial vitality and multicultural composition of Australian higher education institutions. In this regard, learning and socio-cultural experiences of Chinese students can be indicative of many trends in the Australian system of higher education and are likely to be representative of experiences of other international students in Australia (Ryan & Carroll, 2005). Indeed, they provide particular insights into Australian higher education practices that can inform the reflexivity of university educators and administrators. Yet, one's ability to reflect on the challenges of internationalisation can be restricted unless students' experiences are articulated, analysed and made publicly available. The chapter therefore endeavours to explore the ordinary life of Chinese students in order to make some of the challenges and opportunities visible.

Previous research into the learning experiences of Chinese students and other international students have been based largely on the essentialisation of their experiences and identities, focusing on general patterns of intercultural adaptation (Brown & Holloway, 2008; Yu, 2013), cultural assimilation (Best, Hajzler, & Henderson, 2007; Platt, 2014), English language learning (Chang & Strauss, 2010; Yates & Wahid, 2013) and academic learning (Chen, 2014; Tian & Lowe, 2013; Tran, 2013). These studies have helped educators in understanding the life and study trajectories of international students and how education can respond in general terms. Yet, most of the previous studies have not focused on the standpoints of Chinese students in order to examine the diverse perceptions and experiences of international students as they live and study in a host country. Thus, the main objective of this chapter is to explore the standpoints of Chinese students as these emerge from their everyday life and study experiences in Australia. In doing so, we are not attempting to essentialise students' experiences but rather to recognise the diversity of their identities and how they represent and make sense of their lived worlds. We also argue that this approach requires a set of situated and differentiated responses from the providers of higher education.

Understanding the everyday life of international students

Nothing seems to be more transparently obvious, immediate and concrete than our everyday life. The everyday is profoundly related to all our activities, encompassing their repetitive, habitual and monotonous nature, a relative stability of places in which these activities occur, recurrent actions and conversations we engage in and people we meet. As Blanchot (1993) once noticed, our everyday life engulfs us within its insignificance, (non)eventness and banality. Yet, notwithstanding its ostensibly 'ordinary' nature and apparent familiarity, the everyday has attracted a serious attention of many prominent scholars and researchers. This is not just because the everyday is so central to understanding the social world, but rather because it harbours a mystery of social praxis; it has 'a secret life and richness of its own' providing a foundation for our becoming; it is a connective tissue of our social practices and a catalyst for their transformation (Lefebvre, 1991, p. 87). It is for this reason that the studies of everyday life have figured prominently in times of major economic, social and cultural changes and the quotidian has become an analytical tool to tease out economic and cultural processes that result in these profound changes and affect ordinary people's lives.

Internationalisation of higher education has been situated in the context of major global economic, social and cultural changes that affect ordinary work and life of academics, administrators and students. Nonetheless, most researchers of international education have focused on the phenomenon of globalisation, national trends and effects on institutional policies and practices, rather than on the everyday experiences of students and educators. As a result, their everyday lives have remained beneath researchers' attention or separated from the exploration of larger social and institutional processes (Sheringham, 2006). To focus research on the everyday life of international students is to call one's attention to the relationships between the larger processes and the quotidian nature of their experiences, as well as focusing on those events in students' lives that have been left out of historical accounts but are a source of students' becoming and identity work. The concern about everyday life is essentially about tracing complex relationships between the ordinary lives of international students and the institutional, cultural and social domains of practice about which they narrate and through which they represent their understandings of self and others. The ordinary life of students deserves more attention precisely because it provides a window into our understanding of social and educational practices and their logic.

An observation of everyday life needs to go beyond the surface of the immediately observed. In this way, researchers can explore its deeper and often hidden meanings. Lefebvre (2004, p. 90), for instance, used rhythmanalysis to explore everyday life because 'rhythms imply repetitions and can be defined as movements and differences within repetition ... but there is no identical absolute repetition, indefinitely.' Although international students are often represented in general terms as homogenous consumers of 'universal knowledge', as well as consumers of language and culture, the rhythms of consumption in their everyday lives are neither homogenous nor repetitive. The students do not only consume but also produce meanings and understanding in diverse contexts of study and life. They develop their academic, cultural and linguistic capabilities in everyday classroom and social events in which their knowledge(s), languages and cultures collide with the knowledge and culture of an English-speaking country and in which they develop and negotiate similar and different identities. Indeed, everyday life plays a crucial role in explicating one's identity work as international students construct their understandings of themselves and others and, reciprocally, internalise other people's understanding of themselves and others (cf. Jenkins, 2004). Identity is dialogically interpreted and reinterpreted and this social relationality between self and others implies both identity reproduction and its dynamic change. The dialogical perspective on identities of Chinese students can be therefore helpful in overcoming their essentialisation as a homogenous group of learners who share cultural practices, learning styles and attitudes to learning.

In what follows, we focus, in particular, on the institutional identities of Chinese students as these are experienced in their institutional academic life and on their cultural identities as these are experienced in cultural practices in Australia. First, we discuss some methodological issues related to the exploration of everyday life and its relevance to the identity work of international students. Next, the participants involved are introduced and their institutional identity and cultural identity work is presented from the perspective of everyday life. Our analysis demonstrates that some students sustain their ethnic-cultural identities, whilst others develop hybrid identities in Australia. Beyond the discussions of the Chinese students' identity work, we propose a third space and a dialogical communication approach to internationalised pedagogy so that higher education is more responsive to the needs and experiences of international students.

Researching the identity work of international students

Much contemporary research into international students is informed by a so called 'observer' perspective on their study and life. It invites researchers to adopt an outsider standpoint in analysing and representing their study patterns, academic literacy, motivation, and so on, as well as patterns of their cultural adaptation (Atkinson, 1999; Jin & Cortazi, 2006). This type of research has triggered a debate about 'the Chinese learner' as a 'reduced Other' (Grimshaw, 2007), calling not only for a more critical and non-essentialist approaches but also for alternative methodological frameworks in examining international student experiences. Here we suggest a participant (insider) inquiry as a response to the observer (outsider) perspectives that usually either provide a macro-sociological analysis of international students or look at the psychological realm of their study and life. Without going into details of these research traditions, the issue that is at stake here is who can represent the 'truth' of students' reality, observers or participants themselves. This dichotomy, however, does not resolve the problem because, arguably, the problem lies in the process of representation itself. As soon as something that is directly lived becomes represented, it turns into a spectacle detached, as it were, from reality. As such, a spectacle of students' lives presents itself to the observer and to the participant as simultaneously particular and unifying.

In critiquing researchers' strange divorce from the local actuality of people's lives, Smith (1987) calls for rediscovering the underlying social relations and experiences from the point of view of participants. This type of analysis has been attempted by some ethnomethodologists who address the problematic of everyday practices. However, instead of focusing on the analysis of participants' micro-interactions, Smith is more interested in the development a participant-centred method of inquiry that recognises the integrity of everyday life and hence does not reduce the 'lived' character of experience. Smith (1987, 2005) argues that participants have a distinctive standpoint in perceiving their social reality and that this standpoint is situated in particular socio-historical circumstances (i.e., in the institutional or structural context of practice). What this means is that we cannot represent the everyday of students by using general concepts, but rather in relation to the 'particular local historical sites' of lived experiences. What this approach allows us to do is to disclose the everyday as a site of multiple and sometimes contradictory relations (cf. Smith, 2005). To capture the interplay of structural forces and situated actions, we have focused on the role of cultural discourses in the textualisation of everyday experiences, investigating the difference between situated experiences and cultural representations and the ways in which the former becomes transformed into the latter.

This dual sociological focus on the everyday — on the actual practice occurring here and now and on more generalised textual representations that penetrate and mediate this practice — informed our understanding of what participants in a research project do and how their identities are constituted within the context of internationalised education. Seven students from mainland China were selected as participants in the project. Some of them were enrolled in Bachelor degree courses and some in Master degree courses. They represented diversity in terms of their age, gender, place of birth, ethnicity and social status. These participants are represented in Table 1.1.

This study deployed a 'participant–observer' methodology to work with the problem of insider–outsider perspectives on the everyday life of international students. Bin Ai as a researcher and an international doctoral student in the time of research was immersed in the community lives of these Chinese participants. His own multiple identities as a Chinese doctoral student in Australia and a lecturer with ten years of experience in Chinese universities provided him with an insider perspective on the narratives of these participants. Semi-structured interviews generated the detailed empirical data and afforded a great deal of latitude for students to respond to various questions in terms of the lengths of responses and issues they raised. The purpose was to analyse discourses that mediated the

Table 1.1 Project participants

Name	Age	Gender	Birthplace in China	Courses of Study in Australia	Years of Study in Australia
Alex	26	Male	Anhui province	Master of Education	Three years
Baixue	25	Female	Hebei province	Bachelor of Nursing	One year
Ivy	24	Female	Guangdong province	Bachelor of Accounting	Four years
Jordan	26	Male	Anhui province	Master of Sports Management	Three years
Malu	26	Female	Tianjin Municipal City	Dual Master of Finance and Accounting	Three years
Rock	22	Male	Hubei province	Bachelor of Accounting	Three years
Shao	27	Male	Hubei province	Bachelor of Business Information System	Four years

lived experiences of Chinese students and how they made sense of their institutional and cultural identities.

Institutional and cultural identities of Chinese students

Students' narratives about their everyday experiences provided a window into the relational nature of identity work; identities as social constructs and discursive practices do not exist in isolation from others (Rew & Campbell, 1999). Students' identities were continuously made in the course of communication with others, since communicative events involve a simultaneous experience of self and other (Shepherd, 2006). In this section, representations of the institutional identities of Chinese students are first discussed from the perspectives of their self and their real and imagined others. Next, Chinese students' lived experiences of cultural events are examined so as to explore how they participate in Chinese and Australian cultural practices. These research foci enabled us to capture the cultural identity work of Chinese students in their everyday communication with others.

The representations of Chinese students have provided a window into the relational dimension of identity work. This work has involved recognition of reciprocal relations between one's self and other people that are mediated through language and other forms of cultural representations. Hence, self-representations are dialogical in their nature as they emerge from those relations. International students cannot step out of relations, even though they often find themselves in a new social and cultural context that affords some and constrains other communicative opportunities. From this standpoint, students lament that they lack opportunities and cultural literacy to communicate with English speaking students or other local people. Baixue, for example, describes her experiences as follows:

> I, perhaps including most Chinese students, have few interactions in class. Chinese students are not good at communication, though some can do their examinations very well ... Chinese students are not active and they are quiet. (Baixue)

In the group of participants, there has been a general agreement that they often find it difficult to establish friendships with the local students. They attribute this to their own capacities in the first place. Jordan, for example, argues that Chinese students like to communicate with others, but this depends on 'a good command of English ... and confidence to speak in class.' Another student, Ivy, suggests that Chinese students should not be merely regarded as being weak in using English language and relates communicative challenges to how they are perceived by others:

> We cannot integrate into local community ... Many of my friends, including me, wanted to make local friends, but we did not succeed ... Here communication is not as we expected ... since the locals often think that Chinese students' English is not good enough. Perhaps local people do not like to communicate with us. (Ivy)

The group makes recurrent references to a social and cultural distance they have experienced. This distance can be explained by many reasons, including prejudices, differences in lifestyles, interests, social networks, family status and residential locations of students. Nonetheless, it is disappointing that many local students fail to use this opportunity to develop their own intercultural capabilities and understanding.

There is another reason for the communicative distance related to the influence of Chinese cultural and communication practices on identities of students. For example, Malu argues that Chinese students mostly live in a Chinese diasporic community, and they also can avoid communication with local Australians. When it is possible, they prefer to use the services offered by Chinese-Australians and work for them as part-time workers.

> Chinese students usually like to live in a Chinese circle. For example, if they want to buy or repair a car, they will look for a Chinese-Australian business ... A part of their time is spent on part-time work for Chinese-Australians to make money for buying food or eating in restaurants. (Malu)

In terms of academic life, Ivy notes that most Chinese students pay greater attention to academic studies and examination results rather than establishing relationships with others. She clarifies this by saying that 'in addition to English language, our life is different. For example, to Guilao [local students], learning is just an episode in their everyday life. But most Chinese students regard academic learning and examinations as very important'. This comment can be reflective of a more instrumental perspective on learning overseas as a way of obtaining a degree from a foreign university rather than integrating in a foreign culture or a broader community. As she comments further, 'more or less, we integrate a bit, but it is impossible to change the direction. No matter what the process is, the ending is that we want to get that piece of paper — graduation.' At the same time, Ivy admits that their educational success and often higher grades do not mean that they obtain a better understanding of the theoretical knowledge than local students.

The standpoints of Chinese students on their experiences are reflective of their positioning by others as certain type of students and hence involve a performative aspect of identity. This autostereotyping can be used as a strategy of making sense to others and themselves. Indeed, the others not only provide a surplus of vision to self-representations of Chinese students but also affect their identity work as they internalise the representations of others. As Bakhtin (1986, p. 7) once pointed out, 'our real exterior can be seen and understood only by other people, because they are located outside us in space and because they are others'.

This is visible in Shao's discussion of a public perception of international students as those who effectively subsidise the delivery of some tertiary programs in Australia through their fees. He elaborates on this further by saying that 'many local people think that Chinese students are rich. This is their first impression'.

Internalisation of Other-representations of Chinese students can function as a form of autostereotyping — a reproduction of cultural constructs. Rock, for example, says that Australian people think that Chinese students have a strong sense of harmony in communication and social practices, and therefore they usually do not like to argue but accept others. 'The local people usually think that Chinese students are kind. Chinese students would like to embrace others. They try to assimilate'. Another example of autostereotyping refers to students' poor communication with outsiders. Alex says, in this regard, that Chinese students are shy and do not to speak publicly. However, they are effective communicators when it comes to the interaction with insiders:

> Many Chinese students are quiet, and they do not like to speak, so local students often feel that Chinese students are very shy ... Australian students think that Chinese students are smart ... but they do not like to talk. (Alex)

However, the students can also be critical of generalisations and often do not confirm pre-established views. For example, Baixue is critical of some Chinese students who either reproduce bad practices or lack self-discipline. 'Chinese students,' she says, 'have brought bad habits to Australia. The impression that the locals give to me is that they care a lot about the environment ... not like Chinese. On the whole, some Chinese students are not as good as the local people.' Also, she speaks negatively about 'the spoilt

Chinese students' who come from rich families and who do not care about anything, including their studies.

> Some Chinese students forget why they come to Australia; they do not attend classes but just stay at home and play computer games. Their intention to study comes from their family but not from them ... They do not cherish the opportunity to study. Some lack self-discipline and self-dependence capability. They belong to a group with good financial opportunities. (Baixue)

The representations of Chinese students and their standpoints on everyday life reveal that their identity work occurs in the intercultural space of meaning-making. As a result of the tension between various representations by selves and others, some students develop new identities and some students perform identities defined by 'cultural models' (Gee, 1996). Cultural models influence how one makes sense of self and others and what one says and does. Chinese students' institutional identities are products of their communication practices mediated by different cultural models — at least by two cultural models. One is acquired in Chinese cultural and social contexts, and the other one is acquired in Australia. These cultural models carry within them values of different sociocultural groups and mediate perspectives on people and reality. They 'can conflict in their content, in how they are used, and in the values and perspectives they carry' (Gee, 1996, p. 88). As such, the everyday practices of Chinese students contain a number of cultural and social contradictions and these drive their critical and creative ways of meaning- and identity-making.

In particular, the contradictory nature of identity work is most visible in everyday cultural practices of students. In Australia, the Chinese students celebrate cultural festivals as they provide an opportunity not only to follow cultural traditions but also to celebrate their belonging to local and distant Chinese communities. For example, all the participants find their sense of cultural identity is the strongest during cultural events such as the Spring Festival. Alex admits that Chinese festivals provide him with opportunities to share Chinese culture with his classmates. However, he also mentions that he misses his family on these occasions:

> At Chinese festivals, I have a happy mood. I usually distribute little gifts to my lecturers and classmates and introduce Chinese traditional culture to them. I stay with Chinese students, and we wrap Baozi (steamed bun with meat stuffing), Jiaozi, and make dishes and have talks. I feel that I am a Chinese, although I am in Australia. (Alex)

Other participating students have similar experiences. On the one hand they celebrate the traditional festivals enthusiastically and this enables them to build and experience an alternative cultural support networks, as well as 'educating' other international and local students and academic staff about traditional Chinese rituals and food. Yet, this is the time when they experience homesickness most. On occasions like these, they use new technologies more intensively to stay connected with families and friends back in China and 'watch the Spring Festival Party broadcast by the Central China Television' (Ivy). Although, the participating students recognise that cultural festivities, their scale and atmosphere are different in Australia, they neither can nor want to 'escape' their 'primary life'; 'the activities, worries, concerns and interpersonal relationships of day-to-day experience are carried to the second home and influence their life there' (Perkins & Thorns, 2012, p. 87).

In interviews, these participants admit that they usually do not celebrate Australian holidays. Yet, they do not completely ignore them and recall their experiences at these events. Some students explain why they tend not to participate in these events actively, setting themselves apart from the community. First, some Chinese students think that they are 'outsiders' and it is unnecessary for them to celebrate Australian holidays. For example, the participating students feel that in order to celebrate cultural events one should have a sense of belonging to that culture. As Alex says, 'these are not my festivals … Australia Day does not belong to me, since I am a Chinese, and it is meaningless to me'. Another reason for not celebrating Australian holidays or participating in cultural practices is that Chinese students often do not understand popular cultural practices or know Australian history.

> Last May I went to see the Zombie Walk. Almost all the participants dressed up and put blood on their body with stage property. I was just a spectator. I have not celebrated any Australian festivals yet. Last year there was a parade on the ANZAC Day. I went to have a look and took a few photos. (Malu)

However, it should be noticed that some participants show their interest and participate in Australian holidays and cultural practices. For instance, Jordan likes visiting pubs and having beer with the local students. Other Chinese students narrate about their experiences of participating in some social and cultural events practices as well. Alex describes his standpoint on these intercultural experiences by using a metaphor of an ancient Chinese coin:

> A person should be like a Chinese ancient bronze coin — 'Waiyuan Neifang' (round outside and square inside, which implies that one is both smooth and easy going and also is highly principled in life). 'Square' means principles, and 'round' means being able to embrace a lot. Wherever you meet someone with different opinions, at home or abroad, for something not serious, it is fine; yet for something, you can never change at the bottom of your heart. (Alex)

If we agree with the notion that 'being-as-event must be … lived through, and not passively comprehended from afar' (Gardiner, 2000, p. 50), the lived experiences of Chinese students — their becoming-as-experiencing intercultural events — provide them with ample opportunities to develop intercultural or, in some cases, transcultural understanding. It is not difficult to see that some Chinese students experience certain contradictions and tensions when they live and communicate in-between two or more different cultures. Generally, the standpoints of Chinese students are historically mediated by the cultural discourses and practices of mainland China, though they live and study in Australia, as well as by the new social and cultural discourses in which they immerse with different degrees of success. Alex's 'Waiyuan Neifang' reminds us that these forms of mediation are not deterministic or static and Chinese students may develop hybrid identities in Australia. The representations of institutional and cultural identities of Chinese students and their dynamics offer a complex picture of students' everyday life and study experiences in Australian universities. These representations are important as they are linked to study experiences and hence call for a re-examination of 'the Chinese student' as a problematic construct in higher educational practices.

Conclusion

It is important to note at this point that English language plays increasingly a key role in mediating the ways of thinking and acting of Chinese students in everyday life and study events in Australia. Indeed, using the language, and learning it through its use, appears to be closely related to identity reconstruction (Ha, 2007; Norton & Gao, 2008). Norton (1997) uses 'investment' in language to define its value in building one's capability to establish new social relations and to participate in learning and cultural practices. The process of learning the English language is a process of becoming a member of a new community where students are engaged in communication practices, as well as constructing new real and 'imagined' sociocultural identities in Australia (cf. Norton, 2010; Pavlenko, 2003). This is likely to involve 'discursive struggle and transculturation in which hybrid identities are negotiated and contradictory subjectivities are produced' (Grimshaw, 2010, p. 243). Therefore, some caution should be taken while considering the effects of essentialised cultural and educational practices on them (e.g., examination-oriented teaching models, rote learning, lack of creativity and critical thinking in academic learning, etc.).

Living in a new social and cultural context, Chinese students construct diverse identities, reflecting a much more complex, dynamic and sophisticated process than the notion of 'the Chinese learner' implies. Albeit not as apparently as some other international students, Chinese students recognise their identity change and these experiences can vary depending on social, cultural and linguistic constrains and affordances in their lives. On some occasions, Chinese students may adopt strategic essentialism to emphasise their Chineseness or traditional values and beliefs in communication with others. But in other circumstances, they can reflect critically and creatively on traditional worldviews and become open to the worldviews and perspectives of other people. This enables them to re-examine themselves. Some participants develop a transcendental attitude, perceiving themselves as located on the border between two or more cultures — a location where cultural innovations and hybrid identities can emerge.

Such experiences of in-between-ness should be recognised and a new learning space should be established in internationalised higher education to respond to everyday experiences of students in which 'neither the self nor the Other remain the same in a dialogical encounter' (Kostogriz & Doecke, 2008, p. 269). This space, defined by Bhabha (2004) as the space of hybridity, emanates from cross-cultural interaction and manifests itself as a dialogue of differences. It is open and fluid, ready to take in new elements and changes. In it, 'people from different races, cultures and nations come together, communicate and interact with each other. During the process, those boundaries between races, cultures and nations are blurred and communities with no clear boundaries between identities are constructed' (Yao, 2010, p. 19).

Chinese students, as well as local students and lecturers involved in international education, can break cultural boundaries by interacting with each other in a dialogical space. This would help them 'to engage in a pedagogical dialogue [and] to listen and to be open to the Other; ... to be immersed in the discursive space where both teachers and students become responsive and answerable when face-to-face with alterity' (Kostogriz, 2009, p. 147). Equally, the dialogic communication would help lecturers to examine their own professional identities, reflecting on their cultural selves in dialogic communication with international students. This is only possible if academic staff recognise the trap of cultural essentialisms and subject these to critical reflection. If no such space is created in learning and teaching, it is then impossible to address challenges that internationalised education is currently experiencing and make it more responsive to the experiences of international students, particularly to their experiences of constructing new meanings, knowledge(s) and identities.

References

Atkinson, D. (1999). TESOL and culture. *TESOL Quarterly, 33*(4), 625–653.

Bakhtin, M. M. (1986). Response to a question from the novy mir editorial staff. In C. Emerson & M. Holquist (Eds.), *Speech genres and other late essays* (pp. 1–9). Austin: University of Texas Press.

Best, G., Hajzler, D., & Henderson, F. (2007). Communicating with Chinese students offshore to improve their transition and adjustment to

Australia-a pilot program. *Journal of Academic Language & Learning, 1*(1), A78–A90.

Bhabha, H. K. (2004). *The location of culture.* London, England: Routledge.

Blanchot, M. (1993). *The infinite conversation.* Minneapolis, MN: University of Minnessota Press.

Brown, L., & Holloway, I. (2008). The initial stage of the international sojourn: Excitement or culture shock? *British Journal of Guidance & Counselling, 36*(1), 33–49.

Chang, C. E., & Strauss, P. (2010). 'Active agents of change?' Mandarin-speaking students in New Zealand and the thesis writing process. *Language and Education, 24*(5), 415–429.

Chen, R. T. H. (2014). East-Asian teaching practices through the eyes of Western learners. *Teaching in Higher Education, 19*(1), 26–37.

Gardiner, M. E. (2000). *Critiques of everyday life.* London, England: Routledge.

Gee, J. P. (1996). *Social linguistics and literacies: Ideology in discourses* (2nd ed.). London, England: Falmer Press.

Grimshaw, T. (2010). Styling the occidental other: interculturality in Chinese university performances. *Language and intercultural communication, 10*(3), 243–258.

Ha, P. L. (2007). Australian-trained Vietnamese teachers of English: Culture and identity formation. *Language, Culture and Curriculum, 20*(1), 20–35.

Heller, A. (1984). *Everyday life* (G. L. Campbell, Trans.). London, England: Routledge & Kegan Paul.

Highmore, B. (2002). Introduction: Questioning everyday life. In B. Highmore (Ed.), *The everyday life reader* (pp. 1–34). London, Engoand: Routledge.

Hopkins, P. E. (2010). *Young people, place and identity.* London, England and New York, NY: Routledge.

Jenkins, R. (2004). *Social identity* (2nd ed.). London, England: Routledge.

Jin, L. & Cortazzi, M. (2006). Changing practices in Chinese cultures of learning. *Language, Culture and Curriculum, 19*(1), 5–20.

Kostogriz, A. (2009). Professional ethics in multicultural classrooms: English, hospitality and the Other. In J. Miller, A. Kostogriz & M. Gearon (Eds.), *Culturally and linguistically diverse classrooms: New dilemmas for teachers* (pp. 132–150). Bristol, Engand: Multilingual Matters.

Kostogriz, A., & Doecke, B. (2008). English and its Others: Towards an ethics of transculturation. *Changing English, 15*(3), 375–377.

Lefebvre, H. (1991). *Critique of everyday life: Vol.1: Introduction.* London, England: Verso.

Lefebvre, H. (2004). *Rhythmanalysis: Space, time, and everyday life* (S. Elden & G. Moore, Trans.). New York, NY: Continuum.

Martin, J. N., & Nakayama, T. K. (2007). *Intercultural communication in contexts* (4th ed.). New York, NY: McGraw-Hill.

Meiras, S. (2004). International education in Australian Universities: Understandings, dimensions and problems. *Journal of Higher Education Policy and Management, 26*(3), 371–380.

Norton, B. (1997). Language, identity, and the ownership of English. *TESOL Quarterly, 31*(3), 409–429.

Norton, B. (2010). Identity, literacy, and English-language teaching. *TESL Canada Journal, 28*(1), 1–13.

Norton, B., & Gao, Y. H. (2008). Identity, investment, and Chinese learners of English. *Journal of Asian Pacific Communication, 18*(1), 109–120.

Pavlenko, A. (2003). 'I never knew I was a bilingual': Reimagining teacher identities in TESOL. *Journal of language, Identity, and Education, 2*(4), 251–268.

Pavlenko, A., & Norton, B. (2007). Imagined communities, identity, and English language learning. In J. Cummins & C. Davison (Eds.), *International handbook of English language teaching* (pp. 669–680). New York, NY: Springer.

Perkins, H. C., & Thorns, D. C. (2012). *Place, identity and everyday life in a globalizing world.* Basingstock, England: Palgrave Macmillan.

Pink, S. (2012). *Situating everyday life: Practices and places.* London, England: Sage.

Platt, L. (2014). Is there assimilation in minority groups' national, ethnic and religious identity? *Ethnic and Racial Studies, 37*(1), 46–70.

Rew, A., & Campbell, J. R. (1999). The political economy of identity and affect. In J. R. Campbell & A. Rew (Eds.), *Identity and affect: experiences of identity in a globalising world* (pp. 1–36). London, England: Pluto Press.

Ryan, J., & Carroll, J. (2005). 'Canaries in the coalmine': International students in Western universities. In J. Carroll & J. Ryan (Eds.), *Teaching international students. Improving learning for all* (pp. 3–10). London, England and New York, NY: Routledge.

Shepherd, G. J. (2006). Communication as transcendence. In G. J. Shepherd, J. St. John & T. Striphas (Eds.), *Communication as...: Perspectives on theory* (pp. 22–30). Thousand Oaks, CA: Sage.

Sheringham, M. (2006). *Everyday life: Theories and practices from surrealism to the present.* Oxford, England: Oxford University Press

Smith, D. (2005). *Institutional ethnography: A sociology for people.* Latham, MD: AltaMira Press.

Smith, D. (1987). *The everyday world as problematic: A feminist sociology.* Boston, MA: Northeastern University Press

Tian, M., & Lowe, J. (2013). The role of feedback in cross-cultural learning: a case study of Chinese taught postgraduate students in a UK university. *Assessment & Evaluation in Higher Education, 38*(5), 580–598.

Tran, T. T. (2013). Is the learning approach of students from the Confucian heritage culture problematic? *Educational Research for Policy and Practice, 12*(1), 57–65.

Universities Australia (2013). *An agenda for Australian higher education 2013–2016*. Canberra, Australia.

Yao, Y. (2010). *Identity and the Third Space in Michael Ondaatje's Running in the Family, in the Skin of a Lion and The English Patient.* Nanjing: Nanjing University Press.

Yates, L., & Wahid, R. (2013). Challenges to Brand Australia: International students and the problem with speaking. *Higher Education Research & Development, 32*(6), 1037–1050.

Yu, B. H. (2013). Asian international students at an Australian University: mapping the paths between integrative motivation, competence in L2 communication, cross-cultural adaptation and persistence with structural equation modelling. *Journal of Multilingual and Multicultural Development, 34*(7), 727–742.

Chapter 2

Cultural Translations: The Art of Cosmopolitan Learning as an International Student

Carol Reid, Hussain Alsaiari, and Ila Rosmilawati

Introduction

The concept 'cosmopolitanism' has a long history (cf. Delanty, 2012) and is found in many languages. The more recent debates about its meaning centre on understanding its relationship to globalisation. The argument is located around the idea that the increasing movement of people, ideas, media, technology and finance (Appadurai, 1996) is reshaping global dynamics. It is not that globalisation is new, rather it is the pace of globalisation leading to time/space compression (Maguire, 2010) and increasing 'super-diversity' (Vertovec, 2007).

Debates examine the genealogy of the term and its attachment to elite forms of movement, such as processes of colonisation and those who can afford travel. However, more recently this view has been challenged, suggesting that cosmopolitanism takes different forms and is therefore vernacular (Werbner, 2006) and cosmopolitan practices are situated (Sobe, 2009). This chapter extends this usage to an examination of *being* an international student. It does this through understanding how identity is located in relation to the local and global and to the actually existing *different* practical stances taken by students (Sobe, 2009). The reasons that they are vernacular or different, is because of the processes of cultural translation that are undertaken, which are different depending on original *cultural* understandings and practices. They are also different because of place, time and other *social* relations, such as gender and English language capacities. The process of cultural translation is also a process of cosmopolitan learning.

Rizvi argues that globalisation demands new resources of learning about how our lives are becoming re-shaped by global processes and connections, and how we might live with and steer the economic, political and cultural shifts that contemporary forms of global connectivity represent (2009, p. 253). This means a focus on self-realisation and connectedness. Rizvi argues that learning itself needs to become cosmopolitan (ibid) and this means understanding that knowledge is relational and contingent; that is, knowledge about knowledge. How might this learning take place and what kinds of processes are involved? Turner (2002) considers 'virtue' an important element in the ability to respect others and makes concrete this notion through the concept of 'ironic distance' (p. 55). In particular, Turner argues 'cosmopolitan virtue also requires self-reflexivity with respect to both our own cultural context and other cultural values' (2002, p. 57). Rather than seeing national groupings or ethnicities as explanation, a consideration of assemblages of people in particular sites may be what cosmopolitanism focusses on (Spisak, 2009). In this approach, a cosmopolitan disposition seems to be something that can be cultivated through a rational response to difference.

Another approach, that is perhaps less rational and captures the unsettling, transformational and contingency of intercultural relations is that of cultural translation (Papastergiadis, 2011). Here it is useful to quote Papastergiadis in full:

> We must rethink the relationship between cultural translation and cosmopolitanism beyond the mechanist paradigm of interacting entities and the belligerent 'clash of civilisations' thesis. These paradigms can neither explain the tangential energy with which a translation can touch but not follow the path of the original, nor demonstrate how meanings are formed out of the shards of a broken system. Cultural translation is a form of creativity that is joined to the void (Papastergiadis, 2011, p. 89).

In the following section there is an exploration of these processes through two narrative accounts. After these have been presented the implications for practice in relation to the art of cultural translation that occurs in cosmopolitan learning will be outlined.

Hussain: From Tabuk to Sydney

In 2005, the Ministry of Higher Education in Saudi Arabia began King Abdullah's foreign scholarship program. The ministry had a vision that aimed to prepare distinguished generations for a knowledge-based society built on a knowledge economy. The ministry has defined goals for the program, which focus entirely on academic and professional issues for the scholarship student. Also, there is another goal that is no less important — to exchange scientific, educational and cultural expertise and experiences with different countries.

The Ministry of Higher Education orients students who have accepted scholarships before they leave Saudi Arabia in order to introduce them to the country they will head to, as well as to explain the challenges they may encounter there and how to overcome them. However, these sessions focus on providing advice and guidance, instructing students in how to maintain their Islamic practices and values, and showing them how to present a good picture of their homeland. The student is preparing for a new, sensitive period in his or her life and, to be prepared for it, needs to learn how to coexist with the culture of the new country while maintaining their own.

Arrival

It was August, 2006, when I arrived in Sydney, Australia. The journey had begun, going overseas to study a master's degree. It was the first time for me that I wore jeans. I had to learn how to communicate in English with people before the start of my course. On the way, at Dubai International Airport, it already seemed to be a foreign country to me. I remained hesitant to communicate with people in English when I needed to. The challenge continued on the aircraft. The airplane crew used several languages. I was hopeful that someone among them was Arabic as they were Emirates airlines! Learning and understanding English was the first challenge for me and my friend who were travelling together. Before we travelled to Australia, our discussion was mainly based on language acquisition and studying masters in this foreign country. These conversations continued on the airplane until we arrived in Sydney. We were faced with numerous challenges about how to travel to the Gold Coast, where we were to study. We had been advised to board a shuttle bus to the domestic airport. It was unfortunate that this was not well understood by us but we managed to sort it out.

The journey from Coolangatta Airport to our hotel was like a dream to us. The geographical appearance and general topography was stunning. The taxi driver demonstrated a lot of respect and he was knowledgeable and sociable. This helped us deal with our disappointment at the airport where we couldn't even communicate with the check-in people. On arrival to the place where we planned to stay in our first week (hotel in Surfers Paradise), we were faced with further challenges as foreigners in the country. It was difficult for us to explain what we needed as we were not familiar with the language used. For instance, when in hotels we could hardly be understood regarding what we needed. Food and eating points were a struggle as we had to look for places where we could take our meals. Getting familiar foods was a problem as the eating habits in Australia differed greatly from what we were used to in Saudi Arabia. We often found ourselves subsisting on foods such as bread, eggs and tuna as we tried to adjust.

On the second day on the Gold Coast, my friend and I decided to go for a walk around the area (Surfers Paradise). It was in the early hours of the morning, around 7 am and we walked past a group of 4 or 5 people. They started making fun of us and the way we were walking next to each other as our hands almost touched each other. This was common in our culture as it is ok to hold a man's hand and walk. For example, in our culture some people hold hands as they walk as they wish to talk about something important or private. My friend made a comment in Arabic meaning 'who left his home, lost his power'. For our next walk we did not hold our hands as it was against the local cultural practices, at least in public. This is a form of translation adapting to the new culture (Burke, 2011, p. 70–77) but it also required a distancing from one's own culture (Turner, 2002).

The first cultural phase looked to be over when we left the hotel to our homestay families organised by the University Institute. This marked the beginning of a new journey in my life. I was now to face a new cultural set up with different customs, beliefs, and the way of thinking among others. They were completely distinct from those of my home country. For instance, house designs were completely different from those of Saudi Arabia. The furniture and even the fridge door placement was the complete opposite of what I was used to in my original homeland. Again, time for meals looked to be challenging to me. Dining time was set at 6 pm compared to the usual 11 pm I was used to in my home country. In addition, around 5 pm everything had closed with nowhere to go.

As an international student, my first goal and objective of being in Australia was purely academic. I intended to pass in my exams and gain knowledge. Therefore, I had to first study English, which was to aid my masters studies. Improving my English was the main concern at this stage. However, there was a big difference between the academic life (inside the educational institutions) and the life outside the learning centres. In the academy, there is an attempt to understand students' backgrounds, cultures and religions. So they can deal with them according to these cultural values. For instance, the institute that I studied my language course with encouraged the academic staff to read about Islam because of the large number of Muslim students who were studying there.

The concept of the auzlah [void عزلة]

In Arabic, the void is represented by the meanings of auzlah عزلة. Cultural translation, according to Papastergiadis (2011) occurs in this void. Many times I felt I was in a void. Even after being settled in Australia for six years and now studying for my PhD in Sydney I could feel unsettled. A flatmate used to call me 'mad dog' making me laugh thinking that he only meant it as a compliment and not in a nasty way because of the manner in which he said it yet the translation in Arabic meant the complete opposite of what I thought. However, since it was said in a non-threatening manner I adapted and translated the cultural meaning differently (Routledge, 2013, p. 48–58).

There were many other instances of adjustments involving cultural space and interactions. Our cultural greetings mainly involved the cheek-to-cheek kiss. Here in Australia, this was completely strange and extraordinary for people to see, particularly for men. In fact, some of my Saudi friends often fear greeting in public (in our way) for fear of public perception. In addition, Saudi students can be reluctant to participate in activities for religious, cultural, or social reasons. For religious reasons, Saudi students are reluctant to attend any gatherings where alcoholic drinks are served, even when alcohol-free drinks are provided. Similarly, differences in culture and customs may cast a shadow on a number of behaviours, such as the wearing of the hijab (female headscarf), the reluctance of some Saudi women to shake hands with men, and so on. In addition, the Saudi students are not familiar with debates, common in university clubs as they have not being trained in Saudi schools and universities. Some do have debates about controversial issues but it is not common because of the monarchy in Saudi Arabia.

There are other important issues to raise, in particular, about the meaning and possibilities associated with the idea of cosmopolitanism. Appiah (2006) stated that cosmopolitanism can be said to refer to the ideology that all ethnic and cultural groups belong to the same community based on shared moral principles. Cosmopolitan communities are based on inclusive moralities, shared economic values and even political structures (Edwards, 2008). It therefore includes people from many different and varied backgrounds as well as countries. They exist with mutual understandings with respect for their differing beliefs in all sectors of life (Appiah, 2006). Cultural translation is a key conceptual tool for understanding the effects of cross-cultural mixtures and transnational flows. It is also a necessary term for grasping the cosmopolitan forms of agency and collectivity. In this remainder of this section, the strengths and limitations of models of cultural translation that focus on the creativity produced at the point of the encounter with difference are explored.

Cosmopolitanism in Arab Studies

There are no in-depth studies involving cosmopolitanism in Arabic literature, and it is notable that the articles that do address this focus on its political and economic aspects (Khairi, 2014). This focus forms the basis for their accusation against cosmopolitanism: that it dons a political dress in an attempt at political domination, or an economic dress in an attempt, via large corporations, to control and monopolise business worldwide. Here is the equating of cosmopolitanism with colonialism, capitalism and/or imperialism. On the other hand, there are a few literary writings that offer an overview of cosmopolitanism in the Arab world (Shaheen, 2008) and remember nostalgically that cities, such as Aden (Amshoush, 2012), Alexandria (Sayed, 2009) and Beirut (Tay, 2008), were truly cosmopolitan at the beginning of the previous century. Ethnicities with different religions and of different types lived there, and coexistence prevailed at that time. Ibn Khaldun (1377) is among those who were most concerned with the coexistence between human societies, and he investigated intolerance and its effects on national and human development.

From this perspective, the great scholar Bennabi (1970) emphasises the role of culture in creating societies in his book *The Question of Problem of Ideas in the Islamic World*. Bennabi (1970) divided a society into three elements; things, people and thoughts. These elements are how people interact with each other. It is found that Islam, as a religion, is based on a concept of cultural coexistence that accepts all colours, cultures, and classes. The first Islamic undertaking was great with regards to coexistence, involving the fraternity between the Muslims that had immigrated to Medina (Almuhajreen) and those who were already settled there (Alansar). The Muslims already settled in Medina shared their money with the immigrant Muslims who came from Mecca which was known as the pact of brotherhood between Almuhajreen and Alansar (Nuri Topba , 2012, p. 7; Ramadan 2006, p. 92). These few texts reveal that the concept is quite ancient and found in languages other than English.

Cosmopolitan learning in this instance is one that is more than gestures but also a reflexive engagement with understanding the political and economic dimensions of being an international student and the ideologies that underscore differences felt in the void. However, cosmopolitan learning also entails an openness and realisation that we are all now living in a globalised world and that negotiation of contexts is part of cultural translation. Developing ways to support this capacity is the challenge but there is a clear need to work towards helping international students who may be studying in another country but it is not just about learning about that country as it also entails learning about one's own country and knowledge, and entails self-transformation.

IIa: From Jakarta to Sydney

My first visit to Australia was in the winter of 2009 when I had the opportunity to do an academic short-course program, which was funded by an Australian Leadership Award Fellowship. At that time, I visited a university in Queensland from July to September 2009 and studied pedagogy and visited some alternative schools in the Sunshine Coast area. In the first month of the program, I lived with an Australian family, where as part of the program, I practised my English. The second and the third month I moved to an apartment. After a few years, I came back to Australia to undertake a PhD, but in a different state, New South Wales. I started my PhD in February 2012 and now I am in my third year of candidature. I spent one year living in on-campus accommodation and shared the unit with other international students. In the second year I rented my own unit outside the university because my family joined me from Indonesia.

Initial understandings about Australians and their culture had been formed a few years before in Indonesia when I was working with some academics and consultants from Australia on some projects. For instance, at one public university in Indonesia, I received funds for research on illiterate communities and collaborated on other research about education in Indonesia with some Australian professors. From these interactions and collaboration, I felt familiar with Australians, especially with academics, in terms of relating to their language, work habits and daily routine. In fact, a few of them treated me very well, like being a member of their family. However, this does not mean that I fully understand Australia and the culture in general, especially people of non-academic background. In the following section I outline some of the key aspects of my experiences that have required cultural translation.

Cultural translation and the void: Spatial aspects
Australia as an 'empty' place

The second time I came to Australia was quite different. I arrived to commence my PhD on New Year's Day, January 1, 2012. Rather than Australian colleagues welcoming me like my previous arrival at the Sunshine Coast, the only person I met at that time was a (official) driver from the university who left me immediately after we reached the campus. For me, spending two months in the Penrith area in outer Western Sydney before I moved to the Bankstown campus was a totally different experience to the place I lived before, in Jakarta, Indonesia. In Penrith, as well as in the Bankstown area, the shop or mall closes at 5 pm (i.e., except Thursday when open until 9 pm and/or a small shop that opens till late). It means that the only time I have to obtain basic needs such as food or other services is in the morning or afternoon, which for a student like me is studying time. The weekend is worse than weekdays, as most shops close earlier. In Jakarta, everything we need at any hour is easy to find. I am accustomed back home in the middle of the night to break from work and can easily find food vendors if I feel hungry. Indeed, there are a few franchised restaurants in the Sydney area open 24 hours a day but their number is still limited. The population in Sydney suburbs is also much less than in Jakarta, that is why I rarely interact with native speakers. For me, the Western Sydney area, as well as my first experience in the Sunshine Coast, is that they are like an 'empty place', which is totally different to my city in my home country Indonesia.

After several months I came to understand that human capital is more valuable than other capital. Therefore, labour is expensive compared to Indonesia. As a consequence, employers need to carefully calculate if employees have to be paid for extra hours. In contrast, in Indonesia, overtime payments are less common partly as an effect of a monthly salary system. Even so, it depends on the employer's kindness to voluntarily give extra money unless people work in big factory. This Australian practice is influenced by its smaller population. The effect of this practice is reflected in the daily culture of life that is more effective, quick and simple. I consider this circumstance a chance for me to change habits (e.g., wasting time at the shopping centre) and find myself effectively using the time in everyday practice.

Personal versus public space

In eastern countries, especially in Indonesia where the majority of the population are Muslim, it is not common to touch and hug someone from a different sex. Shaking hands is acceptable and common for most of the culture unless groups of people do not practice it because of religious reasons. Personally, when I reach one big achievement in my life journey, my male friends or senior colleagues (except nuclear family members), never hug me to congratulate me (e.g., my graduation day). However, I had a different experience in Australia. One day, one of my senior colleagues, a professor (an older man who I knew a long time before I came to Australia) attempted to hug me immediately after I made a great presentation. At that time I felt confused about what should I do. I admired him very much as this professor influenced me in my academic achievement, but at the same time I also felt awkward, as this is not part of my cultural background.

I clearly remember at that time I was avoiding this action. My response to this situation was not truly a form of withdrawal or denial of the other but for me the situation was unequal. My reaction is also shaped by religion and culture. Mohanty (1991, p. 64) states that third-world women are often written about in terms of 'needs' and 'problems,' rarely emphasising 'choices' or 'freedom' to act but in this case I was not ready to accept the new culture. It might be that I am 'a partial cosmopolitan' (Appiah 2007, p. xvii), who has the ability to live everywhere, but under certain circumstances I limit tolerance of the other (van der Veer 2002, pp. 15–16). Appiah emphasises that in the understanding of cosmopolitanism, there are some values that should be of universal concern, but other values must be from a local perspective (p. xxi).

In contrast with this experience, another concept of 'personal space' in Australia is different. For example, on public transport such as a bus or train, people always keep their distance from others even if full of passengers in order to avoid rubbing against each other. However, in Indonesia, it is common being close to each other in public space as the concept that we adhere to is 'sharing'. For Indonesians, it would be odd if people did not move closer to one another in order to give more spaces for people to board. It is obviously a different concept of physical engagement or personal space between Indonesians and Australians in these particular examples.

In translating these cultural differences I can understand the reason behind this culture, in that Australia has a better public transportation system that facilitates its residents and it affects people's behaviour, but 'life with empathy' becomes a considering factor in my own culture. Even so, I respect the differences, as long as the ideas or values are not bad for people or individuals.

Cultural/religious aspects
Tension between religion and culture
My other experience is about sharing food. Sharing food is common in Indonesia, especially in my own local culture, *Sunda*. Sundanese people like me call sharing food *bancakan*, where people meet in one place and bring their own food (from home or restaurant) and share it. These practices are common everywhere, in the workplace at lunchtime or time at the weekend with family. I found this practice also common in Australia, known as 'sharing a plate'.

As I am a fan of this habit, here in Australia, I feel a dilemma if my colleague from a different religion invites me to share a plate. The issue is about 'halal' (meaning 'lawful' in Arabic and it is a word that describes all food products permitted by Islamic law) food that the majority of Muslims have to abide by. I found a tension between my religion and my cultural background in practising this activity. On one side, I have to gently refuse the food that my non-Muslim colleague is offering me, but on the other side, as Sundanese, it is impolite to reject other people's invitation or offer. As a non-Westerner, it is difficult for me to say 'no' to other people. I remember one night, when I stayed with an Australian family on the Sunshine Coast; they offered me non-halal food for dinner. I refused it with some reasons. However, it felt difficult to explain my words and world, as this was totally different to them. In contrast, when I had a similar experience with a colleague at university, it was much easier for me to give the reasons as they more open-minded.

However, there is a contradiction also when I compare this situation to what I experienced in my home country. I used to live in a share house with non-Muslim students when I was an undergraduate. The tension then was not as strong as the current situation. In my home country, I rarely argued with myself about this issue. I was confident to share their food with them even if the product derived from non-halal food. This tension appears to become stronger when I live in Australia, obviously because I live in a Muslim neighbourhood that might be strengthening my identity as a Muslim relative to non-Muslims. There is a kind of a void in which I have found myself and to connect with other people in the same religion (in a new place) is the factor behind the cause of this tension. In this particular case, in an act of cultural translation, I have created a new sense of my identity. I use a dual level of tolerance/action, whereas inside my own country I might use a universal value (among Indonesian people) whereas here I consider the influence of Australian Muslim immigrants in building my identity.

Academic life: Ethics for research

The shift from 'student' to 'researcher' as a higher degree research (HDR) student obviously needs effort, especially for someone who comes from a different academic culture. For example, when I was applying for ethics approval for my fieldwork in Indonesia, the process took three months from filling in the form. Although the time spent for this process varies among HDR students all research students have to pass with the process. Ethics approval before research aims to encourage and ensure integrity in research. Therefore, commencing a human research activity without ethics approval may constitute research misconduct. Reflecting on my experience in this process, a long list of ethics questions have two different meanings. On one side it leads to reliability of the research process; on the other side it is questioning the researcher about his/her ability in conducting research.

Some sections in the ethics form ask you to predict what will not happen/fit with reality in the field, such as the issue of safety of the research participants. Indonesian culture is based on mutual trust and the responsibility to serve the other. Therefore, from my cultural understanding, the participant (including young people) would not feel threatened during the research process. In fact, lots of students wanted to become my research participants. Mutual trust culturally impacts on the necessity of the consent form for participants. Indonesian researchers rarely give consent forms as proof of confidentiality, therefore, my participants rejected my form. Indeed, in Indonesia we also use permission letters from government bodies and/or university to conduct the research, but this is normally aimed at the institution (e.g., school via principal), not the participants.

It might be true that ethics practices construct international research students as unwitting objects of Western socialisation. Manathunga (2007) argued that this practice has an element of paternalism, which concerns socialising international research students who have a local disciplinary research culture to 'fit in' with the dominant research culture (pp. 213–214). However, supervisors play a useful role in acting as a cultural interpreter. They can interact with their students in the form of cultural exchange, in which the supervisors put themselves in their students' position, and their students will fit themselves into the new academic community.

To reflect the kinds of cultural translation I have made in this section, I have come to a general understanding that 'new knowledge of culture' both inside and outside academic life are continually reshaping my personal/intellectual transformation as an international student. For example, in the process of engagement with others from different entities and cultures, it forces me to move across my original culture. I also come to the movement of new ideas, of rival viewpoints and practices.

Implications and concluding remarks

These narratives emphasise the contingent, local and different scales of cosmopolitanism. They reveal the multiple dimensionalities of self-transformation that come from cosmopolitan learning, as an international student. This learning is both inside and outside the academe. Further, the process of cosmopolitan learning is an unfinished project, in the sense that it is by necessity partial. This sense of cosmopolitanism is not about universalism but engagement in worldliness, meaning that it is not a simple matter of cultural differences but also reflexively understanding the political and economic conditions that structure the power relations in international student experiences. It is knowledge about knowledge.

The implications of a cosmopolitan analysis of international students' experiences includes a number of elements. Drawing on the narratives in this chapter the supervisory relationship is critical. A dialogue that recognises that knowledge is not simply a one-way street but a recognition of 'southern theory' (Connell, 2007). This means sharing ways of knowing between those invested with the power to define what counts as useful knowledge, often supervisors and Western institutions, and the students' own knowledge. This entails a critical analysis of every actor's subjectivity. While it may be important for international research students to fit into the dominant research culture of their institution as Ila noted, it ought to be seen that since 'research is dialogue with other experts' (Wisker, Robinson, & Shacham, 2007, p. 304), there needs to be a space to be provided for dialogue to take place through learning conversations and interactions. In the ethics case raised by Ila the point is made that some 'space' has to be provided for research students to express their own home research culture.

This 'space' and 'voice' will give the ethics committee or university an idea of the context of research and consider student's 'local knowledge' in the approval process. As a result, students get benefits from a new research culture, and the university opens up to the exchange of knowledge from international students. This action also imparts tolerance of cultural difference, which makes the university a more powerful site of both academic research and human cultural understanding. Furthermore as Hussain clearly laid out, there is a rich history of Islamic knowledge and a cosmopolitan worldliness that is often misrepresented. Indeed, as Welch (2014) has commented, 'mobility in Islamic higher learning has a long and illustrious history, having contributed notably to the development of knowledge worldwide' (p. 146).

Finally, there are practicalities that also need attention. The orientation sessions that students often undergo only present information about the rules and regulations of the new country. It is indeed important for students to be introduced to the rules and regulations of the host countries in which they will study before setting foot in them. More important than that, however, is to develop in students an understanding of the void that will be experienced, and with dialogue, that this is productive and creative, for themselves and the host community.

References

Amshoush, M. (2012, September 18.). *Aden madinah cosompolotiah*. [Aden is cosmopolitan city]. Retrieved from *http://www.yemenitta.com/?p=1*

Appadurai, A. (1996). *Modernity at large: Cultural dimensions of globalization*. Minneapolis, MN: University of Minnesota Press.

Appiah, K.A. (2006). *Cosmopolitanism: Ethics in a world of strangers*. New York, NY: W.W. Norton & Co.

Bennabi, M. (1970). *Mushkelat alafkar fi alalem alislami* [The Question of Ideas in the Muslim World]. In B. Barkah & A.Sha'abo, (2002, 2nd ed.). Beirut, Lebanon: Dar alfekr.

Burke, P. (2011). Gilberto Freyre, Hybridity and cultural translation. *Portuguese Studies, 27*(1), 70–77.

Carver, N. (2013). Displaying genuineness: cultural translation in the drafting of marriage narratives for immigration applications and appeals. Cambridge, MA: Harvard University Press.

Connell, R. (2007). *Southern theory: The global dynamics of knowledge in social science*. Sydney, Australia: Allen & Unwin.

Edwards, K. (2008). For a geohistorical cosmopolitanism: postcolonial state strategies, cosmopolitan communities, and the production of the British, Overseas, Non-Resident, and Global Indian. *Environment and Planning D: Society and Space, 26*, 444–463.

Ibn Khaldün, A. (1377). *The Muqaddimah: An introduction to history*. In R. Franz, & D. N. Joseph. (1969). Princeton, NJ: Princeton University Press.

Khairi, M. (2014, April 19). Mudhadat qawmeyah lil awlamah [Nationalism against globalisation]. Retrieved from http://www.ahram.org.eg/NewsQ/278444.aspx

Maguire, M. (2010). Towards a sociology of the global teacher. In S. J. B. Michael W. Apple, Luis Armando Gandin (Ed.), *The Routledge International Handbook of Sociology of Education* (pp. 58–68). Abingdon, England: Routledge.

Manathunga, C. (2007). Supervision as mentoring: The role of power and boundary crossing. *Studies in Continuing Education, 29*(2), 207–221, doi: 10.1080/01580370701424650

Mohanty, Talpade,C, Russo, A, and Torres, L, eds. (1991). *Third world women and the politics of feminism*. Bloomington: Indiana University Press.

Nowicka, M., & Rovisco, M. (Eds.). (2012). *Cosmopolitanism in practice*. Ashgate Publishing, Ltd.

Nuri Topba , O. (2012). *The Prophet Muhammad Mustafa the Elect (s.a.s) — 2*. Smashwords: Erkam.

Palmary, I. (2011). 'In your experience': research as gendered cultural translation. *Gender, Place and Culture, 18*(1), 99–113.

Papastergiadis, N. (2011). Cultural translation and cosmopolitanism. In K. Jacobs & J. Malpas (Eds.), *Ocean to outback: Cosmopolitanism in contemporary Australia* (pp. 68–95). Perth, Western Australia: University of Western Australia Publishing.

Ramadan, T. (2006). *In the footsteps of the Prophet: Lessons from the life of Muhammad*: Oxford University Press.

Rizvi, F (2009). Towards Cosmopolitan learning. *Discourse: Studies in the Cultural Politics of Education. 30*(3), 253–268

Routledge, T. P. (2013). Learner-centred education and 'cultural translation'. *International Journal of Educational Development, 33*(1), 48–58.

Sayed, M. (2009, November 29). *Aleskandriah alati fi bal Nael Altukhi* [Alexandria, which in the mind of Nael Alukhi].

Shaheen, M. (2008). Fi althaqafah [In Culutre]. *Cultural Journal, 71* (4), 4-9. Retrieved from *http://ujnews2.ju.edu.jo/UJNewsPublications/المجلة%20الثقافية%20العدد%2071.pdf*

Sobe, N. W. (2009). Rethinking 'Cosmopolitanism' as an Analytic for the Comparative Study of Globalization and Education. *Current Issues in Comparative Education, 12*(1), 6–13

Spisak, S. (2009) The Evaluation of a Cosmopolitan Identity: Transforming Culture in *Current Issues in Comparative Education, 12*(1), 86–91

Tay, B. (2008, August 30). *Beirut, maqha alasdeqa almahjour* [Beirut, friends' abandoned cafe]. Retrieved from http://www.al-akhbar.com/node/113125

Turner, B S (2002) Cosmopolitan Virtue, Globalisation and Patriotism *Theory Culture & Society, 19*, 45–63.

Van der Veer, P. (2002). Cosmopolitan options. *Etnografica, 6*(1), 15–26.

Vertovec, S. (2007). Super-diversity and its implications. *Ethnic and Racial Studies, 30*(6), 1024–1054.

Werbner, P. (2006). Vernacular cosmopolitanism *Theory, Culture & Society, 23*(2-3), 496–498.

Wisker, G., Robinson, G., & Shacham, M. (2007). Postgraduate research success: communities of practice involving cohorts, guardian supervisors and online communities. *Innovations in Education and Teaching International, 44*(3), 181–195.

Chapter 3

How International Students' Attitudes and Orientations Towards Cultural Differences and Multiculturalism Affect Their Engagement With Learning

Edilson Arenas

Introduction

The past two decades have seen growing interest in international education research. From politics and practices (Paltridge, Mayson, & Schapper, 2012), to everyday experiences (Trahar & Hyland, 2011), wellbeing (Ellis-Bosold & Thornton-Orr, 2013), needs (Roberts & Dunworth, 2012), identity (Hofstede, 2005), multiculturalism (Yang & Noels, 2013), language (Benzie, 2010), stereotypes (Ballard & Clanchy, 1997), academic standards (Rienties, Beausaert, Grohnert, Niemantsverdriet, & Kommers, 2012), and curricula (Dunne, 2011) among others, the common theme is for the provision of more learning-oriented services that genuinely augment international students' learning journey. This journey likens Campbell's (1993) hero in his seminal work on comparative mythology, *The hero with a thousand faces*. The journey may start with a 'Departure' or 'Separation', where our heroes decide to leave their country to face the venture of studying abroad, continuing with an 'Initiation' to overcome hurdles and battles they face during their studies and finishing with a 'Return', where our heroes graduate and come back home triumphantly (Campbell, 1993). This comparison is an applicable and useful analogy when considering the abovementioned number of issues that the research literature documents as facing international students.

This research is designed to address some of these issues, particularly to investigate how students' attitudes and orientations towards cultural differences and multiculturalism may affect their engagement with learning.

Specifically, this chapter aims to answer the following questions:

1. What are international students' knowledge and awareness of cultural differences and multiculturalism?

43

2. What are international students' attitudes and orientations towards cultural differences and multiculturalism?
3. How do international students' knowledge and awareness of, and their attitudes and orientations towards, cultural differences and multiculturalism affect their engagement with learning?

About the study

This chapter draws on an ethnographic study (Arenas, 2012) conducted at two universities in Australia, that explored the behaviours, attitudes, perceptions and conceptions of teaching and learning found within multicultural learning environments that blend online and face-to-face pedagogies.

I collected data from participants located at two qualitatively different sites and from four postgraduate computing courses: Network Security (NetSec) and Systems Analysis and Design (SAD) at Site 1; and Business Analysis and Modelling (BAM) and Fundamentals of Information Systems (FOIS) at Site 2.

Site 1 was located in one of the metropolitan campuses of a multi-campus medium-sized regional Australian university, and Site 2 was located in a large metropolitan Australian university. Site 1's student body comprised international students only, whereas Site 2 was located in a university that catered mainly for domestic students with a relatively smaller population of international students.

The purposive, culturally diverse sample comprised 18 students from nine countries of origin and their respective teachers. Student participants at Site 1 included twelve students. They had diverse educational backgrounds, with different residency time in the country. Prior to the commencement of the semester term, Site 1's students had been residing in Australia for a period of between 3 months and 18 months, with half of them for less than a year and five students for only 3 months. Of the 23 student participants, six were men and six women, including nationalities from Pakistan, China, Bangladesh, Kuwait and India. Before participating in this study, 6 students already held a postgraduate degree and three had more than two years' experience in computer sciences. All students who provided information about their skills reported that they were experts at writing academic arguments in English. They also reported to have expert level knowledge using hardware, software and discussion forums; however, only three students reported to have experience using blogs.

Site 2 consisted of 6 student participants: three men and three women including nationalities from Australia, Oman, Vietnam, Indonesia and China. Prior to the commencement of the semester term, except for one domestic student, Site 2's students had been living in Australia for a period of between one month and two years, with two students residing in Australia for fewer than three months. In contrast to Site 1, where six students already held a postgraduate degree, at Site 2 all students held a bachelor degree before the conduct of this study. Three students had between four to thirteen years' experience working in computer sciences. Only one student claimed to be novice in hardware, software and discussion forums compared to the rest who reported to be experts using collaboration tools. Similarly, two students reported having novice experience writing academic arguments in English, with the rest reporting to be experts in essay writing skills. Only one student claimed to have substantial team work and management experience.

Data collection

The first source of data consisted of digital texts produced by both student and teacher participants during their interactions with the online component of the blended learning environment at each site. During the term, students worked on a number of online learning activities for individual and group work. At Site 1, students required to maintain a blog to reflect on their own learning experiences and perceptions of the course. The blog was based on nine topical questions spread over the last nine weeks of the semester and was assessed. The teaching staff provided structured marking guidelines to ensure each student contributed the nine expected reflections. They also monitored students' progress with prompt feedback. At Site 2, students required to use a discussion forum to extend their engagement with learning activities initiated in face-to-face forums. There were six discussion forums. Three of them designed for individual participation where students had to challenge or critique at least one of the questions raised by the lectures or fellow classmates during the classes. There was a general discussion forum to discuss general issues arising from the course and two group-project-related discussion boards. Of the six forums, only the general discussion forum was moderated by the teaching staff. The other forums were only monitored to check students' progress and prevent language flaming.

I conducted classroom observations at both sites to record reflective notes and descriptions of students' face-to-face classroom activities and behaviours, stimulate personal views of participants in interview, and record events such as student consultations and class participation. The classroom observations were instrumental in the selection of the purposive sample for the student interviews.

I also conducted individual interviews with both teachers and students. The duration of each interview was between 30 and 45 minutes. The purpose of these semi-structured interviews was to gather participants' reflective views of their teaching and learning experiences in the learning environment.

Findings

I iteratively examined data files in search of themes that were meaningful in relation to the aim of the study. This chapter focuses on one of the identified themes: Adapting to a New Learning Environment; and two related dimensions: Culture and Society. The findings associated with this theme and its two related dimensions centred on a wide array of issues affecting international students' learning experience and stemmed from students' cultural, social and educational backgrounds.

Adapting to a new culture dimension

The findings related to the cultural dimension are consistent with those of previous research that reports on phenomena such as *culture shock*, *cultural sensitivity* and *cultural awareness* in association with international students' relocation to a different country.

According to Hofstede (2005), the intercultural encounter between one foreign individual and the new cultural environment is usually accompanied by feelings of bewilderment, anxiety, loneliness, helplessness, distress and hostility, called *culture shock*. In this study, the experience of the feelings that Hofstede attributes to culture shock was apparent in some students. The case of Samuel (Pakistan; Site 1) is an example. During my classroom observations, I noted that Samuel was willing to participate in open discussions when moderated by the teacher. His English was very good, with a great ability to express himself (Observation Notes, Site 1, Observation 7). However, he seemed unwilling to participate collaboratively in peer learning situations where the negotiation of ideas was valued. In fact, during whole class discussions he was sometimes overemotional in supporting his points of views and very critical of peers' opinions, sometimes without sound arguments. He appeared to prefer to work on his own and, when asked to join a group for discussion, he reluctantly agreed. Within the group he remained quiet, contrasting with his relatively active role in open class discussions moderated by the teacher (Observation Notes, Site 1, Observation 7). When asked in the interview about his approach to learning, he reported that he relied solely on reviewing lecture slides and reading textbooks (Samuel; Pakistan; Site 1, student interview excerpt). Asked why he relied so much on authoritative sources like textbooks and the like, oftentimes incomplete, or out of date, he answered:

> When I am reading something which I do not understand and there is no much clarification or when sometimes there is not much explanation, just a couple of sentences, I always go to the Web to find things I do not find clear. (Samuel; Pakistan; Site 1, student interview excerpt)

Chapter 3 How Attitudes and Orientations Affect Engagement With Learning

It was apparent Samuel preferred to learn independently and not collaboratively; and regarding cultural differences, he reported an unwillingness to adapt to the host culture:

> Cultural differences may be a huge problem, but I do not have to worry about it because I am not going to adapt to that culture, I do not have to do with that culture. (Samuel; Pakistan; Site 1, student interview excerpt)

Samuel also reported feelings of loneliness, living away from his family. The data provides a picture of Samuel as a student who is reluctant to engage in the collaborative work valued by the host culture, who reports being resistant to adapting to the new culture and who experiences negative emotions such as loneliness.

The new multicultural environment also appeared to be problematic for Thomas (Vietnam; Site 2); however, unlike Samuel who seemed to actively resist changing his ways, Thomas appeared to be endeavouring to develop greater cultural understandings to adapt to the new environment:

> When there is a problem, I say 'that is okay in my country but I do not know if it is okay in your country'. For example, when I was studying English, I had a conversation with a Chinese guy and there was a misunderstanding as a result of the culture. (Thomas; Vietnam; Site 2, student interview excerpt)

From the quote, Thomas was mainly affected as a result of his lack of exposure to intercultural relations. In fact, he had never operated within a foreign culture before and had not had much time to adapt, having spent only four months in Australia. He also recognised that the process of adaptation had been affected by his English skills and, as documented later, this also affected his studies with a limited number of contributions in the discussion forums and lack of participation in class discussions.

The cases of Samuel and Thomas provide evidence of the phenomenon of culture shock already documented in the literature on international students. However, their orientations differed, with Samuel seeking to insulate himself from the host culture while Thomas sought to adapt to a challenging situation by testing out new behaviours and developing new skills

In contrast to Samuel and Thomas, some students like Jacquie (China; Site 1) and Natalie (Oman; Site 2) did not report or appear to experience any of the negative emotions associated with culture shock during their period of study in Australia. Jacquie, for example, referring to the significance of being an international student, recognised the challenges of, and the need to adapt to, the cross cultural environment:

> For me it is to adapt to the culture especially to language, the environment around me because English is not my first language, I need to learn, study, live here ... and also the culture is quite different from our Eastern world; here is

> Western way of doing things, I have to learn how they behave and get used to them. (Jacquie; China; Site 1, student interview excerpt)

During my class observations, there was evidence of Jacquie's attitude and willingness to volunteer to answer questions posed by the teacher and to happily join the group activities; even acting as a leader. Such an attitude appeared to be in contention with previous research reporting passive behaviour among international students, particularly from Chinese cultural background (Kember, 2000).

In relation to Natalie, it was the high level of acceptance and tolerance of multicultural Australia that was the determinant factor in her adaptation process. There were no feelings of culture shock while studying as a foreign resident in Australia. On the contrary, she felt comfortable enjoying the openness and diversity of this country:

> I have not found any culture shock in Australia ... You can see that in a multicultural environment like here, people are from everywhere, you do not feel weird, and there are no boundaries. Most of people are not originally from Australia and they accept and respect you. (Natalie; Oman; Site 2, student interview excerpt)

Natalie's reported feeling of acceptance appeared to be confirmed by data recorded during my class observations. In fact, in class Natalie was a highly motivated student with a good sense of humour and lively facial appearance. She appeared to be very proud of her cultural background wearing colourful dresses typical of her native country.

In addition to the negative emotions associated with culture shock, some students raised intercultural relation issues of cultural awareness and cultural sensitivity. For example, Rachel (Indonesia; Site 1) was critical of the lack of cultural sensitivity by some of her fellow students and the marked disinterest in understanding and accepting others' cultures and values:

> One of my group members is from a different background of mine and I have found that person is straightforward in expressing the [sic] views. They do not understand others' culture, they ignore you. They are not culturally sensitive and I do not feel comfortable about it. (Rachel; Indonesia; Site 2, student interview excerpt)

However, this sentiment of feeling culturally ignored by others appeared not to have affected Rachel's learning journey. During my class observations, I noted she was keen to participate in class discussions and argue when required. For example, during the presentation of a group assignment, she appeared to be relaxed and comfortable presenting and answering questions from teachers and students (Observation Notes, Site 2, Observation 4).

In essence, as evidenced by the examples discussed, the students' responses to the new cultural environment varied, with some seeking to learn its ways as part of their development and others seeking to insulate themselves by adhering to the cultural values of their home countries.

Adapting to a new society dimension

Within the theme of Adapting to a New Learning Environment, further to the cultural dimensions earlier described, there was also evidence of social dimensions to international students' reported need to adapt to the new host country. Consistent with previous research (Stafford, Marion, & Salter, 1978; Michaildis, 1996), the social dimensions of the students' experience of the new environment included perceiving the host country as being safe and egalitarian, experiencing feelings of loneliness and homesickness due to lack of family support and isolation from social networks, and difficulties rooted in the lack of networking and familiarity with communication protocols.

During the interviews, I asked the students to state the reasons for choosing Australia as the destination for their further studies. The perception of the host country as being safe and egalitarian resonated across a number of students' responses. One of the voices was Jacquie, who enjoyed the style of life of the host country:

> [In my country] people tend to be very anxious or too careful about everything but here people are more relaxed and I have to admit that people enjoy more freedom. (Jacquie; China; Site 1, student interview excerpt)

Moreover, she expressed that in Australia, people had more sense of respect for others compared to her country of origin. From the data, there was no direct evidence how these perceptions of the new environment might have impacted Jacquie's learning experience, but from my observations of her willingness to participate in class and her positive emotions and expressions I assume she enjoyed her study time in Australia.

Like Jacquie, Kathy (Kuwait; Site 1) appeared to have enjoyed the safety and equality of the host country. She particularly highlighted the open-mindedness and tolerance of Australia:

> I enjoy this type of culture and environment because back in my country there is too much of racism. In this country everyone is similar, there is no racism regardless you are a manager, employee or whatever. (Kathy; Kuwait; Site 1, student interview excerpt)

As a mature student living in Australia with her daughter, Kathy found the new environment convivial, with people willing to cooperate, an ideal environment to raise children. Jacquie and Kathy's perspectives were common among the student participants. There were no issues that Australia as a host country was either unsafe or discriminating.

The social dimensions of the theme also included the reported feelings of loneliness and homesickness among some students as a result of a lack of social life and family support. These findings are consistent with those of previous studies like the one conducted by Rajapaksa and Dundes (2002) who identified homesickness and loneliness as major factors affecting students' adjustment to new cultures and their learning journey. Take the case of Katerina (India; Site 1), for example, who despite being happy studying in Australia, also lamented the lack of family support: 'As an international student you feel lonely and homesick, there is not much social life because everyone is very busy' (Katerina; India; Site 1, student interview excerpt). Contrary to Katerina, for whom loneliness was a product of the lack of a social life, for Samuel, as discussed earlier, loneliness was mainly a consequence of the *cultural differences* and his resistance to adapt to the unfamiliar.

Not surprisingly, in some cases, the experience of feelings of loneliness and homesickness as a result of social re/dislocation seemed to be related to the time of living in the host country, suggesting that for some it was a transition issue. This finding is consistent with Pascale's (2006) research on the process of adjustment of overseas students, stating that the longer international students were in the host country, the lesser the impact of feelings of loneliness and homesickness. This was the case, for instance, for Rachel (Indonesia; Site 2), who reported that, after living in Australia for a year and a half, she was not experiencing these sort of feelings, compared to the feelings of loneliness and homesickness she experienced during the first term of her period of study in Australia. She explained that over time she developed social networks that helped her to cope with her emotions.

The social dimensions of the theme also included variations in networking and familiarity with communication protocols, the lack of which was experienced as problematic among some students. For example, as part of a project assignment at Site 2, some students were concerned about the best way of contacting an organisation to conduct an interview. This was a challenging exercise for these students owing to their lack of networking and knowledge of local organisations. As expressed through the discussion forum by one of the students: 'We consider that all of us do not have any working experience at Melbourne, so it is better for us to find an organisation within the university' (Bernard, Site 2, student discussion forum excerpt). Others were mainly concerned about the most appropriate procedure to contact the organisation and collecting the sought information. On behalf of the group, a student posted the following question:

> We are uncertain about the best way to contact the organisation we have chosen. Should we email them and attach the letter? Or should we call them and ask for appointment? (Bernard, Site 2, discussion forum excerpt)

This was a fair question, for which the teacher replied: 'I would recommend either calling them or going and seeing them in person ... a cold email has a good chance to end up not being read' (Sophia, Site 2, discussion forum excerpt).

Undoubtedly for these students, not having any experience with the communication protocol to contact local managers or any networking with local businesses, it would have been easier to contact them by sending an email with a letter of introduction attached to it rather than by face-to-face. In this way, deficits in their connection to the social context provided an added layer of difficulty for these students' completion of the required task.

Although in this study, except for Thomas, it was found that English language issues did not have any major effects on students' learning; communication problems did affect the social interactions of some students. As mentioned earlier, Thomas's contributions to the discussion forum and class participations were limited. As he expressed, the cause of these communication problems was mainly rooted in his 'language barriers', which combined with his short period of time in contact with the new environment, made his adjustment to the new environment more difficult. In the case of Henry (China; Site 2), there was a similar feeling, recognising the difficulties of adapting when facing the host culture for the first time:

> When I first came here, the culture was very different to my home town; I had to learn to cope with it, as well as with the language because it was not my first language compared to the local students. (Henry; China; Site 2, student interview excerpt)

However, two years after, as evidenced by my class observations and the ambience of Henry's interview, he appeared to be fully confident in communicating his ideas and coping well during his stay in Australia.

In essence, there were a number of social dimensions that affected the students' experience of the host environment and their response to this experience. There was a reported feeling of a safe and equal host country across all student participants. All appeared to be happy in having chosen Australia as the country of destination for their further studies. In a similar vein, and consistent with previous research (Pascale, 2006), there was a reported feeling of loneliness and homesickness among some student participants. Finally, students reported problems rooted in the lack of networking and familiarity with communication protocols acceptable within the host society.

Discussion of the findings and conclusions

In terms of students' attitudes and perceptions of the multicultural aspect of the new learning environment, students vary in a number of significant and interrelated ways, including:

- their awareness of cultural differences and their knowledge of different cultures

- their attitudes towards cultural diversity and the extent to which they value such an environment
- their own intentions, convictions, and skills in relation to cultural adaptation.

This study demonstrates how, taken together, these aspects can influence the type of social interactions in which students engage, which can then have implications for their engagement in learning within an Australian university context. Issues such as homesickness, loneliness, culture shock, cultural sensitivity and cultural awareness are well documented in the existing literature on international students.

Homesickness and loneliness

A characteristic of the experience of the international students involved in this study was the homesickness that most reported experiencing during their study time in Australia. This finding is consistent with many previous studies. For example, Stafford et al. (1978), in a study of 747 international students from 71 different countries, report homesickness as the most commonly expressed experience of adjustment to a host culture. This finding was confirmed by Michaildis (1996) in a study of 118 international students, with homesickness as one of the most frequently cited stressors attributable to the adjustment to a new culture. However, despite the comprehensive evidence connecting students' acculturation difficulties to feelings of homesickness, there is less evidence about the impact homesickness may have on students' learning experiences. In this regard, Stroebe, van Vliet, Hewstone, and Willis (2002) has confirmed previous studies linking homesickness to 'cognitive failures, poor concentrations, handing in work late, decrements in work quality and high scores on anxiety and depression measures' (p. 150). In their view, the impact of homesickness on students should not be underestimated, with consequences similar to those found in situations of loss and bereavement.

In addition to homesickness, a number of international students also experience loneliness. These findings are consistent with previous studies like the one conducted by Rajapaksa and Dundes (2002) who reiterate homesickness and loneliness as major factors affecting students' adjustment to new cultures and hence their learning journey. In Stroebe et al.'s (2002) view, the patterns associated with loneliness are similar to the patterns associated with homesickness, both having negative effects on students' learning outcomes.

Knowledge and awareness of cultural difference

Some of the findings of this study are also consistent with, and build upon, previous research about the experiences of, and challenges faced by, many international students as a result of intercultural relations including *cultural shock, cultural sensitivity* and *cultural awareness* (Chataway & Berry, 1989; Michaildis, 1996; Rajapaksa & Dundes, 2002; Stafford et al., 1978). The culture shock-related academic difficulties reported by some students in this study have been extensively investigated in previous research studies. For example, in a study about acculturation experiences, appraisal, coping and adaptation among a group of Hong Kong Chinese, French and English students, Chataway and Berry (1989) found that students' academics difficulties were associated with their willingness to accept or recognise other cultures in relation to their own or original culture. In terms of Berry's (1999) fourfold theory of intercultural relations in plural societies, some students in the study reported here had a strong psychological driving desire to maintain their own cultural identity and behaviours, and a relatively weak compelling desire to participate with those outside of their own culture. For some students, these compulsions, led to what Berry (1999) describes as a *separation strategy*. A separation strategy limited students' explorations of the new world around them and, significantly for this study, deprived them of leveraging the blended approach to learning. For some students their desire to maintain their own cultural values and behaviours, or to isolate themselves from those of the host country, led them not to participate collaboratively in shared learning situations where the negotiation of ideas was valued in accordance with the principles of university learning within the Australian context. For others, their lack of previous intercultural exposure produced feelings of frustration and stress, making it difficult to cope with the new learning environment. In contrast, those students who espoused a desire to integrate with others collaboratively and who exhibited behaviours of cultural acceptance were very well positioned to make gains from the blended learning approach through guided online and face-to-face interactions with their peers and teachers. With reference to intercultural relation issues of cultural sensitivity and cultural awareness, some of the student participants in this study were critical of the lack of cultural sensitivity by some of their fellow students and the marked disinterest in understanding and accepting others' cultures and values.

Perceptions of the multicultural environment

The literature on international students also documents issues due to discrimination experienced by international students, as well as issues arising due to English difficulties and lack of networking. The findings of this study are contrary to some of the dominant messages in the published literature and can be seen as supporting a recent move among some authors to challenge these messages. This study found some students were outspoken in their perceptions of the host country as a safe and egalitarian society where their voices and opinions were valued, heard and regarded, in contrast to the constraints and lesser freedom of speech they had in their native countries. This finding contrasts with the concerns of some Western commentators (e.g., Poyrazli & Grahame, 2007; Wadsworth, Hecht, & Jung, 2008) who have written about the stressful atmosphere international students may have to overcome while undertaking studies because of issues rooted in discrimination and the devaluing of their voices and opinions. Both Poyrazli and Grahame (2007) and Wadsworth et al. (2008) report discrimination experienced by international students. Both of these studies were conducted in the United States and the different national context may explain the contrasting results between the findings of this study and those reported elsewhere. With reference to undervaluing their voices and opinions, reporting on an Australian study of international students' experiences, Ryan and Viete (2009) argue that these students 'want to learn about more than just the content of their course; they want to grow and be valued' (p. 308). In their view, failure to recognise this 'can result in feelings of disengagement and a sense that their own knowledge and experiences are undervalued' (p. 303). This study found that most international student participants emphasised the egalitarian nature of the host country and saw the multicultural context as a positive one.

In contrast to the findings from previous research, in this study there were no major language issues affecting students' learning. In fact, these findings are in contention with the stereotypes held by many Western academics teaching international students that consider poor English as one of the most influential factors affecting international students' learning. In assessing international students' learning abilities, research suggests that there are more influential factors than language to be considered (Ryan & Viete, 2009). For example, there is evidence that academic problems experienced by Asian students in Australian universities may be linked, not to language problems, but to their cognitive architecture (Sweller, Van Merriënboer, & Paas, 1998) that enables them to think and learn differently; and to the way they approach knowledge and authority, which is culturally determined. This perspective is supported by a more recent study of international students (Ryan & Viete, 2009), claiming that the stereotyped misconceptions 'confuse proficiency in English with students' ability to think and know' (p. 304).

This study also identified an issue which is not documented in the existing literature on international students and is possibly specific to areas of study such as computing and business where postgraduate studies in particular often seek to make use of real-life contexts to support students' project work. The findings of this study reveal the difficulties faced by some students when participating in workplace projects in Australian settings as a result of their lack of networking and familiarity with communication protocols in a society new to them. Upon arrival to the host country, international students have to start building from scratch solid and trusting relationships with fellow students and people living around them. It is also in their interest to develop an understanding of the different aspects of conducting business and professional activities in the host country. This is particularly the case when course curricula require them to interact with the business or wider community as was seen in this study and as is common for postgraduate computing degrees.

In conclusion, the array of international students' perceptions of the multicultural aspect of a new environment is wide and diverse; with those perceptions influencing the ways students learn by affecting their interactions with others, with their teachers and with the course content and learning activities. These phenomena, mostly already documented in the literature on international students, have quite particular implications for learning because, on the one hand, they can lead to students' failure to engage fully in the learning activities commonly supported by a blended learning environment (e.g., because of their *separation strategy*), and, on the other hand, blended approaches can potentially be used to ameliorate the situation.

References

Arenas, E. (2012). *Blended learning in a higher education multicultural environment* (Doctoral dissertation). Deakin University, Australia.

Ballard, B., & Clanchy, J. (1997). Teaching international students: A brief guide for lecturers and supervisors. Canberra, Australia: IDP Education Australia.

Benzie, H. J. (2010). Graduating as a native speaker: International students and English language proficiency in higher education. *Higher Education Research & Development, 29*(4), 447–459. doi:10.1080/07294361003598824

Berry, J. W. (1999). Intercultural relations in plural societies. *Canadian Psychology/Psychologie Canadienne, 40*(1), 12–21.

Campbell, J. (1993). *The hero with a thousand faces.* London, England: Fontana.

Chataway, C. J., & Berry, J. W. (1989). Acculturation experiences, appraisal, coping, and adaptation: A comparison of Hong Kong Chinese, French, and English students in Canada. *Canadian Journal of Behavioural Science/Revue Canadienne Des Sciences Du Comportement, 21*(3), 295–309.

Dunne, C. (2011). Developing an intercultural curriculum within the context of the internationalisation of higher education: terminology, typologies and power. *Higher Education Research & Development, 30*(5), 609–622. doi:10.1080/07294360.2011.598451

Ellis-Bosold, C., & Thornton-Orr, D. (2013). A needs assessment: A study of perceived need for student health services by Chinese international students. *College Student Journal, 47*(1), 155–168.

Hofstede, G. H. (2005). *Cultures and organizations software of the mind.* New York, NY: McGraw-Hill.

Kember, D. (2000). Misconceptions about the learning approaches, motivation and study practices of Asian students. *Higher Education, 40,* 99–121.

Michaildis, M. (1996). *A study of factors that contribute to stress within international students (acculturation).* (Doctoral dissertation). University of Lowell, Massachusetts.

Paltridge, T., Mayson, S., & Schapper, J. (2012). Covering the gap: Social inclusion, international students and the role of local government. *Australian Universities' Review, 54*(2), 29–39.

Pascale, E. L. (2006). *A qualitative study of the adjustment process of international students at one private New England University* (Unpublished doctoral dissertation). Capella University, Minneapolis, Minnesota.

Poyrazli, S., & Grahame, K. M. (2007). Barriers to adjustment: Needs of international students within a semi-urban campus community. *Journal of Instructional Psychology, 34*(1), 28–45.

Rajapaksa, S., & Dundes, L. (2002). It's a long way home: International students adjustment to living in the United States. *Journal of College Student Retention: Research, Theory and Practice, 4*(1), 15–28.

Rienties, B., Beausaert, S., Grohnert, T., Niemantsverdriet, S., & Kommers, P. (2012). Understanding academic performance of international students: the role of ethnicity, academic and social integration. *Higher Education, 63*(6), 685–700. doi:10.1007/s10734-011-9468-1

Roberts, P., & Dunworth, K. (2012). Staff and student perceptions of support services for international students in higher education: A case study. *Journal of Higher Education Policy and Management, 34*(5), 517–528.

Ryan, J., & Viete, R. (2009). Respectful interactions: Learning with international students in the English-speaking academy. *Teaching in Higher Education, 14*(3), 303–314. doi:10.1080/13562510902898866

Stafford, T. H., Marion, P. B., & Salter, M. L. (1978). *Relationships between adjustment of international students and their expressed need for special programs and services at a U.S. university: Research and implications.* Presented at the Annual Meeting of the American College Personnel Association, Denver: ERIC Clearinghouse microfiches.

Stroebe, M., van Vliet, T., Hewstone, M., & Willis, H. (2002). Homesickness among students in two cultures: Antecedents and consequences. *British Journal Of Psychology, 93*(2), 147–168.

Sweller, J., Van Merriënboer, J., & Paas, F. (1998). Cognitive architecture and instructional design. *Educational Psychology Review, 10*, 251–296. doi:10.1023/A:1022193728205

Trahar, S., & Hyland, F. (2011). Experiences and perceptions of internationalisation in higher education in the UK. *Higher Education Research & Development, 30*(5), 623–633. doi:10.1080/07294360.2011.598452

Wadsworth, B. C., Hecht, M. L., & Jung, E. (2008). The role of identity gaps, discrimination, and acculturation in international students' educational satisfaction in American classrooms. *Communication Education, 57*(1), 64. doi:10.1080/03634520701668407

Yang, R. P.-J., & Noels, K. A. (2013). The possible selves of international students and their cross-cultural adjustment in Canada. *International Journal of Psychology, 48*(3), 316–323. doi:10.1080/00207594.2012.660161

Chapter 4

International Graduates' Endeavours for Work in Australia: Experiences of International Graduates of Accounting Transitioning into the Australian Labour Market

Ruth Arber and Mark Rahimi

Introduction

Australia's economy in the 21st century is distinguished by broad economic diversification, markedly the spread of skilled services including *education, financial services, scientific research and technological innovation, infrastructure management, energy transmission and many others* (Schedvin, 2008, p. 454). This has led to increasing demand for qualified accountants. With 168,200 employed accountants in May 2012, accountancy is now a large employing profession in Australia (DEEWR, 2012d). A review of recent documents reveals that concerns about international students' outcomes have increased in recent years. University programs in business, management and accounting are highly popular with international students studying at Australian universities, growing from 15,657 international student commencements in 2002 to 32,592 commencements in 2011.

The majority of students in accounting courses are from non-English-speaking countries. Employability of international graduates centres on the general criteria set by the government for international accounting graduates to remain and work in Australia. Birrell and Rapson (2005) note that the 'accounting profession is at the centre of changes in the nexus between immigration regulations, the education of overseas students in Australia and subsequent entry into the accounting workforce in Australia' (p. 18). Apart from attaining an accredited Australian qualification, international graduates face two intertwined issues: (a) obtaining permanent visa status, and (b) obtaining sufficient English language test (IELTS) results[1].

A 2005 study of international graduate employability by Birrell and Rapson analysed data collected by the Australian Bureau of Statistics (ABS) in 2001, and concluded that overseas qualified and trained graduates:

> from the main-English-speaking countries do very well in obtaining professional level work in accounting or in managerial positions. By contrast, those with similar qualifications who come from non-English-speaking countries have struggled to secure professional level work in accounting. However, persons trained in accounting in Australia from non-English-speaking countries do better than their overseas-trained counterparts from the same countries (Birrell & Rapson, 2005, p. II).

A successful transition of graduates to the labour market is the point where graduates' attributes and credentials interconnect with educational and socio-economic contexts (Cappelletto, 2010). In this paper, the analysis is conducted at an individual level, examining the structural and non-structural challenges facing international graduates and the ways they seek to overcome those challenges.

Current demand for accounting graduates

Demand for accountants is driven by multiple groups of employers in *professional service firms, corporations, non-profit organisations and the government sector*. The Department of Education, Employment and Workplace Relations (DEEWR) embarked on research into the accountant labour market in 2011 and 2012 (DEEWR, 2012e). No shortage of accountants was reported in Victoria or New South Wales. Employers in both states faced little difficulty in recruiting suitable candidates. Overall, 88% of vacancies in Victoria and 91% of vacancies in New South Wales were filled within the survey period. The most frequently cited reasons for the unsuitability of applicants in Victoria were reported as: 'applicants' level of experience', 'poor communication skills (in particular their fluency in English)', or 'lack of suitable "soft skills" and corporate fit'. Some applicants did not have working rights in Australia (DEEWR, 2012b, 2012d).

Demand for accountants was different in the other states. For example, according to the DEEWR (2012a, 2012c), there was a shortage of accountants in Queensland. Employers' main reason for rejecting applicants was lack of work experience in some fields, such as mining and agriculture. Some other employers demanded specialist commercial or tax knowledge. Key factors affecting demand for accountants include the general conditions of local and global markets, and changes in national legislation, such as the carbon tax, minerals resources rent tax, and the superannuation reforms (DEEWR, 2012e).

Theoretical framework

Use of Bourdieu's thinking tools

Engaging Bourdieu's work to the theoretical and methodological tools used to link the 'macro processes' or 'structuring structures' provides the framework to mediate the collected data to the micro-events that describe the *situatedness* of everyday life (Blackmore, 2010; Bourdieu & Wacquant, 1992; Maton, 2008). Bourdieu's concepts of *field* is useful as a means to depict the higher education sector, and accounting discipline as a subfield of the higher education sector. A field 'consists of a set of objective, historical relations between positions anchored in certain forms of power (or *capital*)'. The transition of international accounting graduates to professional practice is a shift of individual graduates moving from the field of higher education to the field of professional accounting. In Bourdieu's theory of field, fields are 'as antagonistic, as sites of struggle' among different agents (Thomson, 2008, p. 79). From this perspective, recruitment is seen as an ongoing game that commences at the entering gate of the professional field of accounting. According to Bourdieu, the game in the field is competitive, and players seek their own strategies to play in the field. International graduates who join the game have to learn and follow the rules of the game in order to get the position they want and add to their benefits (Bourdieu, 2005). Bourdieu's notion that the idea of experience can be understood in relational terms with the notion of agency (McNay, 1999) concerns both the acknowledgement of individual experience and the possibility of tracing its connection with social structures that are in tension and in conflict. It explores the ways agents carry out activities normalised as practices and the ways these practices are connected with agents as bodily corporations of social history or *habitus*. It considers habitus in relation to social fields; the environment or habitat within which agent's habitus is expressed as practice (Rawolle & Lingard, 2008). Habitus is understood in relation to social fields; the environment or habitat within which agent's habitus is expressed as practice. Habitus consists of a set of historical relations 'deposited' 'within individual bodies in the form of mental and corporeal schemata of perception, appreciation, and action' (Bourdieu & Wacquant, 1992, p. 16). Further, these historical relations

> tend to guarantee the 'correctness' of practices and their constancy over time, more reliably than all formal rules and explicit norms … For Bourdieu, various forms of capital are embodied in an individual's *habitus*, and the *habitus* is intimately related to an individual's practice; which is 'forever incomplete, immeasurable and always in a state of becoming. (Bourdieu & Nice, 1992, p. 54).

This chapter explores the ways agents carry out activities normalised as practices and the ways these practices are connected with agents as bodily corporations of social history or habitus.

Language and culture

Culture describes the practices and ideas that are made routine in everyday lives; the nexus between everyday objects and events, their embodiment within everyday behaviours and practices, and their manifestation within historically defined social world (Bauman, 2013). Intricately bound with language, the notion of culture contains within it our ways of being and understanding the world frame and the socially accepted principles that define identities and actions within and across contexts. In this respect, language ('concerned with the production and exchange of meaning') and culture ('concerned with the giving and taking of meaning between members of a group') are intertwined (Hall, 1997, p. 131). Language describes the ways that we understand and speak about the social world in which 'we' act and in which 'meaning is produced and exchanged', even as it is the principle means through which we conduct our everyday lives (Hall, 1997, p. 2). The culture of day-to-day practices is negotiated through the commonalities that accrue from shared history and traditions. The world and its history (and the ways that people are positioned, belong, and share in that history) and the implications of a shared past for the present and future are the foundations for and construct the product: culture (Kramsch, 1998, p. 7).

Culture, like language, is reflexive. It simultaneously takes its meaning from its context even as it constructs the very context of what it is to 'mean and be in the first place' (Gee & Green, 1998, p. 127). In Bourdieu's terms, the everyday ideas and practices that make up the habitus[2] of the everyday practice are mediated by the rules and structure of institutions and negotiated within the larger fields of social, economic, and cultural relations. Bourdieu's notion of 'symbolic domination' refers to the ability of certain social groups to maintain control over others by establishing their view of reality and their cultural practices as the most valued and, perhaps more importantly, as 'the norm' (Bourdieu, 2007).

Performance and belonging

In a social world mapped out within the quagmire of unequally empowered and competing discourses, language and culture become the site and subject of the different ways people can behave, are understood, and are included within a society. The character of voice and the bodily performance of language — like physical characteristics such as skin colour — mark who we are and what we can become (Arber, 2012; Rizvi, 2011). The social construction of that-which-we-are-called-to-be is far from merely superficial. Subjectivity is in a sense a 'performance' in which a self-conscious performer chooses an act, which is 'performed'. Power operates through the creation of different subject identities in ways that strengthen and legitimise them through countless acts of reiteration and performance that seek 'to introduce a reality rather than [support] an existing one' (Youdell, 2006, drawing from Foucault and Butler). The identification of individuals and their categorisation as belonging to a group needs to be understood as an 'achievement' that takes place as a matter of 'human activity ... shaped and reinterpreted as a kind of cultural activity conducted together with one's partners and neighbors and negotiated within the various of historical and social contexts' (Bekerman & Geisen, 2011, p. 7)

Space and subject

Feminist theories acknowledge the strength of Bourdieu's notions as a way to develop and explore a metaphoric model of space in which human beings embody and carry with them different volumes and compositions of capital (Adkins & Skeggs, 2004, p. 210). Noting that Bourdieu's model has been useful as a way of moving beyond structuralist models of class theory and the discourse and linguistic turn attributed to much socio-cultural theory, they warn against simplistic comparisons between field and habitus and a deepening of Bourdieu's theories analysis, particularly in relation to the exploration of gender and to change (Atkins & Skeggs, 2004).

The subject of research is engaged within actions negotiated within macro-contextual structural and normative conditions of power that are not necessarily consciously known. The subject is not just engaged in the world but is *in* the world (Atkins & Skegs, 2004, p. 10). The analysis of the subject is understood phonologically and in relation to their structural position but more particularly as a lived relation negotiated within social mores that are conflictual, in tension and changing. This chapter explores statistics emergent within the research and analyses them in terms of the relationship between field and habitus. It analyses case studies about international student work experiences in relation to the transformative and changed relationships that underpin their different cross-cultural and professional trajectories.

With this in mind we would like to extend this analysis by rethinking the characteristics of crucial notions implicated within the analysis: language and culture and identity as it is constructed, gendered and raced in globally interconnected local contexts that are cross-cultural, reproductive and transformative.

Strategies

Strategy as a particular direction of practice that is dependent on habitus has conceptual implications at both individual and institutional levels in this research. It describes the privileged knowledges and capitals that form 'a common sense or orthodoxy' within the field (Blackmore, 2010, p. 102). Portraits of graduates with non-English-speaking backgrounds reveal that they seek to become competitive in a game in which cultural and language capital is a critical asset. Government has a dominant role in setting the rules of the game and interfering in the game through policy. Employability in any discourse is a nexus of individual, educational and socio-economic contexts. International graduates seeking to transition from the field of higher education to the professional field of accounting have to learn rules of the game for getting recruited and make their efforts in compliance with those rules.

Research method and aim

This study considers the perspectives of final year international accounting students in two universities over a three-year period. Longitudinal qualitative data from international students and graduates were collected in the final semester of their study and six months after the expected date of graduation. Nineteen graduates out of a total of 56 international accounting students — who participated in the first interviews — accepted invitations for a second interview. After a series of preliminary focus group, 30 questions were prepared and used in a structured interview format in the first series of interviews with international students. A semi-structured interview format was applied for the second and the third series of interviews. The final series of interviews were scheduled to allow time for graduates to job hunt. Follow-up interviews with 12 volunteer graduates, all from China, were conducted in a semi-structured format within a year after the second interviews. These interviews included follow-up phone interviews.

Data obtained from the interviews at three phases provided the demographic information and participating students' views and narratives. It also included participants' experiences in studying and living in their home country and in Australia, their socio-cultural adaptation experiences in Australia, work experiences (if any), level of English language competency, their short-term and long-term professional goals, and their views on immigration.

The aim was to examine the ways how international students endeavour to overcome the structural and non-structural challenges that mediate the ways students seek to reach their goals. Getting longitudinal data was essential for study aims.

Longitudinal analysis

Data from participants who attended all three phases of data collection were analysed in terms of their final destination and revealed the following results:

- One graduate returned home and was recruited into an insurance company within four months. Being unable to find a relevant job in Australia and her desire to join her parents were her main reasons for leaving Australia.
- Four graduates got irrelevant jobs in: catering, supermarket, a $2 shop and real estate. They were on temporary resident (TR) visas or bridging visas (BV) for temporary residence at the time of their final interviews.
- Two graduates started a professional year program after graduation. They aimed getting extra points via the program to become eligible to apply for a permanent resident (PR) visa.
- Two graduates ended up working full-time at two of the Big Four[3] companies. They got PR visas prior to recruitment.
- One graduate was recruited by a Chinese-owned tax agency. He had obtained his PR visa before applying for this position.
- One graduate left accounting to establish a language training centre for preparing international students for IELTS exams.
- One graduate started a CPA program to get accreditation. He had obtained his PR visa before starting his program.

The five graduates who got PR visas had applied for their visas through a General Skilled Migration scheme. None of the graduates in the cohort were sponsored for their visas by recruiting companies. No-one got the high score of 8 in the IELTS.

Problematising the data

An analysis of the longitudinal data suggested that few respondents secured full-time positions in their professional field at the end of their university programs. The meaning that people give to their everyday experience and actions (Lincoln & Denzin, 1998), and the ways that the contingency of these everyday activities are 'problematised' as they are embodied and negotiated within the complex notional and systemic processes and practices that frame their everyday context needs to be explored (Arber, 2012). The following portraits of two applicants reveal the structural and non-structural challenges the international graduates faced, how they negotiated the systemic and socio-cultural terms and conditions that underpin entry into the Australian job market, and the consequences of this for the ways in which students overcame those challenges to achieve employment.

Case Study 1: Ting

At her first interview, Ting — a female student from China in an Australian university — has few resources to support her decision to get a TR visa and find a job in her area of expertise. She understands that to acquire a job in Australia requires acquiring cultural and linguistic resources related to communication and cultural differences; overcoming the structural challenges posed by the *visa problem* and the IELTS test; and overcoming employers' preference for local people: *I don't think most of them are interviewing international students.*

Despite the academic, cultural and linguistic challenges that Ting outlines, she sees the possibility of getting work as being about motivation, commitment and optimism. She has a part-time job at a Chinese restaurant and her language skills have improved. However, most of her friends are Chinese, she continues to speak mostly in Chinese and she has no non-Chinese friends. Most particularly, she does not believe she has the academic and professional competencies required to have a job:

> Opportunities in Australia? ... I don't see any opportunities at all ... I am not good at study ... Not a well-organised person.

By the second interview Ting has graduated, but is unable to find work. She understands the effort required to obtain work, but has little understanding of what she must do to reach her aspirations:

> You have to put in a bit of effort finding a job ... you can't just give up halfway ... I think I am not so good on that

She also finds herself unable to take on the veneer of someone who belongs:

> I go to those societies and communities, I will get a better friends group. It will help me to get close to many people and communicate better and understand Australia. To be *a fake local* ... It's an expression, to be like. To be like.

Ting's repetition of 'to be like' emphasises her concern that she must take on the attributes of being a local. The term *local* is ambiguous. She sees becoming local as erasing all earlier cultural knowledge and understanding:

> to forget who you are and where you are from ...

and immersing herself within an Australian language culture:

to first just need to be Australian ... Language always and forget where you are from.

By the time of the third interview, Ting is optimistic but still does not have a job. She has found a professional internship at a local company and has just returned from working in a Chinese bank. Her professional year in Australia has been useful. However, she still does not feel that she belongs in Australia. She has no real networks and no local friends.

Ting easily overcomes a major structural challenge facing other of the students: she already has PR. But she finds it difficult to overcome structural barriers that prevent her employment. She came to Australia with few academic resources and with little knowledge of the job-seeking process. She passes her qualifications but her grades are poor and her English skills remain weak. She is unable to gain Australian professional skills and finds the university unhelpful in gaining this experience.

A second level of analysis suggests that Ting's difficulties are underpinned by the difficulties she has accessing the knowledge and behaviours required to become a practising accountant in Australia. Her understanding that the challenge lies in her ability to gain the embodied and meaningful, as well as the superficial characteristics that underpin successful job seeking, is summarised in her insight that she needs *to be like, to be a fake local*. However she has little idea and few strategies to know what she needs to do to help her to take up the notional and performative skills and knowledge she requires to behave in this way.

Case Study 2: Juan

Despite that the majority of respondents being female, of the three students who got a job only two students got a job with the Big Four: one male and one female. Juan, a Chinese female student undertook the first years of an English major in a Chinese university before dropping out because she was dissatisfied with her achievements. Her decision to study commerce and finance in an Australian university was made quickly:

> [I] went to an education exhibition and it said you have opportunities to study abroad. So I thought maybe I should open some other options for myself to do what I want to do. I'm really interested in commerce in general and also finance.

Her prior study proved useful allowing her to achieve a 6.5 IELTS on her arrival in Australia and providing a firm base for her achievement of three 8s (listening, speaking and reading) and one 6 (writing) in the exam.

Her goal direction and the strategies she required to achieve those goals became more focused. In her first interview, Juan defined her long-term goal as:

> To be a business consultant ... in terms of short-term goal, I just want to get involved in ... either accounting or finance department in a company and really gain some understanding.

Juan was well aware of the skills and knowledge she required to achieve this goal and what might help her develop these. By the time of the first interview, Juan felt that her language and communication skills were sufficiently strong to allow her to make friends and to belong. She practised her English with her landlady and she did not try to stick to an all-Chinese community; she tried to mingle with people from everywhere — from all over the world, and she practised English ... in lectures and tutorials — every single possible opportunity you have to really practice.

The university provided Juan with basic skills and knowledge she required to undertake her career, as well as more generalised leadership and teamwork skills:

> The university provided me with the opportunity to learn the knowledge, the degree ... and also in terms of communication skills it gives you a chance to work with your peers ... to work effectively in a team

Juan's ability to cross cultural and linguistic barriers helped her further her skills, knowledge and behaviour. Juan joined the choir where she not only met a lot of friends but she was actively involved in the committee:

> I was social director. So that gave me a chance to practise my leadership skills as well.

Besides this work, Juan has set out a business plan with some other students from the university. She aimed at trying to make the whole international students' experience in Australia much more comfortable and much more interesting.

Moreover, by the first interview Juan had a part-time job as an assistant accountant at the university. The work gave Juan skills beyond those required by the university:

it really gives you some hands-on experience of the thing you have been studying for the past three years …

She got the job through a university job database tailored to university students:

they were updating my résumé there, and … they said there's some positions available on campus,… I went to the interview with the boss and then I just got the job the day after

The structural impediments presented by the changes to the Government policy have made it difficult to plan ahead:

before I came here the immigration policy was quite relaxed … I think after I complete my accounting degree I'd … just get my permanent residency straight after. And you know, one year after getting into your degree you find out, oh, I have to take IELTS, that's fine — but two years after the exam, you find out they changed the immigration policy again. So it's just really not much certainty

A second difficulty is the different notions and behaviours valued by Australian and Chinese societies:

if I go back to China there will be … reverse culture shock. You don't fit into society anymore because you're away for so long. And the way they do things you don't understand anymore

Adapting to Australian cultural norms has made it difficult to return to China in profound ways. It is as if adapting to Australian cultural norms has changed her in ways that leave her unable to behave or understand as Chinese.

By the time of the second interview Juan had worked in Beijing over the summer at a financial credit rating company. In China her international experience and her qualifications were an advantage. Besides this, Juan has found another job:

I was hoping to get into somewhere that would utilise my accounting skills … but in my current position I am basically a consultant, it's more IT sort of thing.

The work provided her with new and useful skills:

Basically it's taxman accounting software, which I had to do training for all the kinds and teach them how to use the software. The training is definitely one of the biggest parts of my job, I track finance on how to use the software [for] whole classes of 15 or 20 attendees …

Most importantly, Juan now has PR:

> Well, I was lucky because I was applying to the new rules... The pain for it was really just getting the extra stuff done, the IELTS test, I was OK for everything else, but for writing I tried a few times

Juan has a strong sense of the strategies needed to get work in Australia:

> Back in China ... students don't have to stretch out to actively be searching for work ... but in Australia ... you should look one year early, keep on working, keep on, you know, searching, keep on applying for jobs and with your work experience, that's important as your lectures

Juan's sense of belonging within the Australian community is somewhat different to Ting's. Juan describes her new workplace and the ways in which she fits into that community:

> My team is quite multinational, we don't have one single Australian, Australian, Australian. They are all ... Australian born, but they have Greek background, or Lebanese background, Chinese background, all different, Italian background, so it's quite mixed. Everybody brings something new to the team ... everybody's different

The final hurdle, that of becoming a fake local, is not one faced by Juan. The social identity to which Juan must take on is something other than Australian, Australian, Australian but rather a polyglot of those who are different. It is mixed and about bringing something new. Asked whether she faces discrimination within the workplace, her response is nothing really because everybody's different.

By the third interview Juan has a job with one of the Big Four. The route she took to obtain the job reflects how the strategies she put in place have come together:

> It was quite informal, when I was at [first company], I used my Saturdays and Sundays just really treating myself as if I was working [on a projected for this company]. It really impressed them ... We had a chat, and I said, 'I'm pretty interested in joining [this company] but unfortunately when I graduated I couldn't get into the graduate program because of my resident status', so she said, 'Oh, such a shame. What about we start from here?' ... We just had a chat and had an informal interview with the partner and that was pretty much it.

Juan understands the barriers to employment:

> It's probably just lacking that stepping stone, because for me, I luckily got into [first company] and they didn't mind that I was on a temporary visa and they took me in ... but not everybody will have this luck. They [can't] get into the graduate program because of the visa status, they [can't] get into the vocational program, the cadetship, when they were in high school, so when it comes to graduation time it's quite daunting. They ... have to compete with

people who started with [this company] ... from as early as cadetship. Added to all that is your English skills, your communication skills and the cultural barriers, but I think the biggest one is ... the lack of work experience.

The hurdle of performing as a local is one which Juan understands she avoids. Once again the workplace is a multicultural one.

Juan is the only woman to find a job — one of only three of the 12 students to find work at the time of the third interview in their field — and only one of two with the Big Four. Juan's English studies in China gave her a strong foundation in English language and culture. Despite her lack of experience in finance and accounting, she sets in place strategies to gain the skills and knowledge she requires to get a job: team building, leadership skills, and so on. The university provides good mechanisms to help students find work and Juan is strategic in accessing these. Her ability to bring together skills and knowledge allows her to reach her job aspirations. However, Juan never tries to belong within the local Australian community. Her friends within the university are international and her employment within an international institution continued her integration into a place where everyone is international.

Analysis

A first analysis of the data makes strong links between the graduating student habitus, the social resources they bring to the field and their strategies to develop them and the social space defined by the higher education and accountancy field. Ting comes to Australia with no tertiary education, little notion of the accountancy field in Australia or China and poor English skills. Despite her hard work, she has little understanding of the academic and professional resources required or the strategies she needs to develop them. She is slow to put in place strategies that would help her develop her sense of social belonging. Juan brings stronger resources to Australia to support her job application search. Juan does not have experience in business or accountancy, but she comes to Australia with a knowledge of the fields and the demands of the task. Her tertiary qualifications in English help her gain the communication skills to belong socially, academically and, by the time of the first interview, professionally.

The knowledge of the demands of the task and the strategies to obtain them can be further understood in relation to the academic and professional provision provided by the different universities. Although happy with her academic qualifications for her university work, Ting finds her university unhelpful in her bid to get professional experience or to gain professional entrance skills and knowledge. Juan has easy access to the university structures and finds them helpful to her in three ways: the university literally helps her find work; the university helps provide the knowledge she requires for her bid; and her university brand adds symbolic value to her bid.

Reconceptualising language, identity and change

The exploration of the disjunct between habitus and field needs to be analysed more comprehensively. Ting describes how her move to gain a local identity requires the complete annihilation of her Chinese self:

> You first need to be Australian and then forget where you came from.

Even so, she believes she will never belong as local — she strives to become *a fake local.*

Juan is cognisant of the linguistic cultural and professional attributes she requires to find work and feels that she belongs. Nevertheless, the identity to which she belongs is multicultural:

> It's actually quite multicultural over here because people from different backgrounds, a lot of Asians here, a lot of Indians, Fijians; different really – not just myself, everybody's from different backgrounds so there's definitely no discrimination.

The different ways in which the students were able to access those understandings were criss-crossed by systemic understandings, particularly those related to race. The participants emphasised that they had not faced racial discrimination at the university or in their job application process. Nevertheless the matter of the interview described the ways in which these students were able to perform as *local* and as accountants.

The students' move to gain employment can be explored more comprehensively. The move to gain English and Australian language and cultural skills can be seen as having several aspects. The move to pass their IELTS and gain professional skills demanded that students become accomplished in understanding and reproducing the signs and structures that provide the symbolic work of Australian citizenship and the accountancy profession. Ting finds it difficult to get good scores in her academic assessments or in the IELTS tests. Juan's existing proficiency in English language vocabulary and grammar enables her to gain access to these areas far more easily.

Language expresses social reality. It describes the ways that people give meaning to their experiences. Despite passing her accountancy exams and improving her IELTS score, Ting's experiences do not provide her with those aspects of language and culture that would allow her to make decisions about the ways that things work and the information she requires to make them work.

Ting's difficulty extends beyond being unable to ascribe meaning to the notion of what it is to be an accountant in Australia. She finds it difficult to understand how to be that person. Language creates experience through language: *it embodies cultural reality*. The notion of embodiment concerns the ways in which the students were able to inhabit the characteristics of what it is to perform as an accountant and as one who belongs as Australian. The work of embodiment and performance is not understood as simply pedagogic (Bhabha, 1994) it is not something simply prescribed and learned. It required hard work and meta-cognition and implementing strategies, but the requirements were *to become an accountant* and *to be Australian*. Although Juan felt able to accomplish the skills required to become an accountant in Australia, she belonged to social groups where the social mores were understood as something other than the local. Juan understood her company as being *international* or *multicultural* and as a place where everyone was *different*.

It is Bourdieu's notion that the person accommodates the field as a process of adaption' that Atkins critiques. She argues that implicit within the process of change is the 'shift in the conditions of social reproduction itself' (Adkins & Skeggs, 2004).

Within the research, students move cross-culturally and at a time of transformation whereby:

> The very terms and contours of these processes have emerged as fundamentally transformed with, for example, social reproduction understood as centrally concerned with shifting forms of female embodiment, social change as concerning those very shifting conditions of social reproduction and processes of individualisation as involving complex new modes of gendered and classed differentiation and division (Adkins & Skeggs, 2004, p. 100).

The students' shift from China to Australia is a move that reflects the ways that selves move from one country to another at a time when the structural and normative terms and conditions of both countries are in flux. Hall's (1997) argument that individuals negotiate their notion of and performance of identity within the normative and structural terms and conditions of local contexts which are unequally empowered in tension and changing, becomes increasingly important as local contexts are globally interconnected. The flows of communication, people, finances, and ideas that underpin global transformation impact on already and always differentiated cultures differently (Appadurai, 2000).

Conclusion

Students come to Australia with notions of professional identity that are both differentiated and in tune with one another. The notion of accountancy as a career in both countries and its place as a university discipline within Australian and Chinese universities is a shared one, even as elements of its process are evidenced differently. The overlay of 'international corporates' which evidence cultural and normative conditions adds a new overlay to these understandings. A simple interrelation between field and habitus explains — but does not properly explore — the trends that explain the data. Subjects never fully occupy or identify with norms. There is '[a]mbivalence at the heart' of identity work (Adkins & Skeggs, 2004):

> Bhabha's work of mimicry ... rejects the view of a simple identification with and adaption to the colonial subject and colonial power ... Bhabha suggests that the practice is far more ambivalent ... raising the spectre that this seeming identification is indeed a parody. (p. 207)

Ting broaches this when she speaks of her need to become a fake local, describing a veneer of being somewhat other. Juan understands and struggles to articulate what is required to become part of the professional sphere, to be what is required: she explains she 'is not an Australian Australian Australian'. Even as she describes the complete disembodiment of her Chinese self, she is alluding to the matter of its absurdity. The matter is both about what is enabled and what is chosen; how Juan is identified and with what she wants to identify. Adkins's second point 'is that Subjects never fully occupy or identify with norms'. The incongruence and ambivalences at the heart of identity work (Adkins & Skeggs, 2004) provide important clues to the ways that international students find employment in Australia.

Acknowledgements

This study draws from an Australian Research Council and IDP Education Pty Ltd funded project "Investigating stakeholder responses to changing skilled migration policies for Australian international graduates" undertaken by Jill Blackmore, Lesley Farrell, Ruth Arber, Marcia Devlin, Cate Gribble and Mark Rahimi.

Endnotes

1. The International English Language Testing System (IELTS) is an international standardised test of English language proficiency for non-English Language Speakers testing listening, reading, speaking and listening skills. Entry into many university programs and into many professional organisations require scores higher than 6.
2. Habitus refers to the commonsense and shared ways of understanding and behaving developed within the everyday conditions of institutional life (Bourdieu, 2005).

3. The Big Four are the four largest international professional services and accountancy networks. They are KPMG, Deloitte Touche Tohmatsu, PricewaterhouseCoopers and Ernst & Young.

References

Adkins, L., & Skeggs, B. (2004). *Feminism after Bourdieu*. Oxford, England: Blackwell.

Appadurai, A. (2000). Grassroots globalization and the research imagination. *Public culture, 12*(1), 1–19.

Arber, R. (2012). *Encountering an-other:* The *culture of curriculum and inclusive pedagogies international handbook of migration, minorities and education* (pp. 461–477). Dordrecht, the Netherlands: Springer.

Bauman, Z. (2013). *In search of politics*. Cambridge, MA: Polity Press.

Bekerman, Z., & Geisen, T. (2011). *International handbook of migration, minorities and education: Understanding cultural and social differences in processes of learning*. Dordrecht, the Netherlands: Springer.

Bhabha, H. K. (1994). *The location of culture*. Abingdon, England: Psychology Press.

Birrell, B., & Rapson, V. (2005). *Migration and the accounting profession in Australia*. Melbourne: CPA Australia.

Blackmore, J. (2010). Research assessment: A calculative technology governing quality, accountability and equity. In J. A. Blackmore, M. Brennan & L. D. Zipin (Eds.), *Re-positioning university governance and academic work* (pp. 67-83). Rotterdam, the Netherlands: Sense.

Bourdieu, P. (2005). *The social structures of the economy*. Cambridge, MA: Polity Press

Bourdieu, P., & Nice, R. (1992). *Le sens pratique*. Cambridge, MA: Polity Press.

Bourdieu, P., & Wacquant, L. J. D. (1992). *An invitation to reflexive sociology*. Chicago, IL: University of Chicago Press.

Cappelletto, G. (2010). *Challenges facing accounting education in Australia*. AFAA: A Joint Accounting Bodies and AFAANZ Commissioned Report.

DEEWR. (2012a). *ANZSCO 2211 Accountant*. Western Australia, Department of Education, Employment and Workplace Relations. Labour Economics Office, Western Australia.

DEEWR. (2012b). *ANZSCO 2211 Accountants*. NSW, Department of Education, Employment and Workplace Relations, Labour Economics Office, New South Wales.

DEEWR. (2012c). *ANZSCO 2211 Accountants*. Queensland Department of Education, Employment and Workplace Relations — Labour Economics Office, Queensland.

DEEWR. (2012d). *ANZSCO 2211 Accountants*. Victoria, Department of Education, Employment and Workplace Relations, Labour Economics Office, Victoria.

DEEWR. (2012e). *Labour market research — Accountants 2011–2012*. Australia Department of Education, Employment and Workplace Relations, Labour Market Research and Analysis Branch.

Gee, J. P., & Green, J. L. (1998). Discourse analysis, learning, and social practice: A methodological study. *Review of Research in Education*, 119–169.

Hall, S. (1997). *Representation: Cultural representations and signifying practices (Vol. 2)*. London, England: Sage.

Kramsch, C. (1998). *Language and culture (Vol. 3)*. Oxford, England: Oxford University Press.

Lincoln, Y. S., & Denzin, N. K. (1998). *The landscape of qualitative research: Theories and issues*. London, England: Sage.

Maton, K. (2008). Habitus. In M. Grenfell (Ed.), *Pierre Bourdieu: Key concepts* (pp. 49–66). London, England: Acumen.

McNay, L. (1999). Gender, habitus and the field Pierre Bourdieu and the limits of reflexivity. *Theory, Culture & Society, 16*(1), 95–117.

Rawolle, S., & Lingard, B. (2008). The sociology of Pierre Bourdieu and researching education policy. *Journal of Education Policy, 23*(6), 729–741.

Rizvi, F. (2011). Theorizing student mobility in an era of globalization. *Teachers and Teaching, 17*(6), 693–701.

Schedvin, B. (2008). Primary Phases of australian economic development in the twentieth century. *Australian Economic Review, 41*(4), 450–455. doi: 10.1111/j.1467-8462.2008.00520.x

Thomson, P. (2008). Field. In M. Grenfell (Ed.), *Pierre Bourdieu: Key concepts* (pp. 67–81). London, England: Acumen.

Youdell, D. (2006). *Impossible bodies, impossible selves: Exclusions and student subjectivities: Exclusions and student subjectivities (Vol. 3)*. Dordrecht, the Netherlands: Springer.

Chapter 5

The 'English Language Question' in Higher Education: Some Reflections on Issues and Strategy

Neil Murray

Introduction

The issue of English language competence has become, in recent years, increasingly prominent in the discourse of English-medium universities, particularly those located in Kachru's so-called 'inner-circle countries' (1985), where English is the native tongue. This is perhaps unsurprising given that higher education has developed into a global enterprise and that English continues to be the world's default lingua franca and thus proficiency in it regarded as a passport to social mobility. The fact is that education in an English-medium university located in an inner-circle country represents an opportunity to obtain a degree within a widely respected higher education system, and to have an educational and intercultural experience that can be life-changing in terms of the individual's personal development, the prestige associated with it, and the often significantly improved job prospects — and, by extension, quality of life — it promises in a world in which English language and intercultural skills are increasingly prized by employers.

The fact that universities see these factors as having created an opportunity to extend their international reach and reputations in an increasingly competitive marketplace, and to secure their financial health through the tuition fees overseas students bring with them, means that the international student body represents a seemingly ever-larger proportion of the total annual intake of students in higher education, particularly at postgraduate level. In 2013, the Organisation for Economic Co-operation and Development (OECD) cited 21.5% of tertiary enrolments in Australia, 15.3% in the United Kingdom (UK), 14.6% in New Zealand, 6.5% in Canada, and 3.5% in the United States (US).

These increases and the associated change to the student demographic of universities has raised a number of fundamental questions about standards of education, teaching and assessment practices, the curriculum and its delivery, English language gatekeeping and support mechanisms, and the nature of the overall student experience. What I seek to demonstrate in this chapter is that these questions have the issue of English language competence at their heart. Furthermore, as universities strive to address them, they almost inevitably find themselves confronting a tension between educational and ethical imperatives. The discussion is premised on a growing sense of concern within higher education over the English language proficiency of international students, a proportion of whom succeed in securing university places, only to struggle subsequently to meet the academic demands of their studies (Bretag, 2007; Murray, 2014). Critically, this lack of proficiency has the potential to undermine their academic and professional success, as well as the reputations of their institutions.

Regulation

The Australian government and higher education sector can legitimately claim to have been at the vanguard of efforts to engage with what I have, elsewhere, referred to as 'the English language question' (Murray, in press), though associated regulatory initiatives, professional discourse, the development of creative systems and procedures, and innovative and theoretically informed interventions in the teaching and learning process.

In terms of regulation, publication by the Department of Education Employment and Workplace Relations (DEEWR) in March 2009 of the *Good Practice Principles for English Language Proficiency for International Students in Australian Universities* (GPPs) was an important milestone, for it prompted Australian universities to review and improve their practices vis-à-vis English language. Broadly speaking, its 10 principles focused on issues concerning assessment, provision and the integrity of pathways into university. Coincidentally, in April of that same year, the UK's Quality Assurance Agency (QAA) published a report titled *Thematic Enquiries into Concerns about Academic Quality and Standards in Higher Education in England*, part of which drew attention to similar issues to those highlighted in the GPPs and similarly made a series of recommendations.

Under the direction of the then newly formed Tertiary Education Quality Standards Agency (TEQSA), the GPPs were later refined and 'rebranded' as standards in a 2012 document titled *English Language Standards for Higher Education* (ELSHE). The switch from 'principles' to 'standards' was significant in that it emphasised the fact, mooted in the GPPs, that universities would be expected to demonstrate, through institutional audits, that their practices were meeting those standards:

> The expectation of the project Steering Committee is that universities will consider the Principles as they would consider other guidelines on good

practice. As part of AUQA quality audits universities can expect to be asked about the way they have addressed the Principles, just as they are likely to be asked by AUQA auditors about their application of a range of other external reference documents for the university sector. (DEEWR, 2009, p. 2)

While, to date, the ELSHE have not been mandated, they and the GPPs have nonetheless served to galvanise the sector into reflecting on the often complex issues with which the remainder of this chapter is devoted and, where necessary, adopt measures to help ensure that students benefit maximally from their educational experience.

The tension between educational standards and business imperatives

The issue of how universities balance educational and business needs has perhaps been the most public face of the English language debate and, in many respects, the most controversial. There have been numerous references in the world's media to international students as 'cash cows' (e.g., BBC News, 2010; Narushima [*Sydney Morning Herald*, Australia], 2008), the implication being that universities are putting their own financial wellbeing ahead of students' educational wellbeing. Whether and to what extent this is true is open to debate; however, in a sector that is increasingly competitive and where funding pressures are increasingly making themselves felt, the attraction of high fee-paying students is undeniable. The income they generate helps pay for developments to institutional infrastructure that keep universities at the forefront of the sector and thereby generate further income through enrolments and research. Furthermore, as students graduate and return to their countries of origin, they disseminate the names of their graduating institutions and enhance their reputations as international universities that are moving with the times, in turn making them an attractive proposition for study and international research collaborations.

Despite business imperatives and the need to outperform their competitors, universities have a duty to find an appropriate balance between remaining financially healthy such that they are able not just to survive but to flourish, and acting in an ethical manner that guarantees the best educational experience for *all* their students. This includes ensuring that those students for whom English is not a first language have the language skills needed to meet the requirements of their degree programmes and successfully graduate having reached their full potential, while also ensuring that those students for whom English *is* their first language likewise have a rich educational experience that allows them also to reach their full potential. For this to happen, there can be no compromises made to the curriculum and its delivery, for that would amount to a lowering of educational standards; and if the curriculum is to maintain its integrity, there need to be effective safeguards that ensure students are able to cope with its demands and thus graduate with a degree that is valued for its rigour. If universities compromise this principle, then, in time, the idea of an English-medium education in an inner-circle country as a mark of quality will dissipate, along with buoyant enrolment figures. In other words, universities need to be wary of the possible long-term dangers of focusing only on short-term benefits.

The frailties of pre-enrolment assessment

It is common practice among English-medium universities in Australia and elsewhere to have in place English language criteria that students for whom English is not a first language are required to meet as a condition of entry. These are typically stipulated in terms of internationally recognised tests such as the International English Language Testing System (IELTS) and Test of English as a Foreign Language (TOEFL). Questions arise, however, as to whether (a) these and similar gatekeeping tests are fit for purpose, and (b) if they are, whether the English language thresholds set by receiving universities are sufficient to ensure that students who meet or exceed them are genuinely capable of pursuing their degree programmes. With regard to this second question, many universities will have committees responsible for recommending thresholds, and those recommendations will often be the result of benchmarking against competitor institutions and, in some cases, taking advice from individual departments. This raises two further and related questions:

- What is the make-up of these committees and what is the extent of their assessment literacy and thus qualification to make determinations of where thresholds should be set?
- How valid are the thresholds being set, given that many universities are setting them in relative rather than absolute terms when they benchmark against competitors' practices?

This second question returns us to ethical concerns, for in reality the process of benchmarking exists, in part, to ensure that institutions are not out of kilter with their counterparts. And this is important, for if they set English language entry standards that are lower than the sector generally, then they risk being perceived as undemanding and academically weak institutions (with implications for their brands), while if they set them higher, they risk being uncompetitive and losing market share; after all, most other things being equal, students will tend to apply to those institutions that present them with fewer hoops to jump through. If universities are to act ethically, they need to ensure that those making the decisions on which tests to employ for gatekeeping purposes and where to set thresholds are suitably assessment literate such that they can make decisions based not on what other institutions do but, first and foremost, on their own understanding of the tests, the nature of their degree programs, and what best serves the students' interests.

In terms of the first question, namely, whether gatekeeping tests are fit for purpose, I have argued that, as tests of general academic English (GAE), they may well be fit for purpose (Murray, 2010; in press), although studies on the predictive validity of such tests have produced mixed results (Cotton & Conrow, 1998; Ingram & Bayliss, 2007; Kerstjens and Nery, 2000; Rea-Dickens, Kiely & Yu, 2007). Where gatekeeping tests, arguably, are flawed is in the fact that they fail to assess students' mastery of the particular academic literacies pertinent to their specific disciplines; literacies that in part define those disciplines and an understanding of which is a prerequisite to being fully conversant in them and bona fide members of their respective communities of practice. This failure may help explain (a) why students who meet English language entry criteria often still struggle with the language demands of their studies, and (b) the typically high attrition rates that characterise in-sessional English language support classes (Lobo & Gurney, 2014). As with gatekeeping tests, these classes tend to focus on general academic English; however, most students have already had their fill of tuition in this as a consequence of having to prepare for such tests in order to secure entry to university. What they now require is tuition in the academic literacies of their disciplines, for many will not have been exposed to these yet have an immediate and pressing need to develop conversancy in them in order to follow their programmes of study and complete assessed coursework. For this reason, there has been growing call in the literature for the embedding of academic literacies in programme curricula in order to make certain that all students develop an understanding of those skills fundamental to their disciplines, within contexts that are most relevant to them (Curnow & Liddicoat, 2008; Wingate, Andon & Cogo, 2011).

The reality is that, in the short to medium term, testing bodies are unlikely to develop a set of discipline-tailored English language tests that can be used for gatekeeping purposes, and would likely only do so if they were confident that universities would employ them and that there would therefore be an adequate return on the substantial investment needed to develop them.

Whether the fact that some students are struggling to cope with the language demands of their studies is due to the nature of gatekeeping tests themselves or their misuse by universities, the fact remains that a proportion of students are entering universities underprepared. This presents the students themselves, academic staff and the institution with considerable challenges.

The challenges for students, staff and the institution

For many international students, the stakes involved in studying overseas in an English-medium university are very high, not simply in terms of achieving their aspirations, but also in terms of what failure can mean for their self-esteem and psychological wellbeing in general, and for their families, who will in many cases have made sacrifices to enable their children to benefit from the experience. For many students, the sense of obligation to their parents and the prospect of returning home to their families and communities as 'failures' weighs heavily on them and can be a source of considerable anxiety.

Clearly, too, there are important implications for their studies. Students lacking proficiency in English can find it hard to integrate at university as well as into society more generally and can feel marginalised and isolated. Inside the classroom, they can find themselves unable and/or unwilling to understand and contribute — something which can lead to resentment among their native-speaker counterparts who, so student satisfaction surveys suggest, may feel that they end up shouldering much of the responsibility in group work activities and that their own educational experience is being compromised, along with their course grades.

For academic staff, poor English language skills among students can leave them feeling frustrated and disempowered; frustrated because they may be unable to teach their courses as originally conceived and in the manner they would wish, and disempowered because they do not have the linguistic knowledge to assist students. Indeed, some would argue that they should not need to if gatekeeping mechanisms were working effectively and entry standards being maintained. As I have indicated, the fact that academic staff feel they need to adjust course content and its delivery in order to make it accessible to those struggling with the language raises questions about standards and, as such, it is right that universities and auditing bodies should be concerned about English.

Post-enrolment language assessment

In response to this situation, a number of Australian universities have considered implementing some form of post-enrolment language assessment (PELA; Dunworth, 2009; Read & von Randow, 2013). While it may feel like closing the gate after the horse has bolted, instituting PELA, whether as a test or a piece of assessed coursework, not only enables institutions to identify those at greatest risk from weak English, it also provides a mechanism for determining who should get priority access to resources that are typically limited. In addition, PELA enables universities to demonstrate cognisance of Good Practice Principles 1 and 7 and Standard 3 of the ELSHE respectively, namely that:

Universities are responsible for ensuring that their students are sufficiently competent in the English language to participate effectively in their university studies. (GPP 1; DEEWR, p. 2)

Students' English language development needs are diagnosed early in their studies and addressed, with ongoing opportunities for self-assessment. (GPP 2; DEEWR, p.2)

The provider ensures that resourcing for English language development meets students' needs throughout their studies. (Standard 3; DEEWR, p. 7)

One of the expectations cited under this standard is that the higher education provider identifies students' individual English language development needs early in their studies and addresses these needs.

PELA is a complex issue. It requires institutions to decide, on a principled basis, whether it should be mandated and if so for whom: All students (so as not to be seen as discriminatory and to avoid students such as domestic NESB students slipping through the net)? International students only? Only those students with proficiency test scores below a certain standard? Assessing all or large numbers of students has implications for how an assessment exercise is administered and marked. For example, limited human resources are an argument for electronic administration and marking, but this brings technological and hardware demands, including a sufficient number of computer suites. Furthermore, if logistical factors mean that not all students can be assessed simultaneously, then what are the consequent risks, if any, in terms of security? Finally, and a point to which I shall return, should PELA focus on general proficiency or instead be tailored locally within the institution so as to test the academic literacy skills students will need in their particular degree programmes?

PELA is also likely to be viewed with caution by university senior management for it can represent a significant risk to the institution's reputation and brand. A university that feels it necessary to assess the language proficiency of its students could be perceived as a university with low standards or which is not thriving and thus is compelled to be less than rigorous in terms of its entry requirements. While these concerns can be mitigated through the strategic presentation of PELA, they remain cause for concern for many, not merely for reputational reasons but because if PELA is mandated, it could again be seen as an unwelcome obstacle to would-be students.

Tuition in academic literacies

I made reference earlier to the increasingly widespread view that academic literacy needs to be embedded within the curriculum in order to ensure that all students benefit from tuition in the particular literacies pertinent to their disciplines. This view is reflected in Good Practice Principle 6 ('Development of English language proficiency is integrated with curriculum design, assessment practices and course delivery through a variety of methods') and Standard 4 of the ELSHE, under which the first 'Expectation' reads: 'The provider ensures that development by students of their English language proficiency is integrated into curriculum design, assessment practices and course delivery'.

Given the increased diversity of the student population in higher education today as a result of internationalisation and widening participation, few assumptions can be made about the literacies with which students come equipped to their degree studies. Yet, while there is a quite compelling argument for embedding academic literacies in the curriculum, this can be a challenging process (see, e.g., Murray & Nallaya, in press). Obtaining the buy-in of those tasked with its implementation can be difficult as academic staff are increasingly skeptical, it seems, about the numerous new initiatives they are asked to engage with, many of which ultimately fail to come to fruition. This means that those driving the initiative need to fully understand it themselves and come with the credentials and thus credibility to muster the support of an often cynical audience. Moreover, they need to be capable of articulating its rationale and benefits in an accessible manner. English language tutors need to work with academic staff to tease out the academic literacies relevant to their programmes — academic literacies of which most will have a procedural but not necessarily a declarative understanding (Anderson, 1983). This is critical, for if academic literacies are a fundamental aspect of being conversant in disciplines then it is academic staff who need to impart them to students as a normal part of the curriculum. For most, this will entail some professional development if they are to do so with the requisite confidence and skill.

Once identified, the relevant literacies need to be located in the curriculum at points where they naturally arise — and thus students require them — and to be scaffolded, on the understanding that they will likely be recycled at different points in the curriculum. As such, as Curnow and Liddicoat (2008) indicate, the mapping of academic literacies onto the curriculum requires careful thought and needs to be closely linked to assessment:

We evaluated the academic literacy practices, which we believed our students should have at the completion of the major (cf. Brown, Bull & Pendlebury 1997, p. 38) and then 'divided up' these practices between the assessment items across the core courses, a 'whole-of-program' approach (cf. Morgan, Dunn, Parry & O'Reilly 2004, p. 211–214; 2008, p. 1).

The nature of English language provision

As I have indicated, if a proportion of students struggle to cope with their studies despite having met English language entry requirements, the receiving universities have a duty to make certain that mechanisms are in place to support them in their efforts to develop their proficiency. Four of TEQSA's 6 standards state respectively:

- The provider ensures that resourcing for English language development meets students' needs throughout their studies.
- The provider actively develops students' English language proficiency during their studies.
- The provider ensures that students are appropriately proficient in English when they graduate.
- The provider uses evidence from a variety of sources to monitor and improve its support for the development of students' English language proficiency.

The fact that the authors of these documents felt it necessary to include the post-enrolment assessment of students and the provision of English language development opportunities in their Principles/Standards, amounts to tacit acknowledgement of the fact that gatekeeping tests are not performing their function sufficiently well.

Two key factors need to shape language provision. The first concerns academic literacies. If one takes the view that language needs to be embedded in the curriculum and taught within the context of the discipline, then there would appear to be a strong argument for providing language support activities that build on that intimate relationship. Thus while the first 'point of delivery' of those literacies should be the academic staff responsible for teaching the curriculum, any additional language support offered, whether by English language specialists or online, should similarly be focused on the particular literacies of the different disciplines. This constitutes an argument for localisation over centralisation of provision; that is, English language tutors should be assigned to particular faculties for this arrangement brings with it the following advantages:

- The fundamental relationship between academic literacies and disciplines is emphasised.
- English language teams are well placed to develop productive working relationships with academic and professional staff in their respective faculties and to develop their discipline knowledge and keep abreast of the literacy requirements of those disciplines within their faculties. Consequently, they are better able to provide more tailored, relevant forms of support.
- English language tutors feel more integrated if they are a permanent feature of the faculty's architecture. They are likely to be privy to

debates and developments within the faculty and therefore better able to make informed contributions according to the local context.
- Closer working relationships with faculties promise to make easier the process of implementing the embedding of academic literacies in the curriculum.

The second factor impacting on provision is PELA, where it exists. There is an argument for saying that if few assumptions can be made about the academic literacies with which students enter university, and if tuition in them should therefore be embedded in the curriculum, there is little point in testing them post-entry and PELA should thus focus instead on general English language proficiency (GAE). Such proficiency not only helps students integrate socially, it provides them with the means to better access the curriculum, and the academic literacy tuition that is delivered through it.

If PELA is to focus on GAE, then those students identified as at risk need access to GAE provision. Such provision can include credit and non-credit bearing electives run during and/or between semesters, online materials, workshops on areas of common weakness or high demand, electronic feedback on written assignments and 1:1 consultations with English language tutors. Importantly, GAE can also be shaped so as to maximise its relevance to students — and thus their engagement — by presenting language and points of learning within contexts that have disciplinary relevance to students. Again local language tutors will be well placed to determine what those contexts are and to identify and adapt texts for this purpose.

I have suggested that the discipline-specific nature of academic literacies is an argument for localising English language provision, as local English language tutors can better understand and respond to students' needs in a way that informs the shape of that provision. If academic literacy tuition in imparted by academic staff via the regular curriculum, this does not mean that English language tutors cannot or should not support such activity; indeed, they can do so via such mechanisms as a cycle of workshops repeated throughout the year and in semester breaks, online materials structured according to faculties and, in time, even broken down to reflect the literacy requirements of *specific* disciplines. Furthermore, resources permitting, limited academic literacy feedback on assignments and 1:1 consultations with English language tutors could be made available. I have suggested elsewhere that PELA could be used as a filtering mechanism, allowing only those students shown to be at risk access to these more resource-intensive forms of provision, irrespective of whether their focus is GAE, academic literacy or both.

Managing linguistic and cultural diversity

I have discussed the professional development of academic staff in relation to the teaching of academic literacies within the curriculum. It can be argued, however, that their professional development needs to extend to the area of intercultural competence, for interacting effectively with a more diverse student population requires sensitivity to different cultural norms and how these are manifested in classroom, seminars etc., as well as to the variation that can exist in the relationship between language and meaning; that is, between what is said and what is meant — what Widdowson (1990) has referred to as semantic and pragmatic meaning respectively. Academic staff need to be aware of and able to manage and accommodate cultural difference, intergroup dynamics, and the tensions and conflicts that can accompany this process (Hockings, 2012; Lee & Herner-Patnode, 2010). They need to understand how such difference can impact pedagogy and student learning, and use that knowledge to shape and manage students' perceptions and classroom dynamics in a manner that produces positive learning outcomes for all. The consequences of failure here can be considerable. In group work, for example, international students may be reluctant to participate or feel that native speakers dominate, due to their language skills but also because of cultural predispositions and their better understanding of local behavioural norms. This reluctance or inability of some international students to engage has been shown in student surveys to lead to dissatisfaction — even resentment — on the part of home students who

- can feel that they end up shouldering much of the responsibility for group tasks and assignments;
- can worry that when assessed as part of a group, their grades will suffer;
- can feel that international students are graded more sympathetically; and
- can believe that their educational experience is compromised as lecturers adjust their material in order to make it accessible to all students.

The knowledge that they are paying handsomely for their education and burdening themselves with a substantial HELP student loan can exacerbate such feelings of dissatisfaction.

For their part, international students can feel left out of activities and ignored, leading to a sense of marginalisation and inadequacy, regardless of their intellectual capacity. Some feel frustrated or embarrassed at their inhibition and inability to contribute and believe that, despite it frequently being one of the factors influencing their decision to study in an English-medium university, they are not benefitting maximally from the opportunity to interact with native speakers to the extent they would wish, and therefore improve their proficiency in the language.

Academic staff today need to be able to manage this situation and to develop the knowledge, understanding and skills for doing so. Importantly, this includes assisting students to develop their own intercultural competence by raising their awareness of its importance to a successful and productive student experience, their employment prospects, and their growth and capacity as global citizens. Students need to develop and perform that competence experientially though opportunities to engage in mixed-culture group work (Summers & Volet, 2008).

Conclusion

There is a palpable sense that English language in higher education is today under the spotlight in Australia (and indeed elsewhere) as never before, as universities are forced to find creative and educationally sound solutions to the various challenges posed by an increasingly linguistically and culturally diverse student body. In this chapter, I have sought, in a necessarily perfunctory manner, to convey some of the complexity and interrelatedness of these challenges and offer some ideas about both how to think about them and how to address them. While most universities share similar such challenges and there are principles that need to underpin all and any responses to them, institutional contexts inevitably vary. As such, there can be — and indeed needs to be — a degree of flexibility as well as great sensitivity and astuteness in how individual universities shape their English language strategies and reconcile tensions between objectives that can appear to be inherently contradictory. And the stakes could not be higher: If they fail, they risk alienating both international *and* home students, discouraging academic staff, and undermining their institutional reputations and brands. Ultimately, their very existence is at stake, for enrolments are likely to whittle away, along with research income that is increasingly dependent on perceived institutional prestige.

References

Anderson, J. R. (1983). *The architecture of cognition*. Cambridge, MA: Harvard University Press.

BBC News. (2010). Foreign students not 'cash cows', says British Council. *BBC News*, 26 March 2010. Retrieved from http://news.bbc.co.uk/1/hi/education/8584819.stm

Bretag, T. (2007). The emperor's new clothes: Yes, there is a link between English language competence and academic standards. *People and Place*, *15*(1), 13–21.

Cotton, F., & Conrow, F. (1998). An investigation of the predictive validity of IELTS amongst a group of international students studying at the University of Tasmania. *IELTS Research Reports 1998*, Vol. 1, pp. 72–115.

Curnow, T. J., & Liddicoat, A. J. (2008). Assessment as learning: Engaging students in academic literacy in their first semester. In A. Duff, D. Quinn, M. Green, K. Andre, T. Ferris & S. Copland (Eds.), *Proceedings of the ATN assessment conference 2008: Engaging students in* assessment, Available online from http://www.ojs.unisa.edu.au/index.php/atna/issue/view/ISBN%20978-0-646-504421/showToc.

Department of Education, Employment and Workplace Relations (DEEWR). (2009). *Good practice principles for English language proficiency for international students in Australian universities.* Canberra, Australia: Author.

Hockings, C. (2010). Inclusive learning and teaching in higher education: a synthesis of research. *EvidenceNet*, Higher Education Academy. Retrieved from https://www.heacademy.ac.uk/resources/detail/resources/detail/evidencenet/Inclusive_learning_and_teaching_in_higher_education

Ingram, D. E., & Bayliss, A. (2007). IELTS as a predictor of academic language performance. Part 1: The view from participants. *IELTS Impact Studies Vol. 7* (IELTS Joint-funded research programme). IELTS Australia & the British Council.

Kachru, B. B. (1985). Standards, codification and sociolinguistic realism: The English language in the outer circle. In R. Quirk & H. G. Widdowson (Eds.), *English in the world: Teaching and learning the language and literatures.* Cambridge, England: Cambridge University Press.

Kerstjens, M., & Nery, C. (2000). Predictive validity in the IELTS test: A study of the relationship between IELTS scores and students' subsequent academic performance. *English Language Testing System Research Reports*, 3, 85–108.

Lee, Y.A., & Herner-Patnode, L. (2010). Developing teacher candidates' knowledge, skills, and dispositions to teach diverse students. *Journal of Instructional Psychology, 37*(3), 22– 235.

Murray, N. (2014). Reflections on the implementation of post-enrolment english language assessment. *Language Assessment Quarterly, 11*(3), 325–337.

Murray, N. (in press). *Standards of English in Higher Education: Issues, challenges and Strategies.*

Murray, N., & Nallaya, S. (in press). Embedding academic literacies in programme curricula: A case study. *Studies in Higher Education.*

Narushima, Y. (2008). Overseas students exploited as cash cows. *Sydney Morning Herald*, December 17, 2008. Retrieved from http://www.smh.com.au/news/national/overseas-students-exploited-as-cash-cows/2008/12/16/1229189622969.html

Organisation for Economic Co-operation and Development (OECD). (2013). *Education indicators in focus.* OECD Publishing. Retrieved from http://www.oecd.org/education/skills-beyond-school/EDIF%202013—%C2%B014%20(eng)-Final.pdf

Quality Assurance Agency. (2009). *Thematic enquiries into concerns about academic qualityand standards in higher education in england: Final Report 2009.* Gloucester, England: The Quality Assurance Agency for Higher Education. Retrieved from http://www.aall.org.au/sites/default/files/FinalEnglishLanguageStandardsMay2012.

Read, J., & von Randow, J. (2013). A university post-entry English language assessment: Charting the changes. *English Language Studies, 13*(2), 89–110.

Rea-Dickins, P., Kiely, R., & Yu, G. (2007). Student Identity, Learning and Progression: with specific reference to the affective and academic impact of IELTS on 'successful' candidates. *IELTS Impact Studies Vol. 7* (IELTS Joint-funded research programme). IELTS Australia & the British Council.

Summers, M., & Volet, S. (2008). Students' attitudes towards culturally mixed groups on international campuses: Impact of participation in diverse and non-diverse groups. *Studies in Higher Education, 33*(4), 357–370.

Widdowson, H.G. (1990). *Aspects of language teaching.* Oxford, England: Oxford University Press.

Wingate, U., Andon, N., &Cogo, A. (2011). Embedding academic writing instruction into subject teaching: A case study. *Active Learning in Higher Education, 12*(1), 69–81.

Chapter 6

International Students and the 'English Problem' in Australian Universities: A Discursive Perspective

Michael Haugh

Introduction

The number of international students in Australia's higher education sector has grown exponentially over the past three decades, from approximately 13,700 in 1983 to over 230,000 enrolments in 2013 (Australian Education International, 2013; Burke, 2002). This rapid explosion in the number of international students participating in higher education has also witnessed a corresponding growth in discourses on problems in relation to international students studying in Australian universities, both in the popular media and amongst academic researchers. Many of these discourses have been arguably negative, ranging from talk of international students as 'backdoor migrants' and 'invaders' through to references to them as 'cash cows' or 'commodities' (Burke, 2002, 2012; Robertson, 2011). One discourse that has dominated debates in Australian higher education, in particular, has been that of the so-called 'English problem', namely, ongoing claims over the past three decades that international students have inadequate English language skills for participating in academic studies, and graduate with insufficient English language skills for subsequent employment in Australia. It has been argued that this not only reflects, but has also led, to academic standards falling in Australian universities (Birrell, 2006; Bretag, 2007; Coley, 1999; Phillips 1987; Watty 2007). The claim that many international students face problems with their level of English language skills is one that has gained considerable traction in influencing recent governmental and institutional policies on entry standards and subsequent English language support for international students in Australian universities (Arkoudis, Baik, & Richardson, 2012; Bradley, Noonan, Nugent, & Scales, 2008; Department of Education, Employment and Workplace Relations [DEEWR], 2009). However, such moves have often been premised on a deficit view of international students, where they are cast as having inadequate language skills and that this deficiency needs to be overcome through various means of English language support (Benzie, 2010). It is commonly assumed that if international students are given sufficient English language support targeting the four skills in academic contexts, along with support in developing their academic literacy more broadly (Benzie, 2010; Harper, Prentice, & Wilson, 2011; Murray, 2012), the problem of falling academic standards in Australian universities will be addressed.

In this chapter it is argued that such views over-simplify the complex terrain of perceptions of and about international students. It is proposed that the subjective understandings of the actual stakeholders in question, namely, international students themselves need to be analysed more carefully with respect to the so-called English problem. A key finding from an analysis of a number of focus groups and interviews conducted with international students about their English language skills and their concomitant interactions with others, is that they are not only a key dimension of the identities they construct for themselves as international students, but they may also constitute the object of affective stances with which other stakeholders may ratify, qualify or dispute. This analysis indicates that the alleged English problem is multi-layered and complex, involving both similarities and differences in the affective stances towards the problem across international students, and thus with respect to the identities they co-construct for themselves. A disconnect between the inherent subjectivity of these discursive representations and their concomitant affective and moral implications, and the way in which the so-called English problem in Australian universities is couched as one of objective, measurable deficiency on the part of international students, thus becomes apparent through this study.

In the next section, the data itself, a set of focus groups and interviews conducted with international students in a large Australian university, and the methods employed for analysing it, namely, content analysis and interactional analysis, are introduced. This is followed, in section three, by an overview of the three key frames with respect to which international students co-constructed their identities vis-à-vis their perceived English language skills. In section four, the ways in which other international students either affiliated with those implicit stances, thereby co-constructing joint stances, or disaffiliated with them through either disputing or qualifying them, are examined in detail. The implications of this analysis for academic research, as well as broader policy debates on international students are then briefly considered in the final section.

Data and method

A total of nine focus groups along with two one-on-one interviews were conducted with international students from a large Australian university that has a significant proportion of international students. The focus groups were carried out with 29 undergraduate students from a variety of countries, including Brazil, Chile, China, India, Iran, Japan, Korea, Russia, Taiwan and Thailand. The focus group facilitators/interviewers followed a semi-structured interview format in asking international students about their experiences studying at the university in question.[1]

The focus group and interview data was then initially analysed using content analysis (Krippendorff, 2013), through which recurrent claims made by international students, or about international students, were classified into a number of overarching themes. The reliability of this content analysis was not tested formally through statistical means given the primarily qualitative focus of this study. However, the said themes were identified in the course of preliminary analyses of the dataset that were carried out independently by two different researchers.[2] Given the importance placed on international student identities in the research literature, the Communicative Theory of Identity (Hecht, 1993, 2009; Hecht, Warren, Jung, & Krieger, 2005) was selected as the conceptual lens through which to carry out this content analysis. According to the Communication Theory of Identity, identities are accomplished through communication in four interpenetrating frames: personal (i.e., 'the ways an individual conceives of self'), enacted ('the performance or expression of identity'), relational ('identities that are invested in relationships, exist in relationship to each other, and are *ascribed* in and through relationships'), and communal (identities that 'exist as characteristics of communities ... held in common by groups rather than individuals'; Hecht, 2009, p. 140, 'original emphasis'). The beliefs and experiences reported by the participants were thus classified according to the frame of identity (or identities) they were enacting on their own behalf, or on the behalf of others (or in some cases both), through their talk in the focus groups. The extent to which the other participants themselves ratified, qualified or disputed the claimed or attributed identity/identities in question (Haugh, 2008) was also examined, with a particular focus on the ways in which other participants affiliated or disaffiliated with the affective stances that were implicit to those identities. Following work in conversation analysis, affiliative responses involves 'actions with which a recipient displays that s/he supports the affective stance expressed by the speaker' (Lindström & Sorjonen, 2013, p. 351), or displays empathy (Stivers, Mondada, & Steensig, 2008). Disaffiliative responses, on the other hand, encompass actions by which a recipient displays that he does not support or rejects the affective stance displayed by the speaker, or does not display empathy with the experiences informing that stance. Given such an analysis requires close interactional analysis, relevant excerpts were transcribed following conversation analysis conventions (Jefferson, 2004), which are listed in the appendix to this chapter.

The discursive negotiation of international student identities

The participants in the focus groups reported a number of beliefs about, and experiences as or interacting with, international students. Through content analysis of these reported beliefs and experiences three key themes emerged with respect to the Communicative Theory of Identity.

The first theme encompassed claims centred on the personal frame of identity, that is, reports that involved the self-concepts or self-images of individuals. One recurrent claim was that many international students lack confidence in speaking English in all spheres of interaction, ranging from in-class interactions with lecturers, tutors and other local students through to interactions with local students and administrative staff outside of classes, as well as in interactions with members of the broader community in which they live. The following excerpts are illustrative of such reports, many of which the participants themselves regarded not as isolated cases, but rather construed as symptomatic of the experiences of international students more generally.[3]

>(1) FG3: 13:15
>
>HK1: International students they always, they afraid of speaking out in front of other people, especially in front of the domestic students. They think their English is not good enough. They will be embarrassed.
>
>(2) FG3: 28:55
>
>HK1: I have some friends that they even don't, when they, like, go to McDonalds and they want to buy a meal, they just say 'Oh, can you help me? Can you help, ah, me to buy meal number 1, for the chicken?', something like that 'Because I don't want to speak to the uhm staff in English', something like that. So they, because their English is not so good, so they feel very embarrassed in speaking before a English speaker. They, they are afraid that they will be laughed by them, or something like that.

This lack of confidence, and related perceived inadequacy in communicating in English was associated with a second recurrent claim, namely, that their English language skills were a source of emotional stress and frustration in various spheres of interaction, as illustrated in the following excerpt.

>(3) FG6: 13: 30
>
>K4: I came here for studying Tourism and Hotel Management. Actually, uhm I, I think I know so many things about management things in, in hospitality

field. For example, marketing, financial control, or managing skills or something like that. But the only problem is I can't express my knowledge, my thoughts. Actually, I really want to talk about so many things, I got so many things behind. But I can't express my real- especially in tutorial class.

In this way, then, the participants enacted on behalf of themselves, or on behalf of other international students, a personal frame of identity as lacking in confidence in their ability to interact with local students and academic staff, as well as members of the broader community, in English. In some cases, they cast themselves as actually having an inadequate level of English language skills in the context of academic interactions.

The second theme encompassed claims centred on the relational frame of identity, namely, various ways in which international students were cast vis-à-vis their relationships with others. On the one hand, these reports involved claims that the interactions between international students and local students, as well as with academic staff, involved displays of empathy and understanding by the latter groups of the difficulties communicating in English sometimes experienced by international students, as can be observed in excerpt (4). In some cases though, international students reported some degree of equivocality with respect to their interpretation of these displays of understanding of or empathy for their troubles, as can be seen in excerpt (5).

(4) FG5: 19:19

J5: You know cause in Australia no one really cares what you are doing. I think that they do, but they are very easy going, like they are very helpful, like.

I: You mean you don't get like criticised you don't get looked down upon or.

J5: Like whenever you make a mistake that's fine.

(5) FG7: 8:05

C3: Last week I take, ah, I took a class in tutorial. And uhm, in, I find, I, uhm, you know misunderstanding the tutorials, the tuto- ah, the teacher. I thought, he, he found me, couldn't understand him. So he said, ah, he said 'I feel sorry about the English is not your first language'. And I don't know if better its better I'm not, I'm not good for study those subjects. I mean-.

Through such reports, the participants enacted identities where international students were construed as having sympathetic and understanding relationships with local students and academic staff.

On the other hand, other reports by participants involved rather more negative experiences in relating with local students, as well as with academic and administrative staff. These included interactions where international students reported feeling they were the target of contempt, discrimination or disrespect from academic staff, local students and administrative staff, respectively.

(6) FG5: 58:43

J6: She is very nice, to Australian. But uhm, she's. There is one Chinese girl who is having difficulties with assignments. And she is not good at speaking English, so it takes time. But the- you know, tutor or lecturer, kind of gives them that face, bad looking, 'Okay so what are you trying to say?', well I understand, but you know. I have seen that situation, so I, from that time, I didn't want to ask her any questions to her cause its very- I was very afraid that, that I will give her a really difficult time, you know, I don't want her to hate me or anything because of my English skills.

(7) FG3: 6:30

HK1: In the tutorial we just separate, I think we have a little bit discriminate by them, because maybe they think our English is not good enough to complete the assignment with a good grade. Uhm, so they always, not all I mean, but most of the domestic students they will refuse to have a group with us.

(8) FG5: 40:03

J6: The very first time I went to the International student- Centre International Office. And I had to ask some questions to some-. But I- because I didn't make an appointment I knew that I had to wait. But I had to wait like more than one hour. And she was, I don't know. She knew that I was waiting, but she just kept talking to the other student. And I felt really miserable, cause it's you know, it's like she doesn't care about me. Well, maybe it was the timing thing. Maybe she didn't think it's such a long time, but for me one hour or more than that is very long, you know. So, (1.0) yeah, I don't really have a good experience.

In this way, then, the participants also cast international students as sometimes experiencing unsympathetic and contemptuous relationships with local students and staff where they were snubbed or were even the target of (perceived) discrimination.

A third theme encompassed claims centred on the communal frame of identity, that is, ways in which participants cast themselves and others as belonging to a larger body of international students. We have seen, in the previous excerpts, how the respondents may cast these reported experiences either explicitly (e.g., excerpts 1 and 7) or implicitly (e.g., excerpt 2, 4 and 6) as representative of the experiences of international students more generally. In the following excerpt one of the participants reported that the reason he only has one Australian friend is due to the hostility he has experienced from Australian students towards international students, a hostility that he now reciprocates.

(9) FG6: 33:57

K4: The students gathers together by very similar area person like that. Yeah, Australian students, seems like don't have attention to us. Obviously, sometimes I feel they dislike us. Basically, I totally I don't like Australian people because just yesterday I was walk along the street at 9am, at night, 9pm. And some Australian girls threw out the eggs for- to me, threw out the eggs.

I: Really?

K4: Yeah, that kind of situation is awkward, really frequently. And I heard that kind of story to my friends, my Korean friends.

I: What? They throw eggs at you?

K4: Yeah eggs. So I hate it. I was really angry and upset, so I yelling 'Hey, come on'. But they just go out, go away, in their car.

I: Did you take a number plate?

K4: No. Some of my Korean friends are hitted by beer bottles.

I: Yeah?

K4: So it is terrible. So basically I, in my mind the anger against Australian people, especially young peoples, is building.

Notably, in the course of this report, the international student construes these as common experiences that are directed towards international students as a collective group.

In the course of analysing the ways in which participants made claims about personal, relational and communal frames of international student identities in the context of these focus groups, it was observed that in the course of enacting these identity claims, international students took also affective stances with respect to those identities. Other participants were found to offer either affiliative responses, where they indicated agreement with the stance in question,, or (mildly) disaffiliative responses, where they disputed the grounds of the stance or even rejected it outright. In the following section, we thus move to examine more closely the ways in which participants both affiliated and disaffiliated with these affective stances.

(Dis)affiliating with the affective stances of international students

In the course of analysing the responses of other international students to the affective stances taken by international students, it became evident that other participants regularly affiliated or disaffiliated with those stances. In some cases, they co-constructed joint stances through affiliating with the prior speaker's stance, by either explicitly agreeing with that stance or by reporting similar experiences. In other cases, their responses were mildly disaffiliative in that the recipient reformulated the scope or grounds of the reported problem in question, or were outright disaffiliative in that the recipient disputed or rejected the legitimacy of the stance in question. In such cases, diverging rather than joint stances were co-constructed.

In the following excerpt from a focus group involving three international students from Taiwan (T1-3), for instance, a joint stance about the way in which international students are excluded by local students is progressively enacted, and affiliated with, by the three international students.

(10) FG2: 25:09

```
1  I:      how did you go with group work.
2  T3:     oh (.) I didn't really have good experience [in working]
3  I:                                                  [o::h o:kay]
4  T3:     (.) wo:rk°ing with° (.)Aussie students
5  I:      mm (.) mm (.) mm
6  (1.0)
7  T3:     u:::hm I think- I don't know maybe they just think I'm DUMb or
8          something >I dunno<, when I (0.5) express my o-hh
9          opinions to people I sawthey don't listen, °o:h okay.°
10         ((looking at T1)) [like just wh]at you said
11 T1:                       [ye:ah ye:ah]
12 T3:     just ignore you=
13 T1:     =ah.=
14 I:      =°mm oh [okay]
15 T3:             [a:nd ] yeah (1.0) and (1.0) whatever
16         you've done you han- yo- you take it to your friends,
17         and they(.) say okay can I have your- okay
18         we can worktogether, and you- when you receive
19         like the result of the=
20 I:      =mm
21 T3:     the homework, and you find out (0.5) your one(.) hh
22         is nOT there=
23 T2:     =YEah.
24 T3:     hhh [not there, and I JUST felt (.) [very disappointed
25 T2:         [HHhhhh                         [HHHhhhhhhhhhh
```

In line 2 and 4, T3 alludes back to T1's prior stance, namely, that they are excluded by local students when doing group assignments, in the course of reporting about her own negative experiences in working with local students, something with which T1 displays emphatic agreement (line 11) and recognition (line 13) (see Haugh, 2008, p. 215). As T3 elaborates in reporting on her experiences, and thereby implements an implicit stance that her contributions are ignored and rejected by local students, T2 also displays emphatic agreement (line 23), followed by affiliative laughter (line 25). In this way, then, the three participants enact a joint stance that their ongoing interactions with Australian students in classroom settings are not positive. Through affiliating with each other in this way, they co-construct a joint

Chapter 6 International Students and the 'English Problem' in Australian Universities

stance that this exclusion is unfair and insulting. Notably, the blame for this problem is implicitly laid with the attitudes of local students rather than any perceived difficulties in communicating in English by the international students in question.

However, while taking affective stances did occasion affiliative responses in some instances, in other cases they prompted disaffiliative responses. In the following excerpt from a focus group that involved two Japanese (J5, J6), a Korean (K1) and a Russian (R2) international student, for example, the Korean student takes the stance that the English language support offered by the university is inadequate. She goes on to claim that academic staff at the university did not offer help or advice when she asked about improving her English language skills. Instead, she reported being told to go and enrol in a TAFE course (see Haugh, 2008, p. 217). She concludes that this reflected a lack of concern on the part of those academic staff, not only for her difficulties in studying in English, but also for her desire to improve her perceived level of English language proficiency. The excerpt begins at the point the other participants respond to the implicit stance she is taking on these experiences.

(11) FG5: 23:30

```
1  I:    but you are at university now.
2        (1.5)
3  K3:   ye:ah
4        (0.5)
5  I:    o::kay.
6        (1.0)
7  R2:   can I °add° just a little bit?
8  I:    ye:ah sure.
9  R2:   I think u:hm, why they like that, and I think L just kind of a:lmost
10       answered the question because when you are at the university
11       you already passed the test, and (.) you're already
12       expected to have certain level of English=
13 J6:   =yeah yeah yeah
14 R2:   and for them to actually, you know, sit down and kind
15       of supervise you on English- people here don't do that.
```

The interviewer (I) responds to the stance K3 takes here by asserting that she is now enrolled at university, thereby implying that expecting support from academic staff to improve her English language skills is not reasonable (line 1). However, K3 does not appear to recognise this response as disaffiliative. After a relatively long pause (line 2), K3 indicates agreement with what was explicitly asserted by the interviewer, but not necessarily with what has implied through an agreement token that lacks utterance-final intonation (line 3). That K3 may not have understood what has been implied is then oriented to by the interviewer when he displays recognition of this lack of uptake (line 5). This is subsequently picked up on by one of the other international students participating in the focus group who offers to elaborate on what has only been implied by the interviewer (line 7), and then goes on to claim that one is expected to have a certain level of English at the point one enters university (lines 9-12), and so academic staff do not need to offer assistance with improving English language skills (line 14-15). R2's response is thus disaffiliative as she undermines the warrant for the Korean student's complaint. Notably, another student (J6) also affiliates with R2's disaffiliative response, thereby co-constructing a joint stance that the reported response from academic staff about which K3 is complaining does not constitute a moral transgression, and that her troubles with communicating in English are primarily her responsibility now that she is enrolled at university.

Implications

The rapid rise in the numbers of international students enrolled in Australian universities over the past fifteen years has been accompanied by a rise in discourse where the English language skills of international students are problematised as inadequate and the cause of falling academic standards. Increased awareness of such issues has prompted the implementation of policies both at national and institutional levels to provide greater English language support for international students. However, in this chapter it has been argued that there are not only similarities, but there are also critical differences, in the ways in which aspects of the so-called English problem are perceived with respect to interactions between international students and local students, academic staff, administrative staff and the broader community. It has also been argued that the affective stances taken by international students with respect to their perceived English language skills and experiences using English in Australia may prompt both affiliative and disaffiliative responses from other international students. Thus, even amongst the key stakeholders in question, namely, international students, there is evidently not consensus about the nature of the so-called 'English problem'. Instead, it has become apparent that in constructing their identities as international students with respect to their perceived level of English, and experiences in using English, these students may take a range of different affective stances, some of which are subsequently co-constructed as jointly shared stances, and others of which are qualified or disputed in co-constructing diverging stances.

The upshot is that any analysis of the perceptions of international students with respect to their English language skills needs to carefully analyse not only how international students co-construct their identities *as* international students through reports about their experiences in using English in Australia, but how such students may co-construct both joint and diverging affective stances with respect to these reported experiences. Indeed, it may prove instructive to track the extent to which international students construct various affective stances with respect to their reported experiences in using English over time, as this may serve as a useful indicator of the relative efficacy of measures undertaken to support English language development amongst international students. In this way, we can move beyond the view that the so-called English problem is simply a matter of an objective, measurable deficiency on the part of international students.

Endnotes

1. The focus groups were carried out in the course of two different projects. One was carried out with support from the then Faculty of Arts at Griffith University (see Haugh, 2008). The other was carried out with support from IELTS (see Humphreys et al., 2012). The author would like to thank Louie Dragut and Elizabeth Stephens for their assistance in conducting these focus groups.
2. The author would like to thank Louie Dragut for his initial assistance in identifying key themes in the focus group data.
3. Participants in the focus groups are identified as follows: the interviewer is identified by 'I'; international students are identified by codes for nationality (HK: Hong Kong; K: Korean; J: Japanese; C: Mainland Chinese; T: Taiwanese; R: Russian) and number (e.g., HK1); academics are coded by 'A' and number (e.g., A1), and local students are coded 'LS' and by number (e.g., LS1).

References

Arkoudis, S., Baik, C., & Richardson, S. (2012). *English language standards in higher education*. Victoria, Australia: ACER Press.

Australian Education International. (2013). International student enrolments in Australia 1994–2013. Retrieved from https://aei.gov.au/researchInternational-Student-Data/Pages/InternationalStudentData2013.aspx.

Benzie, H. (2010). Graduating as a 'native speaker': international students and English language proficiency in higher education. *Higher Education Research and Development, 20*(40), 447–459.

Birrell, B. (2006). Implications of low English standards among overseas students at Australian universities. *People and Place, 14*(1), 53–64.

Bradley, D., Noonan, P., Nugent, H., & Scales, B. (2008). *Review of Australian higher education: Final report.* Department of Education, Employment and Workplace Relations (DEEWR). Retrieved from http://www.innovation.gov.au/highereducation/ResourcesAndPublications/ReviewOfAustralianHigherEducation/Pages/ReviewOfAustralianHigherEducationReport.aspx.

Bretag, T. (2007). The emperor's new clothes: yes, there is a link between English language competence and academic standards. *People and Place, 15*(1), 13–21.

Burke, R. (2002). Invitation or invasion? The 'family home' metaphor in the Australian media's construction of immigration. *Journal of Intercultural Studies, 23*(1), 59–72.

Burke, R. (2006). Constructions of Asian international students: the 'casualty' model and Australia as 'educator'. *Asian Studies Review, 30*(4), 333–354.

Burke, R. (2012). Contesting notions of an 'education industry': media commentary on the transition to a trade-orientated international student program in Australia. *Flinders Journal of History and Politics, 28*, 141–174.

Coley, M. (1999). The English language entry requirements of Australian universities for students of non-English speaking background. *Higher Education Research & Development, 18*(1), 7–17.

Department of Education, Employment and Workplace Relations (DEEWR). (2009). *Good practice principles for English language proficiency for international students in Australian universities.* Retrieved from http://www.innovation.gov.au/highereducation/ResourcesAndPublications/HigherEducationPublications/OtherPublications/Pages/GoodPracticePrinciples.aspx.

Devos, A. (2003). Academic standards, internationalisation, and the discursive construction of 'the international student'. *Higher Education Research & Development, 22*(2), 155–166.

Harper, R., Prentice, S., & Wilson, K. (2011). English language perplexity: Articulating the tensions in the DEEWR 'Good practice principles'. *The International Journal of the First Year in Higher Education, 2*(1), 36-48.

Haugh, M. (2008). The discursive negotiation of international student identities. *Discourse: Studies in the Cultural Politics of Education, 29*(2), 207–222.

Hecht, M. (1993). A research odyssey: towards the development of a communication theory of identity. *Communication Monographs, 60*, 76–82.

Hecht, M. (2009). Communication theory of identity. In S. Littlejohn & K. Foss (Eds.), *Encyclopedia of communication theory: Volume 1* (pp.139–141). Thousand Oaks, CA: Sage.

Hecht, M., Warren, J., Jung, E., & Krieger, J. (2005). The communication theory of identity. In W. Gudykunst (Ed.), *Theorizing about intercultural communication* (pp. 257–278). Thousand Oaks, CA: Sage.

Humphreys, P. Haugh, M, Fenton-Smith, B., Lobo, A., Michael, R., & Walkinshaw, I. (2012). Tracking international students' English proficiency over the first semester of undergraduate study. *IELTS Research Reports Online Series, 2012/1.* Retrieved from http://www.ielts.org/pdf/Humphreys2012_ORR.pdf.

Krippendorff, K. (2013). *Content analysis: An introduction to its methodology* (3rd edn). Thousand Oaks, CA: Sage.

Lindström, A., & Sorjonen, M. (2013). Affiliation in conversation. In J. Sidnell & T. Stivers (Eds.), *The handbook of conversation analysis* (pp. 350–369). Malden, MA: Wiley-Blackwell.

Murray, N. (2012). Ten 'Good Practice Principles' . . . ten key questions: considerations in addressing the English language needs of higher education students. *Higher Education Research & Development, 31*(2), 233–246.

Phillips, D. (1987). Language proficiency assessment and tertiary entry for non-English speaking students. *Journal of Tertiary Educational Administration, 9*(1), 77–88.

Robertson, S. (2011). Cash cows, backdoor migrants, or activist citizens? International students, citizenship, and rights in Australia. *Ethnic and Racial Studies, 34*(12), 2192-2211.

Stivers, T., Mondada, L., & Steensig, J. (2011). Knowledge, morality and affiliation in social interaction. In T. Stivers, L. Mondada & J. Steensig (Eds.), *The Morality of Knowledge in Interaction* (pp. 3–24). Cambridge: Cambridge University Press.

Watty, K. (2007). Quality in accounting education and low English standards among overseas students: Is there a link? *People and Place, 15*(1), 22–29.

Appendix

Transcription conventions

[ ]	overlapping speech
(0.5)	numbers in brackets indicate pause length
(.)	micropause
:	elongation of vowel or consonant sound
-	word cut-off
.	falling or final intonation
?	rising intonation
,	'continuing' intonation
=	latched utterances
underlining	contrastive stress or emphasis
CAPS	markedly loud
° °	markedly soft
.hhh	in-breathe

Hhh	out-breathe/laughter
↓ ↑	sharp falling/rising intonation
> <	talk is compressed or rushed
< >	talk is markedly slowed or drawn out
( )	blank space in parentheses indicates uncertainty about the transcription
(( ))	double brackets indicates extra contextual or non-verbal information

Chapter 7

Towards a Pedagogy of Experiential Thirding in Language Education

Alistair Welsh and Alex Kostogriz

Introduction

The political context in Australia has been marked by a significant investment into the development of Asia-relevant capabilities through schooling and higher education to increase the county's economic competiveness as well as cooperation in the Asia-Pacific region. In part, this aim has been realised through initiatives that foster intercultural understanding, communication and experiences of students through their inbound and outbound mobility. Since the inception of the Colombo Plan for Aid to South and Southeast Asia in 1951, the Australian system of higher education has seen a steady flow of international students from the region, contributing to 'constructive engagement with Asia' and 'promoting mutual understanding with Asian peoples' (Lowe, 2010, p. 16). One can argue that the Colombo Plan was particularly instrumental in mediating some important shifts in cultural politics and languages education in Australia in the 1950s and the 1960s. As a result, the need for teaching Asian studies and languages emerged in the early 1970s as one of the central issues in educational policy-making.

From the outset, this need was linked to the growing emphasis on Australia's economic engagement with Asia as a new, at that time, national priority. The Auchmuty Report (1970, p. 7), in particular, articulated a set of practical arguments for Asian languages and studies of Asia, recognising their importance for the 'steady growth in the economic, political and military links between Australia and Asia.' Education was identified as a key in establishing a parity of esteem between languages taught in Australia, as well as in transforming the traditional attitudes towards Asia. The subsequent language and curricula 'policy parade' (Lo Bianco, 2009) in the 1970s and the 1980s acquired increasingly a more distinct economic character, prioritising only languages and cultures of the major trading and political partners. The economic rationalisation of language and curricula policies culminated in the Rudd Report (1994) that paved the way for a long term plan of building an Asia literate society in order to boost economic performance and 'export culture.' Analysing the historical significance of the Rudd Report, Henderson (1999, p. 203) argued that this document 'would only achieve political endorsement if it was presented in terms which addressed the economic well-being of the nation.'

The primacy of economism in educational policy-making in the 1990s and the 2000s has set a broad agenda for building Asia literacy and, in doing so, has posed limits on the concepts of 'Asia-related capabilities'. Economic rationalism has arguably reduced the cultural 'gift' that such a literacy can offer to the relational dimension of teaching and learning and to the development of critical 'world-mindedness'. The ongoing and deep-seated challenges of building the Asia literate society through education remind us that the prejudice against the Other has by no means disappeared in contemporary Australia. Its communal sub-consciousness may still have the sediments of old narratives and discourses that represented the Asians as a yellow peril, as 'physical, racial and social pollutants' who threatened the civilised West (O'Neill, 2009). Similarly, the seven decades of restricting migration from Asia through the White Australia Policy and implementing state and federal legislation that discriminated against Asians may still influence current attitudes to Asia and Asian languages (Jakubowicz, 2011). It is partly for this reason that the Asia literacy project should be conceived as a large-scale cultural-linguistic project that not only addresses the primacy of economic concerns but also raises ethical sensibilities towards Asia and develops intercultural capabilities.

Hence, we argue in this chapter that the building of the Asia literate society requires a shift from a project that seeks to understand Asia as the object of Australia's economic desires to a project that enables students to engage in a dialogue with the Other. Asia literacy, beyond knowing about Asia, demands a redressing of the relational balance between the Self and the Other; it demands openness to the Other beyond the Same and a more ethical way of recognising and engaging with difference. It is argued that these capabilities can result from educational endeavours, including the learning of Asian languages in and through study programs in Asian countries. Recognising the importance of such learning experiences, the current Australian Government has initiated and funded a 'New Colombo Plan', sometimes also referred to as a 'reverse Colombo Plan'. The concept of supporting student mobility is similar to the original Colombo Plan (1950), but now the new plan focuses on the outbound mobility of Australian students to Asia by providing an impetus through scholarships for them to undertake in-country studies or internships.

It is against this backdrop of the 'New Colombo Plan' and the project of building an Asia literate society in Australia that we draw attention to the underpinning assumptions of Australia's perception of Asian countries as competitors or even a threat. We interrogate the logic of regarding the Asian Other as a threat by exploring perceptions and language learning experiences of university students who study Indonesian language. In doing so, we question the narrow focus attributed to language education as being instrumental in maintaining a competitive economic advantage or as a tool of knowing about the Other. In contrast, we present a more ethical approach that aims to assist learners overcome an essentialised view of Asia so that they may question both social and personal prejudices towards difference. In particular, the proposed alternative seeks to enable students to ethically respond to the Other through a dialogical approach to learning the language and culture of Indonesian people. This approach does not seek to ignore or dissolve differences, but rather to recognise them and to find a pedagogical approach where alternative and opposing perspectives can co-exist. This dialogic practice is referred to in this chapter as Thirding. Based on intercultural dialogism, the proposed approach invites students to question their own selves in a social interaction with cultural Others. It welcomes opportunities for Australian students to study abroad as an integral component of their language learning experiences. We propose a pedagogy of Experiential Thirding that draws on students' in-country experiences as an opportunity to interrogate assumptions about others and themselves and to create a space of radical openness in relations with others.

Perceiving a cultural Other

In considering how a cultural Other is perceived, our attention habitually turns to the relational nature of human existence and, more specifically, to the relationship between Self and the Other. This relationship is mediated by textual representations produced and consumed in a living space of communication. This is the semiotic space of culture with a plenitude of finalised and unfinalised meanings that signify relational symmetries and asymmetries (both imagined and real). All cultures produce text about selves and others that help them to either deny the alterity of others by insisting on their sameness and assimilation or recognise them as radically different and often in negative terms as hostile, underdeveloped, primitive, traditional and so on (cf. Levinas, 1969). In discussing how differences between people are commonly viewed, Kristeva (1991) describes the Other in terms of being a stranger or foreigner. When people confront Otherness, she argues, the Self typically responds with one of two kinds of logic, either assimilation or repression. If the Other is perceived as being sufficiently similar it can be seen as equal, thereby reflecting a logic of assimilation. However, if the Other is perceived as being different, and if that difference cannot be assimilated, then the difference of the Other is regarded as being inferior. This reflects a binary logic of repression (Barclay, 2010; Kristeva, 1991) where opposites are represented through such value-laden characteristics as good and bad, superior and inferior, right and wrong, and so on.

The cultural representations of sameness and difference imply the notion of boundary between us and them, Self and Other, our culture and foreign culture. The boundary separates, as it were, 'our' space which is safe and ordered from 'their' space which is hostile and chaotic. Besides this function of ordering and organising cultural reality, the boundary is also a mechanism of communication with others as cultural Othering. It is a semiotic location where the Other is translated and reduced to an object-like status. It is here that the strange and unfamiliar object becomes essentially hierarchised through its depreciation and marginalisation. In the process of Othering, the dominant subject attempts to secure a privileged place in the relational hierarchy; a position that is predicated on the idealised image of the self as superior against an inferior representation of the Other. Othering therefore habitually results in essentialist representations of the Other (e.g., stereotypes) that are applied to all members of a group, society or nation. Holliday (2011) argues in this regard that Othering is common in popular perceptions of difference through which a positive sense of self and a collective identity are produced. This mechanism of producing prejudices by the Western self is so obscured and perpetuated by societal, media and political discourses, that Othering is also commonly enacted in languages education (Holliday, 2011).

So how is it possible then to disrupt Othering in language education and start to think and learn about difference otherwise? If boundary divisions are so powerful and pervasive in creating asymmetrical differentiations, then seeking new ways of relating to and communicating with others becomes a project for languages education. Acts of Othering can persist only when others have unreciprocally been 'the Other' in our eyes. To imagine the Other otherwise in and through language education is not simply a matter of understanding other people and their cultures. Learning experiences are first and foremost experiences of encountering the Other that call for new frames of thought and conduct, demanding an ethical response. This ethical demand of recognising the Other as irreducible to the Self is about calling into question our own selves. It is tempting in learning languages and cultural practices of other people to render their strangeness and foreignness assimilable into our own worldviews, rather than questioning our own worldview and making the familiar strange. Encountering the Other demands dialogical ethics in responding to the uniqueness and particularity of others and social contexts.

In order to achieve this through language education, first, one should recognise language as a dialogical and social phenomenon that 'lies on the border between oneself and the other' (Bakhtin, 1986, p. 279). This dialogical notion of language applies equally to our being as a deepest form of communication where our thoughts and words are laden with traces of the words of Others:

> I am conscious of myself and become myself only while revealing myself for another, through another, and with the help of another. The most important acts constituting self-consciousness are determined by a relationship towards another consciousness ... To be means to communicate. (Bakhtin, 1984, p. 287)

In case of learning a foreign language, the dialogical architectonic of relationships between self and the Other is constitutive of one's intercultural becoming. Byram (2003) suggests, in this regard, that to become intercultural, one must develop a greater awareness of the relativity of one's culture by locating their own location in experiences of (an)other culture(s). Being intercultural is about learning to see one's own culture and Self through the eyes of the Other so that students and teachers can reflect on their own knowledge and meaning-making practices and, in turn, 'learning to unlearn' ways of thinking about and representing the Other (Andreotti and Souza, 2008).

A study of intercultural becoming

The empirical data for this chapter is based on a study that investigated Australian university students' perceptions of Indonesian culture, their intercultural interaction with Indonesian speakers and the pedagogical implications (Welsh, 2014). All student participants in the study were learners of Indonesian language in an Australian university. There were two cohorts of student participants. One cohort had only learned Indonesian in Australia, while the other cohort had undertaken part of their language study in Indonesia through an in-country study program accredited by their Australian university. This study abroad experience was either a short or long term program, ranging from six week intensive language study programs to long term stints of one year. In-depth interviews were conducted with all students. Two interviews were conducted with students who studied in Indonesia; the first interview was conducted in Indonesia during their in-country study, and the follow-up interview was conducted six months after their return to Australia. There were eleven student participants in this study, who came from four different Australian universities. The study also included in-depth interviews with lecturers of Indonesian from three of the

Australian universities where student participants were enrolled. Select data from several participants are used for this chapter, and, to protect participants' identities, all references to participants use pseudonym names.

Student participants of both cohorts perceived Indonesian culture to be represented by various characteristics that have been used to formulate the following three categories: traditional values; diversity of society; and norms of social interaction. Key factors that shaped students' perceptions were formal study and social interaction. The results of formal study were linked to knowledge, that is, cognitive or intellectual awareness of what Indonesia and Indonesians are like. Knowledge about the country, its history, religion, institutions and traditions led students to extrapolate the human dimensions of Indonesian culture, that is, what Indonesian people are like.

Conversely, when articulating an understanding of the cultural Other, students who had studied in Indonesia tended to emphasise human dimensions. Drawing from experience of social interaction, they tended to focus on Indonesian people to extrapolate what Indonesian culture is like. Social interaction during in-country experience had led these students to challenge pre-existing essentialised notions of Indonesian culture and to view culture as multi-faceted, complex and often contradictory. Students with extended experience in Indonesia reflected a more nuanced understanding of diversity of the cultural Other. For example, after one year of studying in Indonesia, Jane reflected on how her cultural perceptions had changed: 'I think you come with certain interpretations and when you get here it's a lot more complex than you could possibly imagine'. The experiential dimension of social interaction enabled students to reassess pre-existing perceptions of Indonesia, which had been acquired through formal study. After extensive experience in intercultural social interaction, student participants tended to see the cultural Other at an individual level rather than as an over-generalised collective. In arguing the benefits of experiential learning, Jane added: '... until you meet and talk to Indonesians themselves you don't realise just how many contradictions there are within this culture'. This suggests that students acquire a different kind of understanding of culture from interaction with native speakers, than they do from formal study, and reflects that culture is embedded in context and is socially constructed (Nieto, 2009). With this in mind, we examined the effects of experiential learning from in-country language study.

Student participants' experiences of intercultural engagement were highly variable, even for those who had extended experience in Indonesia. Students reflected a variable range of identity positions, and alternated between monologic and dialogic stances towards the Other. After studying for a year in Indonesia, Anita described how she responded to the cultural Other:

it really does depend on my mood, the location, the person I'm talking with. If I've had a really crap day ... I'm not going to make any adjustments. I'm just going to be me, I'm just going to speak English ... I'm going to be that cocky Western tourist ... If someone is really nice and genuinely interested ... I'm going to make allowances for them. I'm going to speak their language, I am going to act in a way I feel will make them feel more comfortable ...

Anita's response reflects an ambivalence for both Self and Other as she variably adopts a monologic and dialogic stance towards the Other. This kind of variable response to the Other was also evident in other students' reflections of their intercultural encounters. Monologism posits Self and Other as closed, finalised identity positions, and essentialises the Other, in order to maintain cultural boundaries between the Self and Other. By contrast, a dialogic stance is more responsive, and positions the encounter at the edges of, or across, cultural boundaries to engage the Other in a more open and dynamic manner. Dialogic encounters with the Other transforms culture into a dialogic act that engages otherness and dissolves clear boundaries between Self and Other, leading one to a space of in-between-ness, or thirdness.

However, intercultural engagement is not always entirely dialogic as individuals can switch to dogmatically restore a monologic, distinctive identity position, by rejecting others (Kristeva, 1991). Alternating between monologic and dialogic stances, as described by Anita above, demonstrates how voices of the Indonesian Other can struggle to compete with the dominant voices of the Australian Self that position the Indonesian Other as inferior and as a threat. Anita used the terms 'old self' to describe her monologic positioning in relation to the Other and the term 'new self' when she enacted the dialogic practice of thirding. She was well aware that she shuttled between different identity positions of her 'old self' and 'new self', and while recognising that her 'old self' was problematic in terms of being aloof and selfish, she still valued being able to retreat to that position. In contrast, she saw her 'new self' as being more polite, patient, responsive and mindful of others. She clearly attributed the transformation to her 'new self' to the cumulative effects of her experiences of sustained social interaction with the Other, in Indonesia.

The transformative potential of intercultural encounters is further evident in this study where Australian students in Indonesia experienced what it was like to be the minority Other of the dominant Indonesian Self. This experience reversed power relations between the Australian self and the Indonesian Other, and was conducive to Australian students engaging in the practice of what Bakhtin (1981) refers to as out-sidedness, where they could see the Australian Self through the eyes of the Indonesian Other. Out-sidedness enabled Anita to critically self-reflect, when in a follow-up interview 6 months after returning from study in Indonesia, she said: '...we have the most closed minded people ... It boggles the mind how Australians think about migrants...'. The cumulative effects of Anita's dialogic intercultural encounters led her to critically reappraise her sense of self in the following way: '... the biggest change that has come over me [is] not how I view Indonesians, but how I view Australians viewing everyone else ...'. This is dialogism at work, where Anita engaged in the practice of thirding to look at the Indonesian and Australian identity positions from an outside perspective, and in doing so, she was able to position herself at the margins of both. This reflects Anita's 'new self' where she questioned previously-held cultural assumptions that the Australian Self was somehow superior, in dialectical opposition to the inferior Indonesian Other.

Data of this study show a clear tendency for student participants to initially view the cultural Other as inferior, but also that students came to challenge their repressive views after a sustained level of social interaction in Indonesia. As a result of experiences in social interaction, participants demonstrated enhanced self-reflexivity and the ability to enact out-sidedness, where they decentred from the Self and stepped into an alternative reality, to look at their own culture through the eyes of the Other. In the space of out-sidedness, student participants were able to split 'the self' into the individual self and the collective Australian self. By adopting an outside view of themselves they were more readily able to position their individual self separately from the collective Australian self. These acts of thirding were dialogically constructed in relation to the Indonesian Other. Students' reflections of their intercultural engagement suggest that social encounters had the most profound effects, although social interactions were momentary events involving temporary identity positionings.

Despite the temporary and variable nature of intercultural dialogic encounters, the notion that the transformative effects of thirding can be cumulative is well recognised (Fitts, 2009; Gutierrez, Baquedano-Lopez & Tejeda, 1999; Kostogriz, 2009). More specifically, dialogism offers transformative potential due to a 'surplus of vision' that the Other offers for the Self in terms of learning; 'an excess of seeing through the eyes of the Other contributes to the recognition of my limitations, particularly the limits of my own worldview' (Kostogriz, 2009, p. 145). Transformative effects are evident in this study, where students demonstrate an ambivalence for both Self and Other, an enhanced critical perspective on their own cultural background, and an enhanced appreciation of the Other that enables them to see common ground between the Self and Other. These transformative effects resulted from a breadth and depth of intercultural third space encounters that students experienced whilst studying in Indonesia.

In a follow up interview six months after studying in Indonesia, Steve noted how he now is 'more tolerant' and has 'a respect for different cultures' and a greater 'understanding of other cultures in general'. This was a point of self-reflection that consistently emerged in follow up interviews with students who had studied in Indonesia, where they reported a new openness to others and cultural difference, something that they did not have before. These students also commented how other Australians, who had not had an overseas study experience, lacked such openness and tolerance of cultural difference. Several students expressed their frustration and disappointment at the monological, closed-mindedness of some of their fellow Australians. This was typified by Steve, who reported how he was 'offended by people who are ignorant of other cultures' and that his heightened awareness enabled him to 'pick up more of the … racist comments … by people that have never been there and don't understand and have no basis for what they say'.

Similarly, Anita was disheartened to see other Australians express negative stereotypical views towards foreigners, such as towards Indonesian Muslim women who she socialised with back in Australia. She reported encounters in her home town where she felt other Australians were glaring at her for being with and speaking the language of the foreign Other. In this instance, she identified more closely with the foreign Other and distanced herself from fellow Australians. She attributed such negative reactions from other Australians to prejudices that result from fear and ignorance of the Other, and to the cumulative effects of being brought up in a place where those attitudes are the norm.

With a heightened sensitivity to how the Self responds to the cultural Other, Anita expressed a strong sense of displacement since returning to Australia. She yearned for the intense social interaction that she had experienced in Indonesia, and for social norms that she called 'communalness'. Anita lamented a sense of loneliness that she felt since living back in Australia, which she suggested to be an individualistic society. However, during the interview, she demonstrated alternative voices of dialogism in recognising that the social norms of Indonesian and Australian societies both had their positive and negative dimensions. In this dialogical monologue, Anita was demonstrating a fluid and unfinalised view of social and cultural norms, as the practice of thirding.

All student participants who studied in Indonesia recognised that their intercultural experiences had enhanced their self-reflexivity, which helped them avoid adopting a repressive stance towards the Other, as had previously been a kind of instinctive initial reaction. They recognised that their awareness of Self and Other is an important part of how they react to the Other, and that how they act in an intercultural context is something that they can cognitively monitor and partially control. They had come to recognise aspects of Otherness within their own Self that had been previously obscure to them. Heightened self-reflexivity also enabled participants to view differences between Self and Other more as being equal, rather than as a superior-inferior dichotomy.

It was evident in the data that identity shifts occurred not only as an immediate result of specific social encounters, but also as a cumulative effect of multiple encounters. Identity positions were also found to be influenced by past voices, histories, memories and discourses. For example, the collective Australian self was used by participants in two ways, to either align with a stance that they viewed as being Australian, or to establish new identity positions using the Australian collective self as a referential point for differentiation. In many instances, students alternated between what they perceived to be Australian and Indonesian identity positions. They also adopted identity positions that were shaped dialogically, from contact with the Indonesian Other, which represented unique hybrid identity positions.

Several students who studied in Indonesia reported practicing linguistic hybridity, where they code switched between English and Indonesian. This was highlighted by Marie who said '… a lot of the time I can't really speak Indonesian or English because I'm always speaking half — somewhere in between. With my friends … I'll chuck in Indonesian words into English or I'll chuck English words into Indonesian'. This act of linguistic hybridity could only have been communicatively effective with people who had an adequate grasp of both languages. It shows how Marie engaged in-between-ness where clear boundaries between self and others were dissolved. This is an example of thirding where out-sidedness enables one to anticipate how the Self will be perceived and understood and dialogism enables one to uniquely respond to the Other.

In-between-ness was also noted by Margaret, one of the lecturer participants in this study who commented on how Australian students conducted themselves in intercultural encounters: '… they learn about ways of interacting in Indonesian … try to do it in an Indonesian way, but of course aren't quite. But they're not necessarily doing it in an Australian way'. This suggests that in their efforts to interact, students adjust social and cultural norms in unpredictable ways, to create unique intercultural spaces. Such spaces are characterised by fluid relationships where difference enacts its enriching potential to create new and dynamic intercultural dialogue that generates and negotiates new identity positions (Kostogriz & Tsolidis, 2008). The three lecturer participants in this research were unanimously, yet independently, of the opinion that their students demonstrate transformation as a result of their intercultural engagement, and that this is especially evident in students who undertake in-country study in Indonesia.

Tony, another lecturer participant, reported seeing some of his Australian students experience an 'intercultural awakening' as they develop the ability to appreciate and accept the strangeness of a cultural Other, and become curious about difference. Tony referred to borders associated with cultures that are often used to identify strangeness of the Other; strangeness that is viewed as threatening and inferior. He referred to subtle or obscure traits of Australian culture that students become increasingly aware of, as part of what he calls an 'intercultural awakening' where students develop the ability to see one's self through the eyes of the Other. As a result of extended experience in social interaction in Indonesia, heightened self-reflexivity and an increased awareness of self at a dialogic intra-personal level, students come to recognise subtle qualities of the self that they have seen in others.

Towards a pedagogy of experiential thirding

Considering the Bakhitnian notions of out-sidedness and dialogism between Self and Other, there are striking similarities with Kristeva's (1991) notion of reconciling one's self with otherness as a journey into the strangeness of the Self and of the Other. She describes this as being 'toward an ethic of respect for the irreconcilable' (Kristeva 1991, p. 182) whereby one can only tolerate the foreigner if one can tolerate one's self. Kristeva addresses the dynamics of a 'polymorphic' culture and suggests that in the context of living together people are required to take into account otherness within the self. She suggests that a culture does not merely assimilate difference, but that it dissolves the clear boundaries between self and others, creating a space of in-between-ness. This is consistent with what we term as thirding, as this study has found to be experienced by Australian students as a result of sustained and intensive contact with the cultural Other, during in-country language study. However, Kristeva recognises that this does not always occur and that individuals can dogmatically restore their distinctive identity positions by rejecting others. This, too, is consistent with data of this study where student participants are found to alternate between a binary logic of opposed identity positions of Self/Other and a dialogical in-between-ness.

What is required then is a framework in which the politics of seeing the Other and the 'us–them' binarism in language education is rethought productively to formulate a pedagogy of thirdspace. The starting point here is to approach language learning experiences as the domain of life, the unfixed, the dialectic, the dynamic — an intercultural space of action and meaning. Students need to learn how power–knowledge relationships saturate their lived experiences within the boundaries of constructed, multiple, 'real-and-imagined' spaces (Soja, 1996). They need to know how binaries are constructed in these asymmetrical relationships. The aim of a pedagogy of experiential thirding is to transcend socio-cultural binarisms by deconstructing the essentialised representations of meanings and identities through experiences that present 'other-than' choices. 'Thirding' is not a simple combination of the dominant and the marginal cultural understandings and practices but, rather, an open alternative that is both 'strikingly similar and different', radically open to difference and otherness and to a continuous production of new identities and meanings (Soja, 1996, p. 61). Without providing this kind of critical experience, language pedagogy will continue to be nothing more than another apology for demanding the Other to assimilate to the Self. Adopting a position that enacts assimilation or repression is 'ethically bankrupt' (Brandist, 2002, p. 48).

To overcome the phenomena of repression and assimilation, we argue the value of in-between experiences in language learning for students to start a journey into their selves, welcoming the stranger within themselves through an 'ethic of respect for the irreconcilable' (Kristeva 1991, p. 182). In this regard, we would define the pedagogical thirding as a space of language learning in which difference is respected, but at the same time as a movement, involving the re-construction and hybridisation of learners' identity which is generated in a communication with difference. This perspective recognises that students can establish a porous boundary between Self and the Other in intercultural communication and, in turn, a new set of possibilities in learning and meaning-making. Within such a space of in-between-ness it is necessary to hold a number of differences together, to arrange them in multidirectional and fluid orders, and, most importantly, not to render the identity of one as the negative of the Other. The main critical aim of third-space pedagogy is then to rupture the prevailing cultural codes and discourses that have already determined the trajectory of learning experiences in terms of neutralising the Other, by means of either assimilation or, worse, abjection. In-country language learning experiences, as the study demonstrates, do not involve a total upheaval but, rather, a radical shift in emphasis to those aspects of the Self and the Other that have been essentialised.

In arguing against essentialised views of identity, meaning and knowledge, a third-space pedagogy articulates language learning as an are(n)a of negotiation and representation of new expanded knowledge and identity. This model argues for a shift from the modes of neutralising difference in meaning-making to new modes of difference inclusion — the modes of pedagogic practice in which differences coexist and teaching does not rely exclusively on shared knowledge or fixed meanings. A Third-space pedagogy aims to decentre the singularity of unexamined knowledge and to dismantle the skewed binarism in relation to the Other by making sure that the perspectives brought to learning are not those of just the dominant cultural group, but that other perspectives are included and legitimated. Consequently, the pedagogic third-space relies on creating conditions in which students can have rich learning experiences of dialogical engagement with the Other, including those that are afforded through their out-bound mobility and in-country language learning programs.

In line with Dewey's concept of experiential learning (Ord & Leather, 2011), the data of this research suggests a cumulative effect of third-space encounters whereby students who have a longer duration of in-country experience tend to undergo a more profound transformation. This is consistent with the findings of Keenan and Miehls (2008) who suggest there is longer term transformative potential of engaging in intercultural third-space and that 'repeated third space experiences and re-examinations of one's subjectivity can result in psychological development over time' (Keenan & Miehls, 2008, p. 166). As a form of experiential learning, the cumulative exposure to intercultural social interaction during in-country study is likely to have a transformative effect on students and equip them with Asia related capabilities. The importance of thirding as a relational process injects a critical dimension to the concept of Asia literacy. The transformative potential of experiential thirding manifests itself in student participants in this research who demonstrate a shift in mindset from that of maintaining cultural boundaries to one of boundary crossing.

Such a shift in mindset can be unsettling and confronting for the individual who experiences a sense of displacement upon returning to their 'home culture' where they encounter boundary maintenance. Student participants in this study were aware that they had become more critical of their own culture and community since returning to Australia where they felt confronted by a mindset of dogmatic closure and boundary maintenance. While such transformation can be unsettling, leaving one feeling no longer belonging in one's community, it is also inspiringly productive as demonstrated by more fluid relations with other people and the ability to construct new spaces of interaction. Some participants reported being more open to otherness, which they demonstrated through a more welcoming attitude towards foreign others who they encounter in Australia, as well as through greater self-reflexivity, at both an individual and collective level.

Conclusion

In this chapter, we have proposed a pedagogy of thirding that seeks to enable practices of dialogic intercultural encounters in language education. This form of pedagogy is an attempt to articulate a framework for language education of university students which transcends the economic rationalism of current approaches to building Asia literacy through languages education. Third-space is a way out of essentialist and reductive perceptions of Asia. Critical of essentialist positions of identity and Asia literacy as knowing about others, it enables other positions and literacies to emerge. As a lived space, third-space is a mode of articulation of new identities and meanings, blurring the limitations of existing boundaries and calling into question established categorisations of culture, identity and Asia literacy. Despite the exposure of third-space to contradictions and ambiguities, it provides a spatial politics of difference that is inclusive rather than exclusive or assimilative. Third-space is not about a resolution of contradictions between differences but is itself a way of living and learning with difference(s) and ambivalence in systems of cultural representations and practices of representing. Thirding is construed as a political strategy of languages education where power relations are dialogically re-inscribed. Exposure to this type of language teaching is likely to make a contribution to students' critical world-mindedness, to become more open to difference and to act responsively in relation to the Other.

Critical world-mindedness, as proposed by Lo Bianco (2009), is evident in the data of this study where individual students, through experiential thirding, have developed their capabilities to critique stereotypical, essentialised representations of others, and to be open to the unfamiliar and the strange. In this way, students see culture as representing relational human traits, some of which are common to the Self and Other. This is a transformative realisation, as opposed to conceptualising culture merely as representing static notions of categorical difference such as religion, race, ethnic group, artifacts, traditional practices or customs. By recognising shared humanity, students are better enabled to view the Other as equal rather than as inferior. By engaging otherness ethically, they recognise common ground between Self and Other, despite unresolvable differences remaining. Through dialogic reflexive thinking and critical world-mindedness, students can also attain a better understanding of the cultural complexities of their individual and collective selves, and how they position themselves and are positioned in the world. The opportunity to experience the Other through a genuine dialogicality of unmerged voices can lead to third-space literacy, something that goes well beyond the binary logic in teaching and learning the languages and cultures of Asian others.

References

Andreotti, V. & Souza, L. (2008). Translating theory into practice and walking minefields: lessons from the project 'Through Other Eyes'. *International Journal of Development Education and Global Learning,* 1(1), 23–36.

Auchmuty, J. (1970). *The teaching of Asian languages and cultures.* Canberra, Australia: AGPS.

Bakhtin, M. (1981). *The dialogical imagination: Four essays by M. M. Bakhtin.* Austin: University of Texas Press.

Bakhtin, M. (1984). *Problems of Dostoevsky's poetics*. Minneapolis, MN: University of Minnesota Press.

Bakhtin, M. (1986). *Speech genres and other late essays*. C. Emerson and M. Holquist (Eds.). Austin: University of Texas Press.

Barclay, F. (2010). Kristeva's stranger within: The question of the foreigner in Daniel. *Paragraph, 33*(1), 1–19.

Brandist, C. (2002) *The Bakhtin Circle: Philosophy, culture and politics*. Sterling, VA: Pluto Press.

Fitts, S. (2009). Exploring the Third Space in a dual-language setting: Opportunities and challenges. *Journal of Latinos and Education, 8*(2), 87–104.

Gutierrez, K., Baquedano-Lopez, P. & Tejeda, C. (1999). Rethinking diversity: Hybridity and hybrid language practices in the Third Space. *Mind, Culture, and Activity, 6*(4), 286–303.

Henderson, D. (1999). *The Rudd Report: An anatomy of educational reform* (Doctoral dissertation). Griffith University, Brisbane, Australia.

Holliday, A. (2011). *Intercultural communication and ideology*. Los Angeles, CA: Sage.

Jakubowitcz, A. (2011). Empires of the sun: Towards a post-multicultural Australian politics. *Cosmopolitan Civil Societies Journal, 3*(1), 65–85.

Keenan, E. & Miehls, D. (2008). Third space activities and change processes: An exploration of ideas from social and psychodynamic theories. *Clinical Social Work, 36*, 165–175.

Kostogriz, A. & Tsolidis, G. (2008). Transcultural literacy: Between the global and local, *Pedagogy, Culture & Society, 16*(2), 125–136.

Kostogriz, A. (2009). Professional ethics in multicultural classrooms: English, hospitality and the other. In J. Miller, A. Kostogriz, & M. Gearon (eds.), *Culturally and linguistically diverse classrooms new dilemmas for teachers* (pp.132-150). Clevedon, Engoand: Multilingual Matters.

Kristeva, J. (1991). *Stranger to ourselves*. Hemel Hempstead, England: Harvester Wheatsheaf.

Levinas, E. (1969). *Totality and infinity: An essay on exteriority*. A. Lingis (Trans.). Pittsburgh, PA: Duquesne University Press.

Lowe, D. (2010). *The Colombo Plan and 'soft' regionalism in the Asia–Pacific: Australian and New Zealand cultural diplomacy in the 1950s and 1960s*. Geelong, Australia: Alfred Deakin Research Institute.

Lo Bianco, J. (2009). Dilemmas of efficiency, identity and worldmindedness. In J. Miller, A. Kostogriz, & M Gearon (eds), *Culturally and linguistically diverse classrooms: New dilemmas for teachers,* (pp. 113–131). Clevedon, England: Multilingual Matters.

Nieto, S. (2009). *Language, culture, and teaching: Critical perspectives*. New York, NY: Routledge.

O'Neill, B. (2009, October 10). Peril refuses to go away. *The Australian*.

Ord, J. & Leather, M. (2011). The substance beneath experiential learning: The importance of John Dewey for outdoor education. *Australian Journal of Outdoor Education, 15*(2), 13–23.

Rudd, K. (1994). *Asian languages and Australia's economic future*. A report prepared for the Council of Australian Governments on a proposed National Asian Languages/Studies Strategy for Australian schools. Brisbane, Australia: Queensland Government Printer.

Soja, E. (1996). *Thirdspace: Journeys to Los Angeles and other real-and-imagined places.* Oxford, England: Blackwell.

Welsh, A. (2014). *Language teaching for the Asian century: Indonesian in Australian universities* (Unpublished doctoral dissertation). Deakin University, Geelong, Australia.

Chapter 8

Arabic Language Interferences in ESL Among International Students in Australian Language Centres

Abe W. Ata

Introduction

Language learning is a most complex system of communication — one which triggered a large number of theories associated with various positions. Although it is beyond the scope of this chapter to survey these theories in a concise and clear fashion, their contribution is not to be dismissed. Knowledge about these theories, estimated to be in excess of 20, will help us to understand and explain better how learners of L2 succeed or fail; the subtleties of intercultural communication; the variation between language and meaning; differences of learning between individuals and the relationship between them. A clear comprehensive view of these and other roles such as the functionalist, pragmatic, cognitive, social are found in the work by Mitchell and Miles (2004); Herschensohn & Young-Scholten (2013); Cook (2013); and Doughty (2003).

Language acquisition, often considered an act of mere imitation and memorisation, is, in fact, a very complex activity. Scholars in the field, led by Krashen in the 1980s, made a subtle distinction between *acquisition* and *learning*. They propose that the former is both subconscious and anxiety free; that is, when a child constructs a grammar of his/her native language by listening to linguistic data and forming generalisations which come to function unconsciously and automatically, as grammatical rules for the language. To extend this point to a classroom setting, this 'natural' approach emphasises communication, and places decreased importance on conscious study of grammar and explicit correction of student errors (Krashen and Terrell, 1983). The fact that a child produces unacceptable forms such as 'foots' for 'feet' and 'goed' for 'went', which he cannot have learnt by imitation, means that he is involved in a complex activity of hypothesis verification. At a later stage, when the child discovers by further observation and socialisation by others as the child participates in discourses in one's native language that his or her rules for forming the plural and the past are too general he/she modifies them to account for irregularities.

By contrast, it is suggested that learning is a conscious effort; that is when a child studies and practices what the learner needs and wants and what is perceived as relevant.

In this regards Harmer (2011) says that the language that is learnt tends 'to get in the way' of the how the acquired-language production and may inhibit spontaneous communication ; and that one is to keep monitoring from the acquired language store that what is coming from it is 'O K' (Harmer, (2011, p. 47).

Having said that, the link between attitudes and language acquisition was found to be so strong that they way learners attitudinal leanings; that is, how they feel about language, and teacher's largely determines a successful acquisition and performance. Subsequently, one could assume that if second language learners initiate their language learning while they have negative attitudes towards the target language and the people using that language, they are not expected to make considerable progress in their process of language learning. This assumption was held as far back as 1995 when Truitt (1995) hypothesised that students' beliefs and attitudes about language learning may vary based on cultural background and previous experiences. Thus, it can be argued that positive or negative attitudes do not develop accidentally but have some reasons for their emergence. Malallaha (2000) investigated the attitudes of Arab learners towards English and discovered that they have positive attitudes toward the English language and their proficiency in tests was positively related to their positive attitude to English. Hence, it can be argued that having positive or negative attitudes towards a certain language can exert considerable effect on the learners' performance on a language test.

Several linguists proposed the idea that the transfer implies a process in which the learner tends to assume that the system of L2 is more or less the same as his/her L1, until the learner discovers that it is not. In other words the learner senses or assumes that there is some kind of influence on the transfer of language for it to actually happen. In other words, one's native language influences the language being studied, with the result being one of transfer. If a skill is transferred from the L1 results in production that is different from target language expectation (L2) it is called negative; and when the skills leads to a smoother transfer it is called positive. (Odlin, 2005; Allard, Bourdeau, & Mizoguchi, 2011).

The same process of hypothesising and rule formation is employed in acquiring a second language. However, for reasons not completely understood, the capacity for language acquisition diminishes with age. It is generally recognised that a learner commencing second language acquisition after puberty will be unlikely to achieve native competency in the second language. It is also recognised adult second language learners can learn a second language at a fast rate initially by utilising knowledge of their first languages, and by the same token knowledge of their first language is a source of interference. This change constitutes a handicap against the learner who is often exposed to his second language, under artificial situations in the classroom, years after he has gained control of the system of his first language. The learner of a second language also has an added complication in the form of interference from the system of his native language which has been internalised. It is this type of interference which is at the source of recurring and stubborn structures in the English of Arab students.

With this brief description, one might attempt to explain the errors that a native speaker of Arabic makes when speaking or writing in English. Naturally, one finds errors such as misspellings, mispronunciations and grammatical usages which are not the result of Arabic interference. Such errors are due to improper generalisations or insufficient exposure, and are also made by speakers of languages other than Arabic. By and large, the majority of the errors analysed is lexical and grammatical.

First language interference, which varies in degree with the individual's incompetence in his second language, is manifested at all levels of linguistic structure. Even though the number and nature of linguistic levels is subject for argument, one might assume the existence of the following levels:

(a) phonological
(b) grammatical
(c) semantic
(d) stylistic.

Each of these will be discussed separately, keeping in mind that the separation is artificial and solely intended to facilitate the analysis.

Methodological design and data analysis

The sampling method involved the selection of 90 Arabic speaking candidates drawn at random from Monash, Melbourne RMIT and Deakin University language centres. (These centres have a large cluster of Arabic speaking students who are funded by their governments including Saudi Arabia, the Gulf, Kuwait and Libya to study English prior to, and as required by these universities, to enrol in a future graduate or postgraduate degrees.

A structured questionnaire was administered to these students consisting of pre and post International English Language Testing System (IELTS) candidates to collect data on their knowledge and attitudes to IELTS. The questionnaire was designed largely to elicit responses as to why Arabic speakers of English formulate incorrect parts of speech in writing, and under what conditions. What kinds of grammatical, phonological, semantic and stylistic interferences exist between English and Arabic including intonation, stress, and rhythm features; and the manner in which contrastive features cause semantic confusion and unintentionally triggered responses.

The second task involved participants to write an essay of their choice on a select subject that are interested in writing. Participants who completed this task early were asked individually to read a paragraph from their essay. This was recorded so as to capture the sound segments for further phonological analysis.

Analysis of findings in this paper is largely qualitative and is based solely on the second task. Administration of the questionnaire was completed over a period of 8 weeks.

(a) Phonological interference

Each language has its own inventory of sound segments — consonants and vowels, which are combined, according to systematic patterns, to form syllables and words. In addition, a language has 'supra-segmental' features (e.g., stress and rhythm) which superimpose on the segmental sounds. By comparing these phonological aspects in English and Arabic, it is possible to identify the problems which the speaker of one of these languages will face in learning the other. In English, for instance, there is no sound which is equivalent to the Arabic / ^ /; and consequently, a native speaker of English will substitute for this sound the closest sound available in his language which is /a/.

The Arabic speaker learning English will have to deal with a number of distinctions which Arabic does not employ in its system of segmental sounds. Thus, the most common mispronunciations involve the following distinctions /p-b/, /f-v/, /k-g/, the vowel sounds in 'boat' vs 'bought', and the vowel sound in 'nut' vs 'not'. Other problems are caused by the sounds represented by the italicised letters in thin, then, thing, and by the different phonetic quality of English and Arabic /t/ /dl/ /rl/ and /i/. Even though these problems are mainly manifested in speech, they are sometimes transferred into writing as shown by the examples below. These were drawn from the essays which were written by the participants of this study:

1. He brayed to the God for merci.
2. I did not bitch well in my baseball game.
3. I was advised not to put my eggs in one pasket.
4. My father infested 1200 dollars in the bank.
5. We may pull Shakespeare out of his crave.

6. Ulysis was bold in battle.
7. Jonson was too fund of Shakespeare.

Example number 3 poses an interesting question as to the reason behind writing and pronouncing the word 'basket' as 'pasket', when the speaker is expected to do the exact opposite. The answer lies in the fact that this student, after being repeatedly corrected for substituting /b/ for /p/, is unconsciously using this information in inappropriate situations in an effort to be correct. This process is known as hyper-correction.

Another possible source of interference is the pattern according to which syllables are formed. When an Arabic student pronounces 'springe' 'sipring' or 'spiring', it is because Arabic generally does not allow for a cluster of three consonants in one syllable. However, contrary to English, Arabic does allow for a sequence of two identical consonants. Hence an Arabic speaker often pronounces the double consonants in words such as 'appointment', 'account', 'arrest', and 'umbrella'.

The supra-segmental features of a foreign language are probably the most difficult to learn and they are often the clues that betray a foreign accent. In fact many people who have mastered these segmental sounds of English run into some difficulty with rhythm, pitch and stress. To compare and contrast the supra-segmental feature; Arabic and English is a talk which is beyond scope of the present discussion. Some examples of stress patterns, however, should clarify point. The word '*dic*tionary', which has a primary stress on the first syllable, is often pronounced 'dic*tionary*', with stress on the second syllable. The wrong placement of stress is clearly due to interference from the Arabic stress pattern of words such as *madrasati-* (my school), which contains same number and type of syllables as in 'dictionary'. Other common examples are 'develo'pment' for 'deve'lopment', which is analogous with saala'thum (she asked them), and 'seco'ndary' for 'se'condary', which is analogous with *sa'altani* (you asked me).

(b) Grammatical interference

Grammatical interference from Arabic to English is undoubtedly one of the main factors contributing to the high consumption of aspirin among teachers of English as a second language. The result of such interference is often manifested in unintelligibility, ambiguity or unintended meanings. But even when the meaning is clear, it is difficult to get at because of the foreign structure that carries it. One source of challenges for learners is grammatical construction; that is the syntactic string of words ranging from sentences over phrasal structures to certain complex lexemes, such as phrasal verbs. Here, grammatical construction differs in a number of respects from Arabic to English. Here are some examples:

1. There is a large school consists of nine buildings.
2. Freedom is a meaningful term cannot be understood.
3. I did not read the book which I borrowed it from you yet.
4. He wrote a brilliant way which he reached the top by it.
5. It is a play about a man which pretends to be dying from hunger.
6. But Satan who God postponed his punishment, was very rebellious.

If translated verbatim into Arabic, the above sentences could be perfectly grammatical.

They illustrate four points of interference from the grammatical rules which govern the relative construction in Arabic:

i) Sentences 8 and 9 follow the Arabic rule which requires the absence of a relative pronoun just in case the noun modified by a relative clause is indefinite (e.g. *madrasatun,tata'-llafu min* ... vs *al-madrasatu llati tata'allaju min* ...).

ii) Sentences 10 and 11 are the result of applying an Arabic rule which requires that an object pronoun referring to the modified noun be included in the relative clause (e.g., *alkitaatuu lladhi ak-kadhtuhu ... tariigatum wa sla biha*).

iii) Sentence 12 shows that the distinction in English between the human and non-human forms of relative pronouns (who-which) has no equivalent in Arabic. Hence, the two forms are sometimes used interchangeably.

iv) Sentence 13 is the direct transfer of an Arabic structure functioning as a substitute for an English structure (possessive form of the relative pronoun) which has no equivalent in Arabic (e.g., *Ashashaytaamu lladhi ajjala llaahu ga saa sahu*).

Another major area of interference is detected in the verb system — particularly with regard to agreement of tenses, agreement between subject and verb, infinitive forms, and improper use of tense. The examples below will hopefully illustrate these points without subjecting the reader to any further grammatical jargon. Arabic speakers will no doubt be able to identify the source of these problems by translating the sentences into Arabic:

1. He looked to the people as if they are beasts.
2. We hear Jonson says, 'men fear death'.
3. He signed a paper which let Shylock to take one kilo of Antonio's flesh.
4. We must to learn in order to succeed.
5. He asked people to don't fear death.
6. He told his wife that he has not eaten since two days.
7. Several of these problems has no solution.

8. In Spencer's poems we notice it deals with human nature.
9. I cut my hair (meaning: I had my hair cut).

Other common errors, though not restricted to Arabic speakers, are to be found in verb-adverbial combinations such as 'turn off', 'turn out', 'turn in', 'turn up', 'turn down', and so on. Such distinctions, which have no corresponding forms in Arabic, seem to be difficult to learn. Thus, we often find people 'filling up' application forms, but 'filling in' glasses; 'wiping out' baby's face, and 'wiping' the water on the floor, 'picking out' garbage, and 'picking up' a nice colour. The writers of the two sentences below intended to use 'take off' in examples 1 and 2, below:

1. He took out his shoes to rest his feet.
2. A good teacher should rub what he writes on the board before he leaves the class.

The use of prepositions (almost all of them) is a particularly difficult aspect of second language hearing. The problems which stem from first language interference from the later sentence examples are:

- the addition of a preposition where it is not needed (e.g., sentence 3)
- the election of a necessary preposition (e.g., sentence 10)
- the use of the wrong preposition (e.g., sentence 5).

1. I met with a pretty girl on my way to the school.
2. I am in favour with his ideas.
3. I chose science because it concerns with the mind.
4. He got married from a woman older from him.
5. He was angry from his wife.
6. I paid to him five pounds and thanked him.
7. Let me do to you a favour.
8. I'll try to reach to my aim.
9. I left to Beirut by the plane.
10. I went to London after noon.
11. I agree with George for how he looks to the freedom.
12. Most of the writers in that time admired him.
13. I am responsible about my actions.
14. He did it by his own.

The remaining examples in this section illustrate the problems with the verb 'to be' (1–3); indirect questions (4 and 5); the distinction between 'too' and 'very' (6), the distinction between 'for' and 'since' (7), and the use of the article (8 and 9).

1. He lyrics can sung be the people today.
2. This literary creation worth reading.
3. He is will succeed in all his life.
4. I don't remember how many plays did Shakespear write.
5. It is difficult to ask what is literature.
6. His children were too happy when he returned.
7. She didn't see her husband since 3 years.
8. A poet must admire the beauty.
9. George also wrote poem.

(c) Semantic interference

The most striking instances of semantic interference are likely to be found in idiomatic usages and in common and useful expressions such as greetings. The use of 'welcome' as an initial greeting corresponds to the use of *ahlan* in Arabic. The answer to 'How are you?' is often 'thank God'. 'How much is your age?' has been for 'How old are you?' and 'How much your watch?' for 'What time do you have?' The list of such errors is inexhaustible.

Another instance of semantic interference involves the use of a word in an inappropriate context which usually requires a different word with a similar meaning. This often happens when two or more words in English correspond (at least in the mind of the individual) to one word in Arabic, thus obscuring some meaning distinctions. Examples of this nature (1–9) includes sets of words such as 'do-make', 'shallow-superficial', 'steal-rob', 'agree-approve', and so on, and so on.

1. Everyone does mistakes because nobody perfect.
2. He was capable of making the job.
3. Most of the lakes in Lebanon are superficial.
4. The carpenter worked a nice table for her.
5. He saw a person stealing a shop.
6. We don't approve with him about the things which he said it.
7. John shows how God made the world in six days and then he retired.
8. We can take many informations from it about the human beings.
9. If someone speak something wrong, he feels sorry.

The use of malapropisms (mistaking one word for another) is not specifically an Arabic interference problem. Nevertheless, it is quite common, as suggested by the following examples:

1. Shakespeare's plays are still wildly read.
2. Julius Caesar is a hysterical drama.

3. The play is empty from the feminine sect.
4. Swift wrote 'Tales of a Tub' which is a satire about religious sex.
5. Thomas Gray wrote the Alergy in a country church yard.
6. Wordsworth wrote 'Immitations of Immorality'.
7. Another reason for the decline of the medieval church was the immorality of the clergymen.
8. I plan to study petroleom theology in the Australia.
9. Nearly every religion has been connected with a profit.

Examples of incorrect word form are:
- he wants to get marriage
- a famous musician band
- his economical problems
- it was a failure marriage;

and of incorrect context:
- bring a boy (= give birth to a boy)
- lose dignity (= lose virginity)
- finish business (= do business)
- carrying her baby (= pregnant with her baby);

and of incorrect choice of words:
- repair his mistake
- Al-Qaidah arrangement
- pray the prayers
- work your work
- destroyed houses (= broken homes)
- hurts the mind (= harms the brain).

(d) Stylistic interference

One may master the grammatical and semantic systems of a foreign language, yet fall into the stylistic trap of the first language. The type of interference is quite apparent in the English of many Arabic speakers for whom the distinction between descriptive and creative writing is non-existent. Consequently, poetic elements and flowery expressions find their way into letters and composition papers, with effects ranging between the humorous and the pathetic. The samples below are taken from a composition paper (1), and application form for an MA program (2), and a letter to the editor of a TESL magazine (3):

>1. Is there something its beauty more than love? No and a thousand times, no.

2. In the absence of enlightenment in our Arab world and due to the lackness of knowledge and justice, one can't stumble on a torch to scatter the arrows of darkness better than education.

3. Dear the editor,

I can't say what I felt when our darling 'ESL' came at my hand, I came at the highest of my spirits and soon began to swallow what is richly and cleverly put down on 'her' ...

Again I hope I could continue to be one of your forever friends; and 'ESL' would get more success and prosperity; with my dearest wishes and greetings. Thanks very much again.

Conclusive summary

This chapter aims at addressing the problem of cultural and Arabic language interference and we would be able then to build an instructional system to help students overcome these patterns of errors which precipitate in the acquisition English.

Several broad and detailed learning difficulties and analysis of underlying concept difficulties were presented — both for teachers to create new cultural aware teaching scenarios, and students to understand and interpret them as they are required to demonstrate higher levels of English proficiency.

Several implications arise in presenting the various categories of classic errors encountered through second language learning as in the case of Arabic-English. A key one is to provide a 'culturally-aware' education (see also, Blanchard & Allard 2010). This kind of direction may provide a stronger case for education that is responsive to cultural and linguistic differences. In this regard, the starting point of such responsiveness is not much a deficit view of international students but rather an understanding of linguistic/cultural origins of difference. Errors then can be perceived differently and work can be done in the space inter-language — an interim language system which is attributed to Larry Selinker (see also Van Patten & Benati, 2010).

The principle behind inter-language theory is that the language of second-language learners is governed by systematic rules as in any other language, and that these rules are different from those of the language being learned and from those of the learner's native language. Hence at every stage of learning, language learners do not merely copy what native speakers do, but create an entirely new language system unique to themselves. Selinker (1972) proposed then that inter-language is based on three basic principles: (a) over-generalisation from patterns found in the language being learned; (b) transfer from patterns found in the learner's native language, and (c) fossilisation, the phenomenon of a learner's language ceasing to develop (Van Patten & Benati, 2010).

The focus on learner errors is arguably useful to language teachers as a means of enhancing teaching methodology, with the caution that teachers avoid overgeneralisation and the search for a unitary source of an error. An awareness of the types of errors Arabic speakers tend to commit is necessary for language teachers so that they are able to properly and timely correct inappropriate and unacceptable utterances.

Finally, whether one reacts to errors of linguistic interference with laughter or with dismay, one must never be unsympathetic. Such errors should be viewed not as a result of stupidity, but rather a natural consequence of the interaction between two extremely complex linguistic systems. Some errors, though, defy linguistic analysis and can only be attributed to individual genius: for instance, the statement of an English Language Intensive Courses for Overseas Students (ELICOS) postgraduate student, who said he had read with great interest 'The Rape of the Pope' by Alexander Locke.

Learning and teaching a second language are activities which require a lot of time and effort, and, above all, a good sense of humour.

References

Allard, D., Bourdeau, J., & Mizoguchi, R. (2011). Addressing cross-linguistic influence and related cultural factors using computer-assisted language learning. In E. Blanchard & D. Allard (Eds.), *Handbook of research on culturally-aware information technology: Perspectives and models* (pp. 582–598). Hershey, PA: IGI Global.

Al-Salmani, A. (2002). *Collocations and idioms in English-Arabic translation* (Master's thesis). University of Salford.

Bhela, B. (1999). Native language interference in learning a second language. *International Education Journal, 1*, 22–31.

Blanchard, E., & Allard, D. (Eds.) (2010). *Handbook of research on culturally-aware technology: Perspectives and models*. Hershey, PA: IGI Global.

Channell, J. (1981). Applying semantic theory to vocabulary teaching. *English Language Teaching Journal, 35*, 115–122.

Cook, V. (2013). *Second language learning anf language teaching*. London, England, Routledge.

Doughty, C. (2003). *A handbook of second language acquisition*. Oxford, Engoand: Blackwell.

Ellis, N. (1997). Vocabulary acquisition. In N. Schmitt & M. McCarthy (Eds.), *Vocabulary: Description, acquisition and pedagogy*. Cambridge, England: Cambridge University Press.

Emery, P. (1987, July). *Collocation: A problem in Arabic/English translation?* Paper presented at the BRISMS Annual Conference.

Emery, P. (1991). Collocation in modern standard Arabic. *Journal of Arabic Linguistics, 23*, 56–65.

Farghal, M., & Shunnaq, A. (1999). *Translation with reference to English and Arabic.*

James, C. (1998). *Errors in language learning and use.* London, England: Longman.

Harmer, J. (2011). *How to teach English.* Essex, Pearson Education.

Herschensohn, J., & Young-Scholten, M. (Eds.). 2013. *The Cambridge handbook of second language acquisition.* Cambridge, Engoand: Cambridge University Press.

Kharma, N., & Hajjaj, A. (1997). Errors in English among Arabic speakers. Beirut, Lebanon: Librairie du Liban.

Krashen, S.D. & Terrell, T.D. (1983). *The natural approach: Language acquisition in the classroom.* London, Engand: Prentice Hall Europe.

Mahmoud, A. (2003). The inter-lingual errors of Arab students in the use of English binomials. *Journal of Documentation and Humanities, 15,* 9–22.

Malallaha, S. (2000). English in an Arabic environment: current attitudes to English among Kuwait University students. *International Journal of Bilingual Education and Bilingualism, 3,* 19–43.

Mitchell, R., & Myles. F. (2004). *Second language learning theories* (2nd ed.). London, England: Arnold.

Myles, F (2010).The development of theories of second language acquisition, Language Teaching, *43*(3), 320–332.

Odlin, T. (2005). Crosslinguistic influence and conceptual transfer: What are the concepts? *Review of Applied Linguistics,* 25, 3-25.

Our World Through English (Series 2002–2004). *The English language course for the Sultanate of Oman.* English Language Curriculum Department. Ministry of Education.

Ringbom, H. (1987). *The role of the first language in foreign language learning.* Philadelphia, PA: Multilingual Matters.

Selinker, Larry. 1972. 'Interlanguage.' *International Review of Applied Linguistics in Language Teaching, 10*(1–4), 209–232.

Sheen, R. (2001). Contrastive analysis in language teaching: Time to come from the cold. *Academic Exchange Quarterly, 5,* 119–125.

Taiwo, R. (2004). Helping ESL learners to minimize collocation errors. *The Internet TESL Journal, 10*(4). Retrieved from http:// iteslj.org.

Truitt, H. (1995). Beliefs about language learning: A study of Korean University students learning English. *Texas Papers in Foreign Language Education, 2,*12–28.

Van Patten, B. & Benati, A. (2010). *Key terms in second language acquisition.* London, England: Continuum. p. 100.

Chapter 9

Reconceptualising the Academic Writing Difficulties of International Students

Linda Y. Li and Yanyin Zhang

Introduction

International students from non-English speaking background (NESB) encounter a wide range of academic challenges at Australian universities. Research on international students' academic experiences suggests that the adjustment to a new learning environment where expectations, requirements and approaches to teaching and learning are different is a challenging process for most international students (Lin & Yi, 1997). At Australian universities, the expectations of independent learning, active participation in the learning process, and taking responsibility of learning are new requirements for international students from educational systems where more teacher-centred approaches are still dominant. The linguistic demands of learning in English as a second language and cultural differences further compound their difficulties. In particular, research suggests that most international students experience tenacious difficulties in academic writing even though their confidence in other academic language skills such as listening, speaking and reading has improved after some years of study (Zhang & Mi, 2010). Evidence from research highlights academic writing as a heightened challenge for international students. It has been identified as a **significant** predictor of academic performance (Li, Chen, & Duanmu, 2010) and a main factor impacting learning and academic performance (Matters, Winter, & Nowson, 2004; Phakit & Li, 2011).

Academic writing is central to a student's success in higher education. What makes it particularly difficult for international students? The challenges presented by the ever larger number of international students have generated considerable research. However, a deficit view of international students is prevalent in the existing literature. In the deficit mode, international students are portrayed as difficult and passive learners: they lack independent, critical thinking skills, cannot write in proper academic English, tend to learn by memorisation and plagiarise in assignments (Ballard & Chanchy, 1991). Previous research on the academic writing of international students, which is often framed within the deficit model, tends to focus on the inadequacy of English language as the major source of difficulties. Earlier studies have identified English proficiency as the best predictor of perceived level of academic difficulties (Xu, 1991), the major factor causing academic stress (Wan, Chapman, & Biggs, 1992), and the major source of difficulties in managing the demand of study and time, and assignment preparation (Burns, 1991; Lin & Yi, 1997).

Academic writing in a second language is a complex, developmental process that can be impacted by multiple factors, both contextual and personal (Richards, 2003). The focus on language-related problems, as prevalent in existing literature framed within the deficit model, has failed to provide a full account of the difficulties arising from the complexity of academic writing in a second language. A holistic and contextualised approach should be taken to gain a comprehensive understanding of the academic writing difficulties of international students.

In this chapter, we argue that the academic writing difficulties of international students go beyond language-related problems. Drawing on second language writing theory and relevant research on international students, we reconceptualise academic writing difficulties by exploring the complexity of academic writing in a second language in light of the linguistic, rhetorical, cultural, educational and individual differences that may impact on the academic writing processes of international students. We contest the deficit view by examining evidence from research that reveals the successful strategies used by international students in tackling academic writing difficulties and the factors conducive to success in academic writing. We propose that the bilingual/multilingual, educational and cultural resources of international students should be drawn on to turn the sources of difficulty into resources useful for developing their academic writing capacities.

Factors contributing to the academic writing difficulties of international students

'Learning to write in a second language is one of the most challenging aspects of second language learning' (Hyland, 2003, p. xiii). For NESB international students, academic writing is not only linguistically demanding, but also highly cognitively taxing as they have to express complex ideas in a second language following unfamiliar academic writing conventions. The complexity of academic writing in a second language involves a number of factors that may impact on the academic writing process of international students. These factors reflect the nature of academic writing in a second language that is different from writing in the native tongue. They include linguistic, rhetorical, cultural, educational and individual factors, a combination of which contributes to the heightened challenge of academic writing for international students.

Linguistic factors

Comparative research into first and second language writing shows second language writers take longer time to compose, tend to write more slowly and produce few words of text (Hyland, 2003). Compared with native-English speakers, NESB international students have limited linguistic resources in English as their second or third language. Their linguistic knowledge base of English is different. For example, compared with native-English speakers, second language writers have a much smaller vocabulary base and they do not have the intuitive ability for grammar and vocabulary when writing academic assignments (Hyland, 2003). Lack of control of sufficient vocabulary may slow down students' reading, impact their understanding of texts, and restrict their writing output (Schmitt, 2005). Second language writing research also reveals that first language linguistic conventions may interfere with writing in the second language; the grammar or the orthography of the writing system itself may pose considerable barriers (Richards, 2003).

The linguistic issues of international students have been well recognised in numerous earlier studies that focused on language-related problems. Research shows that NESB international students require a lot more time and efforts to complete academic writing assignments: they required extra time to read their textbooks and other materials for their assignments (Lin & Yi, 1997); they struggled to convey their ideas in appropriate and correct English (Campbell & Li, 2008). In Hee and Woodrow's (2008) study on international students' approaches to academic assignments, the students' low self-perception in English language proficiency affected their confidence in interacting with both peers and academic staff, thus impacting on their assignment preparation.

Although linguistic factors seem to be the most immediately obvious causes of difficulties for international students, academic writing does not involve just technical skills. Proficiency in English language surely provides a solid linguistic base for writing, yet accuracy in grammar and good control of vocabulary do not necessarily lead to effective academic writing. Some international students coming from educational systems where English is the medium of instruction in schools (e.g., students from Asian countries such as India, the Philippines, Singapore, or African countries such as Nigeria), still struggle with meeting the requirements of academic writing though

English does not seem to be a problem for them. It is therefore necessary to examine factors beyond the linguistic difficulties.

Rhetorical factors

Research in contrastive rhetoric offers insights for understanding another aspect of academic writing difficulties for international students from first language backgrounds of different rhetorical conventions from English. Originated from Kaplan's (1966) work on examining the patterns of presenting ideas and organising texts in different languages, contrastive rhetoric maintains that each language has rhetorical conventions unique to it, and first language conventions may impact on second language writing in English (Connor, 1996). For example, Kaplan identified one salient difference between English writing and Oriental writing: while English writers started by making the point following an essentially linear pattern, Oriental writers tended to use an indirect approach and came to the point only at the end. Although Kaplan's original findings have been widely criticised for being too prescriptive and ethnocentric, research informed by the principles of contrastive rhetoric has yielded findings that have useful insights for understanding the academic writing difficulties of NESB students. For example, the lack of a clear thesis statement in the introduction of essay writing by international students is commonly highlighted by subject lecturers, and students struggle with the requirement of including a thesis statement in essay writing. The influences of first language rhetorical patterns of the English writing of Chinese postgraduate students are clearly revealed in Ren and Hitchock (2013).

The distinction between writer-responsible versus reader-responsible language delineates another salient rhetorical difference across languages, which can account for the difficulties second language writers experience in English academic writing. Hinds(1987) suggests that in writer-responsible languages such as English, it is the writer's task to ensure reader understanding by guiding readers through the arguments with explicit 'signposts' or signals in the text. In reader-responsible languages such as Japanese, the writer deliberately does not spell out everything, but gives hints for the reader to dig out the meaning. While clarity and explicitness are valuable features in English writing, subtlety is appreciated in Japanese and some other reader-responsible languages. Such rhetorical differences can be drawn on to explain the frustration second language writers may have when their teachers comment that their writing is not clear because of lack of explicit statements, whereas the students regard it as clear enough because they think the reader should follow the hints to draw out the inherent meaning. This calls for the need for lecturers of international students to recognise different writing styles (Charnock, 2010).

The importance for international students to understand the nature and structural conventions of English academic writing in Australia is highlighted in the findings of Green's (2007) study on Asian international students' approaches to essay writing. In this study, the students who had limited understanding of the discursive structures of the essay genre struggled with essay assignments: they were confused about the nature and purpose of academic writing; they tended to take a surface approach and equated essay writing as information gathering. On the other hand, those students who made efforts to seek understanding of the discourse conventions of academic writing developed a sense of argument, structure and reader in academic writing, and tended to actively engage in the essay writing process. The findings of this study point to the importance of developing cross-cultural awareness of the differences between academic writing in English and in international students' first language, thus highlighting the significant impacts of cultural factors on academic writing.

Cultural factors

Apart from language, cultural differences are commonly viewed as another major cause of academic writing difficulty for international students. Educational practices are shaped by the cultures in which they operate (Ryan & Carroll, 2005). The cultural values and beliefs about learning and teaching differ in different educational systems. Students coming from diverse linguistic and cultural backgrounds bring with them their own cultural schemata about teaching and learning. Since what is known and valued by students from their prior learning might contrast or conflict with what is encouraged and valued at Australian universities, cultural differences may arise to exert influences on international students' academic writing in English.

The influence of cultural differences on international students' academic writing is evident in research that compares cultural patterns of thinking in English writing and other languages. A considerable body of literature in second language writing research on contrast rhetoric, as discussed in the preceding section, has revealed cultural variations in the rhetorical patterns of structuring and presenting ideas in texts across different languages (Connor, 1997). More recent research on international students' academic writing experiences provides further evidence for the significance of cultural impacts on how students structure academic writing. For example, Ren and Hitchcock (2013) examined the features of discourse organisation in the English academic writing of native Chinese students, focusing on the different ways of placing the thesis statements in English and Chinese writing.

Zhang (2011) also revealed Chinese international students' awareness of the differences between Chinese (a reductive approach) and English (a deductive approach) academic writing in terms of the methods used to develop arguments. Such findings suggest the influence of cultural thinking patterns on the discourse organisation of the texts and point to the need for increasing awareness of cultural discrepancies between the native and the English language to improve the English writing ability of international students.

Lack of knowledge of academic norms and conventions in English academic writing is another cultural factor that contributes to academic writing difficulties for international. Naya and Venkatraman (2010) explored the influence of home country academic culture on the performance of Indian international students studying business courses at an Australian university. The study found that the students' lack of familiarity with academic writing assignments constituted one of the main academic cultural gaps challenging the students. In particular, the notion of a critical voice in English academic writing is unfamiliar to many NESB international students coming from learning traditions where this notion is not emphasised, or interpreted differently. The study by Campbell and Li (2008) revealed that Asian students were not uncertain what should be an appropriate voice to adopt as a student in an English speaking academic environment, and they struggled to express their ideas using their own words.

Related to the notion of critical voice is the concept of critical thinking, which is fundamental to Western thinking and essential for academic writing in English, yet it is a concept that has caused a great deal of confusion for international students. The Chinese international students in Zhang's (2011) study identified the requirement of critical thinking and critical analysis as a key barrier in academic writing. The students found it difficult to express critical viewpoints about published works because in China, published works represent authoritative bodies of knowledge to which students should pay high respect; it is not meant to be critiqued. Compounding this challenge are the disciplinary specific requirements of critical thinking, thus causing uncertainty for students as to what is required in their writing in order to demonstrate the crucial element of critical thinking. This study highlights the challenge for international students from different educational systems and learning traditions where critical thinking is either not endorsed or endorsed differently.

Another cultural difference lies in the conventions of incorporating others' research into academic writing, which is a distinctive feature of English academic writing, but not commonly practised in the academic writing of some other languages. For example, the Chinese international students in Zhang's (2011) study expressed particular concerns about the rules of citation and references in English academic writing. These are salient features in academic writing in English, but less appreciated in Chinese academic writing, and they had to make extra efforts to learn and practise how to follow such academic writing conventions in their English academic writing.

Educational factors

Educational factors are related to the teaching and learning contexts which may facilitate or pose challenges for international students. International students coming to a new learning environment encounter differences in the way teaching and learning are conceptualised and practised. At Australian universities, students are expected to study independently, think critically, research and read widely, and write with confidence in academic English. These may be different from those in their home educational systems, thus requiring significant adjustments. Research shows that differences in teaching styles and academic expectations of students in classroom participation were among the main causes of academic difficulties for Asian international students (Lin & Yi, 1007). Green (2007) highlights the important role lectures play in facilitating international students' understanding of disciplinary expectations and participation in disciplinary practices. Among the factors that caused difficulties for international students are inconsistent and unclear explanations of academic expectations from lecturers and mismatches in the display of knowledge presented to the students. All of these make it more challenging for students to understand what is required of them in their specific disciplines. The significant role of lecturers' teaching approach in facilitating learning and development for international students is also evidenced in Kette (2006).

Mismatching understanding and expectations about academic writing between discipline lecturers and international students further complicates the difficulties involved. Arkoudis and Tran (2007) examined the approaches taken by Chinese international students in adapting to the academic discourse and practice in their course of study. Interesting discrepancies were observed in the concerns about academic writing difficulties between students and their lecturers. While the students were primarily concerned about the content of their writing and did not consider their English language ability to be an issue, the lecturers' concern tended to focus on linguistic and referencing aspects of the students' writing. Such discrepancies reflect a predominant concern with the language-related problems of international students.

Individual factors

International students are not a homogenous group. They are individuals with different personal motivations, perceptions of learning, preferred learning styles, and different knowledge and skill sets from their prior learning. Individual factors should be taken into account when looking at the difficulties they experience with academic writing in English. Arkoudis and Tran (2007) observed individual differences in international students' struggles with academic writing even though they came from the same culture and studied in the same discipline. The students' own attitudes towards their first language writing, their understanding of academic writing in English, their personality, experiences and motivations all contributed to the approaches they took to adapt to the disciplinary requirements. Individual factors such as academic English proficiency, self-regulation, motivation, self-efficacy, formal learning experience and academic adjustment were also identified in the study by Lin and Yi (1997). Hee and Woodrow (2008) also noted the students' low self-perception in English language proficiency affected their approaches to assignment preparation.

Plagiarism and academic integrity are issues of keen concern which have generated much discussion about international students (Pecorari, 2008). Recent research has identified various reasons for plagiarism. Although students generally understand the concepts of academic honesty and plagiarism, there are individual difficulties in applying the concepts in new learning environments. The study by Tran (2012) contests the prevailing view that links plagiarism with cultural norms, values and behaviours in international students' background. It contends that a host of complex personal and situational factors may account for the tendency to plagiarise, including the students' English proficiency, the inherent writing style in their home country, their motivation and learning style. In addition, the difference in the approaches to referencing adopted by different lecturers also significantly affected the students' management of citing and referencing in their writing assignments.

It should be noted that language problems were not recognised as a main problem by international students a number of studies (e.g., Arkoudis & Tran, 2007; Green, 2007). Evidence from second language writing literature and research on international students' experiences, as analysed and discussed earlier, renders support to our argument that the sources of academic writing difficulties for international students should be viewed in light of multiple factors rather than just language-related problems. As Green (2007) states, for the majority of international students studying in Western universities, language competence is seen as 'part of a wider issue of managing language and learning in specific disciplinary contexts' (p. 340). The academic writing difficulties of international students should be examined holistically and contextually. In particular, instead of focusing on their problems, it is more constructive to look into the strategies used by international students to tackle academic writing difficulties, and reveal some of the more positive aspects of international students' experiences with academic writing.

International students' strategic responses to the challenges of academic writing

Instead of looking at the problems and sources of difficulties, recent research on the academic writing experiences of international has started to explore the strategies international students take to come to terms with the academic writing requirements in their disciplines of study (e.g., Arkoudis & Tran, 2007; Green, 2007; Leedham, 2012; Mu, 2006; Tran, 2008, Zhang, 2011). A review of the major findings from research along this line provides support to our argument against the static views of stereotyping international students as bearers of problems.

Evidence from research suggests international students use various strategies to participate in disciplinary academic writing practices. There are discipline specific expectations and discourse conventions for academic writing, and these are often implicitly rather than explicitly communicated to students (Hyland, 2000). A clear understanding of the academic requirements of writing in the discipline is a crucial start for successful assignment writing. Tran's (2008) study on the different ways Chinese international students' sought to make sense of academic expectations in their disciplines of study reveals various strategies the students used to facilitate understanding of disciplinary academic writing requirements: they followed the writing guidelines and assessment criteria; they studied the writing models provided by their lecturers; they sought chances to contact their lectures and ask for feedback on assignment drafts; they made use of writing support services, and they took time to revise writing. All of these demonstrate the students' initiative and problem solving skills. Such findings defeat the popular view of international students as being passive and inactive learners.

Research also reveals that international students are capable of making use of effective strategies and taking appropriate approaches to tackle academic writing. In a recent United Kingdom study based on corpus analysis of student writing assignments, Leedham (2012) found that Chinese international students made significantly more frequent use of tables and lists as strategies in their writing assignments than their English counterparts. In Green (2007) on the approaches to essay writing by Asian international students in Australia, the students who had a clear understanding of the knowledge transforming nature of academic writing in the Western academic context viewed academic writing as knowledge constructing; they attended academic writing programs and advising sessions to seek understanding of the discourse conventions of academic writing; they developed a sense of argument, structure and reader in essay writing; they were able to take an independent approach to engage actively in the essay writing process; they were able to see the interconnection between academic writing and development of disciplinary knowledge; they developed cross-cultural awareness of the differences between academic writing in English and in their first language; they were able to draw on their reflection on cross-cultural differences in terms of learning cultures, learning style and academic writing; they adapted mostly readily to the learning culture and writing practices in Australia.

Such positive findings of international students' strategic responses to the challenges of academic writing are also corroborated in other studies (e.g., Arkoudis & Tran, 2007; Kette, 2006; Ryan & Viete, 2011). The qualitative study by Arkoudis and Tran (2007) examined the individual differences in Chinese international students' perceptions of academic writing and their choices of strategies in responding to academic essay writing as they progressed in their learning. The findings showed that after a semester's study in the course, changes could be observed in the students' enhanced understanding of the nature of academic writing, and in particular, the role of reading and critical thinking in academic writing. While the students' participation in the course practices required new skills, new ways of thinking and viewing the world and new interaction patterns, they responded strategically to the new challenges.

Findings of the research reviewed above challenge the deficiency perceptions and static stereotyping of international students from non-Western countries in the research literature and popular discourse. It is clear that the cultural stereotyping of international students is not conducive to enhancing the learning of these students. Then what factors are conducive to facilitating the development of the academic writing capacities of international students? What can be done by teachers and students alike to address the challenges of academic writing for successful disciplinary studies? Such questions will be addressed in the next section.

Developing academic writing capacities of international students

The literature on international students' experiences with academic writing as reviewed above demonstrates that English language is only one of the factors contributing to their academic writing difficulties. What is revealing from the more recent literature is a range of factors that can facilitate international students' development of academic writing capacities for success in their disciplinary studies. These factors should be made known to inform all involved with international students in higher education.

From the international students' perspectives, what is done by the lecturers that is helpful for assisting international students to address their academic writing challenges? The following suggestions are summed up from research findings reflecting the perspectives of international students:
- interactions and dialogues between lecturers and students
- individual or group consultations to discuss writing issues
- clear and specific explanations of the expectations and assessment criteria of writing assignments
- guidelines and writing models for specific assignments,
- early and timely feedback on writing
- comments on written drafts.

At the teaching and learning forefront are discipline lecturers whose assumptions and perceptions of international students, teaching styles and pedagogical approaches may have a direct impact on students' learning experiences. The significant role discipline lecturers plays in facilitating international students' responses to academic writing challenges is evidenced in research (Tran, 2008). It is important to keep in mind that international students do not have the background knowledge and experiences that we assume of our students, and they do not yet possess the sophisticated language needed to express ideas and demonstrate their abilities when they are new to the country, but they are capable of exercising their agency for change. A positive view on international students is of utmost importance. Teachers of international students are often so preoccupied with the problems international students seem to manifest in their adjustments to studying in an unfamiliar language and learning context that they fail to see the positive aspects in their students' struggles. A positive view on international students sees them not as bearers of problems, but resourceful individuals with multilingual knowledge and skills, cultural beliefs and learning strategies from their first language learning that can be conducive to success in learning in a new language and culture.

It is important for international students to have a positive view of their own backgrounds and experiences and develop self-confidence to tackle the challenges they face. It is encouraging for international students to recognise that they can utilise their multilingual knowledge and skills and prior learning to adapt to their new learning. They should be encouraged and guided to:
- understand the disciplinary requirements and expectations of academic writing
- develop awareness of the disciplinary discourse conventions and practice

- develop cultural awareness of the differences in academic writing between English and first language
- maintain self-motivation and self-regulation
- communicate and establish mutual understanding and relationships with academics
- seek help and support from available services.

At the institution level, writing support for international students should not only focus on study skills and language skills as the language is not the only source of difficulties. The focus should be on student learning, capitalising on what international students bring from their linguistic and cultural backgrounds. Academic writing is situated in disciplinary contexts (Hyland, 2000). The current research on academic literacy development advocates embedding development of academic writing into the curriculum (Ferman, 2004). Green (2007) calls for an 'embedded, holistic, and cross-cultural approach' to the development of academic writing for international students. In the embedded approach, the development of academic writing is considered holistically as part of the students' acculturation process. Students are encouraged to engage in cross-cultural reflections on learning cultures, academic writing practices and learning styles and strategies. Developing the academic writing capacities of international students requires multiple response and collaborative efforts from institutions, discipline lectures, writing support staff and international students themselves. It is everyone's responsibility.

Conclusion

In this chapter, we have reconceptualised the academic writing difficulties of international students by exploring the complexity of academic writing in a second language in light of the linguistic, rhetorical, cultural and educational, and individual factors that may impact on the academic writing processes of international students. By presenting research evidence about the successful strategies used by international students in tackling academic writing difficulties and the factors conducive to success in academic writing, we contest the deficit view of international students as difficult and passive learners. We agree with Carroll and Ryan (2005) that international students should be seen as 'bearer of culture, not bearer of problems'. The positive attributes of international students should not be overlooked. Their prior learning experiences should be acknowledged and valued. International students bring with them a set of skills and experiences from their prior learning. These skills and experience have made them successful in the past, but may not be fully useful in the new setting. What is required is for those of us involved in teaching international students to embrace change and welcome international students as bearers of alternative knowledge, perspectives and life experiences. The multilingual, educational and cultural resources of international students should be drawn on to turn the sources of difficulty into resources useful for developing academic writing in a new language. A holistic and contextualised understanding of the academic writing difficulties of international students should inform teaching and support for international students for developing academic writing capacities in English as a second language.

References

Arkoudis, S. & Tran, L. T. (2007). International students in Australia: Read ten thousand volumes of books and walk ten thousand miles. *Asia Pacific Journal of Education, 27*(2), 157–169.

Arkoudis, S. & Tran, L. T. (2010). Writing Blah,blah, blah: Lecturers' approaches and challenges in supporting international students. *International Journal of Teaching and Learning in Higher Education, 22*(2), 169–178.

Burns, R. B. (1991. Study and stress among first year overseas students in an Australian university. *Higher Education and Research Development, 10*(1), 61–78.

Balard, B. and Clanchy, J. (1991) *Teaching students from overseas: A brief guide for lecturers and supervisors,* London, England: Longman Cheshire.

Campbell, J. & Li, M. (2008). Asian students' voices: an empirical study of Asian students' learning experiences at a New Zealand university. *Journal of Studies in International Education, 12*(4): 375–96.

Charnock, K. (2010). The right to reticence. *Teaching in Higher Education, 15*(5), 643–552.

Connor, U. (1996) *Contrastive rhetoric: Cross-cultural aspects of second-language writing,* Cambridge, England: Cambridge University Press.

Ferman, T. (2004). Ways forward for development the writing skills of international students. In A. J. Liddicoat, S, Eisenchlas & Trevaskes (Eds.) *Australian perspectives on internationalising education* (pp. 39–51). Melbourne, Australia: Language Australia.

Green, W. (2007).Write on or write off? An exploration of Asian international students' approaches to essay writing at an Australian university. *Higher Education Research & Development, 26*(3), 329–344.

Hee, L. S. & Woodrow, L. (2008). International students' out-of-class interaction during the preparation of academic assignments: the case of six Korean TESOL postgraduate students. *University of Sydney Papers in TESOL, 3,* 35–72.

Hinds, J. (1987). Reader versus writer responsibility: A new typology. In U. Connor & R. B. Kaplan (Eds.), *Writing across languages: Analysis of L2 Text* (pp. 141–152). Reading, MA: Addison-Wesley.

Hyland, K. (2000) *Disciplinary discourses: Social interaction in academic writing*, London, England: Longman.

Hyland, K. (2003). *Second language writing*. Cambridge, England: Cambridge University Press.

Kaplan, R. B. (1966) Cultural thought patterns in intercultural education. *Language Learning, 16*, 1–20.

Kette, M. A. (2006). *Agency, discourse and academic practice: reconceptualising international students in an Australian university* (Doctoral dissertation). The University of Queensland, Brisbane, Australia.

Leeham, M. (2012). Writing in tables and lists: A study of Chinese students' undergraduate assignments in UK universities. In Ramona Tang (Ed.), *Academic writing in a second or foreign language: issues and challenges facing ESL/EFL academic writers in higher education contexts* (pp.146–164). New York, NY: Continuum International.

Li, G, Chen, W. & Duanmu, J. (2010). Determinants of international students' academic performance: a comparison between Chinese other international students. *Journal of Studies in International Education, 14*(4), 389–405.

Lin J-C G & Yi, JK (1997). Asian international students' adjustment: issues and program suggestions. *College Student Journal, 31*(4), 473–451.

Matters, H, Winter, J. & Nowson, C. (2004). Enhancing learning for culturally and linguistically diverse (CALD) students. *Focus on Health Professional Education, 6*(1), 26–36.

Mu, C. (2006). *An investigation of the writing strategies three Chinese postgraduate students report using while writing academic papers in English* (Doctoral dissertation). Queensland University of Technology, Brisbane, Australia.

Nayak, R, R, & Venkatraman, S. (2010). A pilot study into international students' academic culture: the context of Indian business students in an Australian university. *E-Journal of Business Education & Scholarship of Teaching, 4*(2), 1–12.

Pecorari, D. (2008). *Academic writing and plagiarism: A linguistic analysis.* London, England: Continuum. Plagiarism Tran (2012).

Phakit, A. Li, L. (2011). General academic difficulties and reading and writing difficulties among Asian ESL postgraduate students in TESOL at an Australian university, *RELC Journal, 42*(3), 227–264.

Ren, Z, & Hitchcock, R. (2013). Influences of Chinese cultural patterns of thinking on discourse organisations in English dissertation writing. In T. Coverdale-Jones (Ed.), *Transnational higher education in the Asian context* (pp. 149-160). Basingstoke, England: Palgrave Macmillan.

Rochecouset, J., Oliver, R, Mulligan, D., & Davies, M. (2011). The English language growth project. *Australian Universities Review, 53*(1), 102–104.

Ryan, J. & Carroll, J. (2005). 'Canaries in the coalmine': International students in Western universities. In J. Carroll & J. Ryan (Eds.), *Teaching international students: improving learning for all* (pp. 3–10). London, England: Routledge.

Ryan, J & Viete, R. (2011). Chinese international students in Australia: creating new knowledge and identifies. In J. Ryan (ed) *China's higher education reform and internationalisation* (pp. 151–168). Abingdon, England: Routledge.

Schmitt, D. (2005). Writing in the international classroom. In J. Carroll & J. Ryan (Eds.), *Teaching international students: Improving learning for all* (pp. 63–74). London, England: Routledge.

Tran, L. T. (2008). Unpacking academic requirements: international students in management and education disciplines. *Higher Education Research & Development, 27*(3), 245–256.

Tran, L. T. (2012. The perceptions and attitudes of international students towards plagiarism. *ACPET Journal for Private Higher Education, 1*(2), 15–23.

Wan, T-Y, Chapman, D.W. & Biggs, D. A. (1992). Academic stress of international students attending US universities. *Research in Higher Education, 33*(5), 607–23.

Zhang, Z. (2011). A nested model of academic writing approaches: Chinese international graduate students' views of English academic writing. *Language and Literacy, 13*(1), 39–59.

Zhang, Y. & Mi, Y. (2010). Another look at the language difficulties of international students. *Journal of Studies in International Education, 14*(4), 371–388.

Xu. M. (1991). The impact of English-language proficiency on international graduate students' perceived academic difficulty. *Research in Higher Education, 32*(5), 557–570.

Chapter 10

Exploring the Consequences of IELTS Through International Students' Personal and Academic Experiences: A Qualitative Analysis

Catherine Montes and Megan Yucel

Introduction: The consequences of language testing

Australian Higher Education (HE) determines international students' suitability for academic study in English in various ways. Of these, the International English Language Testing System (IELTS) is most commonly used by universities in Australia for this purpose (IDP, 2014). The dominant status that IELTS holds in Australia and other countries is further supported by the reported 2 million candidates who took the exam worldwide in 2013 (IELTS, 2014). As a gateway to study in Australia, success on the IELTS is thus a focal point for many individuals planning to study abroad.

In Australian HE, maintaining equitable practices demands that the impact of high-stakes exams such as IELTS be subjected to continuing research, focusing on washback, validity, and test use. Online marketing materials assure stakeholders (students, teachers, institutions and government departments) that the test offers a reliable and rigorous measure of academic proficiency in the four macro-skills (reading, listening, writing, and speaking; IELTS, 2014). Significant amounts are thus invested in test development and validation, as evidenced by the IELTS Joint-funded Research Program that offers funding for IELTS-related projects (IELTS, 2014). However, research investigating the validity of IELTS in predicting academic success has produced mixed results (Woodrow, 2006). The inconclusiveness of investigations in this area suggests that social and personal factors have an impact on testing and academic success (Benzie, 2010). Coaching and experience in taking the test are also linked to IELTS success, impacting on the test's effectiveness as an assessor of academic language proficiency (Green, 2007; Walker, Redmond & Morris, 2010).

Meeting language proficiency requirements 'on paper' does not necessarily equate to the capacity to successfully and independently manage academic tasks in English (Agosti & Bernat, 2009; Ahern, 2009; Benzie, 2010; Walker et al., 2010). For some students, success on IELTS allows them to access a doorway into a new academic culture, only to encounter significant language shock on the other side. The reverse is also true, as it can be argued that some students may not have the capacity to achieve on the test despite having the adequate academic language proficiency. The focus on IELTS thus has consequences that reach beyond the achievement of the target score, leading to questions which have not yet had the benefit of prolific research. How concerned should test developers be about how stakeholders use English language proficiency tests such as IELTS to make life-changing decisions? Are there ethical issues surrounding a test being used for purposes that are perhaps beyond the original intentions of the test developers? And what of the assumptions and aspirations of the test-takers? What are their perceptions of the IELTS test? Do they believe it is a fair measure of their abilities and a reliable predictor of their future academic or career success?

In 1996, Messick reconceptualised test validity to incorporate the notion of consequence. This has shifted research attention towards the fairness of how tests are used. Accordingly, evidence of the consequences of tests (positive/negative; intended/unintended) contributes to what Messick described as the consequential aspect of construct validity. The stories recounted by the participants featured here elucidate two broad categories of consequences: academic and personal. This chapter thus aims to use the concept of consequence as a lens to discuss high-stakes language testing through the personal and academic experiences of four international students seeking IELTS success.

Perspectives from the literature: Washback and validity

Preparation for the IELTS test influences the emotional and learning experiences of international students seeking to enter Australian universities. IELTS' academic impact is evidenced by *washback* (Cheng & Curtis, 2004; Qi, 2004, 2005) or *backwash* (Dahlin, Watkins, & Ekholm, 2001), which are terms used in research to articulate the extent to which tests affect teaching and learning. Washback can be categorised in two ways. First, washback can be minimal or profound, depending on the emphasis placed on the test (Green, 2007). Washback can also be harmful or beneficial, depending on how closely it matches teaching and learning objectives (Hughes, 1989). Definitions are not limited to the impact of IELTS on the academic experiences of students. Bachman and Palmer (2010) extend the boundaries of washback by situating it within the broader context of the consequences of assessment on individuals, education systems, and society. Shohamy (2001) goes further still, positioning washback as an institutional mechanism of power that controls the lives of teachers and students.

Researchers have explored the impact of IELTS in a variety of ways. Hawkey (2006) examined the global impact of IELTS, focusing on a range of stakeholders, such as test takers, teachers, materials writers, examiners, and institutions. Moore, Stroupe, & Mahony (2012) explored the impact of the IELTS test in Cambodia and found that while the IELTS test had had little impact on Cambodian society as a whole, the impact on the lives of candidates was substantial. There have also been numerous washback studies in the past decade on the influence of IELTS on classroom practice (Badger & Yan, 2012), preparation materials (Colman & Everett, 2003), and candidates' study methods (Mickan & Motteram, 2008). For example, Mickan and Motteram (2008, p. 20) found that while the IELTS test is designed to test language proficiency, candidates demand and receive instruction not only in developing their language, but also in improving their 'test-wiseness' or test-taking techniques. IELTS thus has a significant impact on stakeholders directly involved with the test, such as teachers and test-takers, affecting their teaching and learning practices.

Traditionally, validity was confined to the test developer's role in ensuring that the test 'measures what it purports to measure' (Ruch, 1924, p. 13). Validity was thus defined in terms of test items being reasonable exemplars of the knowledge and skills that candidates were expected to have mastered. Messick (1996) linked washback to test validity by arguing that the consequential aspect of validity should include evidence of 'unfairness in test use, and … positive or negative washback effects on teaching and learning' (p. 251). This suggests that the responsibilities of the test developer may also extend to how the test is used to make decisions about test candidates (Fulcher, 2010). In the case of international students in Australian HE, test use is determined by hosting universities. The focus on 'social consequences' (Brualdi, 1999, p. 1), has been argued in the research as 'cluttering' the notion of validity, leading to 'confusion, not clarity' (Popham, 1997, p. 9). It is perhaps for this reason that the issue of personal and academic consequences stemming from a strong focus on IELTS has received scant attention from researchers.

Research setting

Conceptualising the consequences of IELTS necessitates understanding the multifaceted and longitudinal nature of the setting in which the phenomenon occurs. The participants' perceptions of IELTS developed across time and in various settings, including the home countries where IELTS preparation was undertaken, and the Australian university where they ultimately aimed to study. Interviews were conducted at various stages of their journeys, spanning from the early stages of their English for academic purposes (EAP) studies in their home countries, to preparing for the IELTS test, to completing their Australian university degrees.

Methodology

This chapter examines how international students at one Australian university experienced the IELTS test. Drawing on interviews with a selection of international students who were taking the test for university entrance purposes, the authors focused on two main questions. Firstly, how did preparing for a high stakes English language proficiency test such as IELTS colour the students' perceptions of the academic knowledge and skills required to be a successful student in an Australian university and what were the linguistic and academic challenges that these international students faced as they interacted with standards and assessment?

Two data sets were accessed to provide the stories that are presented here. Five participants were recruited through an IELTS test centre at an Australian university. Another eight participants were recruited through the Chinese student association at the same university. Through a process of purposive sampling, participants with substantive IELTS experience were selected. Table 10.1 presents the basic demographic data of the participants.

The researchers employed qualitative research methods, including narrative inquiry and case study approaches, to analyse and interpret the data. Individual narratives were generated and the experiences of the group were compared in order to uncover themes and patterns.

Emerging themes

A number of striking themes emerged from interviews with international students in Australia regarding their experiences of IELTS. These are summarised in the sections following.

Table 10.1 Demographics Variables of Participants

Pseudonym	Gender	Nationality	Age Range	Faculty	Ugrad/Pgrad
Pamela	F	Columbian	Mid-20s	EAI*	Postgraduate
Toshi	M	Japanese	Early 20s	HSS**	Undergraduate
Xiao Xiao	F	Chinese	Early 20s	BEL***	Undergraduate
Eve	F	Chinese	Early 20s	BEL	Undergraduate

Note:* EAI = Faculty of Engineering, Architecture & Information Technology
** HASS = Faculty of Humanities and Social Sciences
*** BEL = Faculty of Business, Economics & Law.

Enduring challenges

The levels of stress associated with taking the exam were a common point of discussion with participants. IELTS was generally perceived as a hurdle to be overcome. Experiences of extreme difficulty were tempered by optimistic attitudes and the hope that they would ultimately achieve the score that they needed. The perceived variability and thus reliability of the exam was another emergent theme, with the participants citing examples of friendly or unfriendly examiners, or easy or difficult writing topics. A case-in-point was one Chinese participant who told the story of an IELTS examiner referred to as '5.0 Lady', infamous for never giving a higher score than 5. They shared rumors that they had heard about the test and talked of predictions that had been made about test content.

The time, energy, and money invested to prepare for the test was also an important consideration. For example, the Chinese participants' investment in achieving on IELTS was such that it was reported that students living in metropolitan areas would travel to rural areas to take the test. This was due to perceptions of higher competition in metropolitan areas, leading to harsher scoring. Furthermore, participants commonly engaged in strategies such as enrolling in specific IELTS preparation courses, purchasing IELTS test preparation books, and taking the test multiple times. Interestingly, the participants framed their experiences with IELTS as 'passing' or 'failing', despite the reality that the test in fact places candidates on a continuum.

Perceptions of test validity

There were differing perceptions as to whether the IELTS score was a valid reflection of students' language proficiency. IELTS was seen by some of the participants as having been a vehicle for real language proficiency development. In terms of what IELTS actually assesses, some felt that the academic version of the IELTS test tested a fair sample of the language and skills required to function in a university setting, while others felt that IELTS did not reflect real English. Many felt that they couldn't give their best because of the lack of time given to complete various tasks. Similarly, there was evidence in the interview data of students' perceptions of the impact of construct-irrelevant variables (Taylor, 2012) on their test performance such as nerves or poor use of test strategies.

IELTS as a business venture

Many students took a cynical view of the test, saying that IELTS was a money-making venture, and voiced suspicions that it was in the IELTS test partners' interests for candidates to take the test over and over again.

The following paragraphs draw specifically on the participants' data to exemplify some of the stories of students preparing for and taking the IELTS test. Some of these feature the personal consequences of IELTS on students' lives, while others elucidate the academic consequences of focusing on IELTS.

The following four stories are presented: Pamela, Toshi, Xiao Xiao, and Eve.

Pamela: 'No exceptions'

Pamela's story exemplifies the plight of those international students who somehow fall through the cracks by failing to reach the language requirements of their chosen university, despite their aptitude and desire to study there.

Unlike some students who may not have formulated clear ambitions before commencing their university studies, it was immediately apparent that Pamela had a strong sense of her professional identity and her research goals. In other words, she had a definite purpose for being in Australia and a clear scholastic goal that she wished to achieve. She had a conditional offer to do a Master's degree, having already found a supervisor and begun to collect data for her research project back in her country. Pamela, a geological engineer, was being sponsored to study by her employer, a large multi-national firm. The research that she was to complete was destined to feed in to a multi-million dollar mining project in Columbia. Pamela had also presented at an international conference and co-authored a paper in a peer-reviewed journal on the aforementioned project. Attaining the required IELTS score to commence her studies was the final hurdle. Unfortunately, this hurdle became a seemingly insurmountable one. As she took one test after another, the pressures on Pamela — both from within and without — began to mount.

Understandably, Pamela felt a sense of obligation to her employers to succeed in IELTS. She was conscious of the costs involved in her Australian sojourn and she was also cognisant of the potential scale of the mining project that her research was contributing to, and the effect that this project could have on the local economy if it proceeded. A sense of bewilderment became apparent, as Pamela tried to reconcile her lower-than-expected IELTS scores with her confidence in her knowledge of her chosen field and her ability to successfully carry out research. She frequently referred to the stress that she experienced when taking the test and wondered if this response was normal. She noted that tasks, quickly and easily completed in her English class, became much more difficult under exam conditions. She concluded, humorously, 'maybe I don't need more English courses ... maybe (I need) yoga to manage my stress!'.

At the end of her English course, when it was time to return home, Pamela had still not attained the overall IELTS band score that she needed, falling short by 0.5. After taking the test on five separate occasions, she remained in limbo. Pamela spent her final days in Australia dealing with university officialdom, unsuccessfully trying to find a way around the IELTS hurdle, only to be told to come back when she had an IELTS score. She articulated her feelings thus:

> So frustrating. I know I can do this. That's the frustration. I know I can do this. But they [university admissions] won't even look at it, (her current IELTS score]) they won't look at me. It's the idea that, is there any exception? But of course they don't make exceptions.

Pamela's story illustrates the disconnect between university admissions departments wishing to have a clear and unambiguous set of requirements for entrance, and prospective international students who feel that they have the ability and the credentials to undertake their chosen course of study but are being kept out by an unnecessarily narrow definition of language proficiency.

Toshi: 'Never say die'

Toshi's story is somewhat typical of the many international students who strive to meet the language requirements of the university that they have chosen. These students refuse to be disheartened by their inability to reach the language requirements, studying diligently and taking the IELTS test again and again until they are successful.

Toshi was an exchange student from Japan. He had originally hoped to study at The University of Queensland (UQ) for two semesters, but a lower-than-expected IELTS score meant that he spent one of those semesters studying English intensively and taking IELTS preparation classes at the language institute attached to the university. Toshi saw the positive side of this, explaining that as he hoped to become an English teacher one day, the experience had been beneficial in giving him an insight into the latest English language teaching methods used in Australia. Nevertheless, during our interviews, Toshi expressed his eagerness to begin his university studies as soon as possible. Like Pamela, Toshi had taken the test on multiple occasions and had come very close to the required band score to enter UQ, but still needed an overall average of 6.5 on one test. Despite this predicament of being so near and yet so far, Toshi displayed unfailing optimism in our interviews. He was fully aware of his strengths and weaknesses and was convinced that with enough hard work in the right areas, he would achieve his goal. He frequently referred to this hard work (e.g., 'I'm trying very hard for almost 10 weeks, yeah. I've been trying very hard and studying every day and talking').

Toshi spent a lot of time in our interviews talking about each skill tested in the IELTS test, and the strategies that he was employing to improve his results. He gave an amusing example of one such test strategy that he had used in his most recent speaking test. When asked about a particular type of hobby, he found himself with nothing to say because he had no interest in it. 'But I had to say something', he went on, 'so I told a lie. It's a kind of strategy. One of my friends likes that hobby so I just talked about that. But in my heart I was like, I'm so sorry for telling lies'.

In our penultimate interview, Toshi had good news — he had achieved the 6.5 he needed to begin his university studies. However, this was not without some difficulty. When he first received his scores, Toshi had received a lower score than expected. After some deliberation, he exercised his right to a re-mark and was awarded a higher mark in one of the skills, which was enough to give him the overall score that he needed. We met again some months later, just before he was about to return to Japan. He had had a wonderful semester and had achieved good marks in the assessment for his university subjects.

Toshi's story illustrates how success may be achieved through diligence, motivation, and a positive attitude towards tests. Rather than see the IELTS test as an unnecessary hindrance, Toshi accepted its existence and worked steadily and optimistically towards reaching his goal of 6.5. He spoke of the connection between preparing for the test and seeing an improvement in his language skills. Toshi, therefore, is typical of those international students who accept the need for universities to ascertain English language abilities through language proficiency tests and are prepared to work within those parameters to gain a place.

Xiao Xiao: 'Stepping outside the comfort zone'

Xiao Xiao's story perhaps typifies the experiences of many international students in that she achieved the necessary IELTS score and was able to access study in Australia, only to subsequently encounter moments of extreme language difficulty.

Xiao Xiao made the decision to study in Australia through a 2+2 program, linking partner universities in China and Australia. Xiao Xiao had always been 'crazy' about English. She was a fan of English language movies and 'Western' music and would often walk down the street practising English conversations in her head. Xiao Xiao was attracted to the prospect of being able to communicate with others from different cultures. So, after finishing high school, and with strong support from her family, she enrolled in a university in Beijing so that she could eventually study abroad and improve her English. Achieving this goal could not happen without success on the IELTS.

Xiao Xiao's experience of IELTS was ultimately successful but punctuated by stress and frustration. Having 'failed' the exam three times, her point of weakness was always the written component, leaving her struggling to hold onto her dream of studying abroad. Xiao Xiao was baffled by the difficulty that she encountered, as she had learned a battery of strategies to help her pass the written exam during an IELTS preparation course. The most important strategy was to memorise a sample text, which could then be adapted to what was required by inserting topic-specific vocabulary. Xiao Xiao recognised that using that strategy in the exam would enable her to achieve a satisfactory score, but never a high score. A pivotal moment arrived when an English language teacher, Peter, told her to just 'throw those things [the strategies] away'. Xiao Xiao became aware that it would be better to create her own text as opposed to repeating someone else's words. This allowed her to 'open' her mind and pass the written component of the exam.

Through her 2+2 program, Xiao Xiao had access to EAP classes in China for one semester. Interestingly, IELTS was seen to penetrate the EAP curriculum, which Xiao Xiao felt was reasonable because it was a fact that in order to study in Australia, it was crucial to first pass the IELTS. However, the consequence of this was that her academic discourse competence did not extend beyond what was needed to achieve on IELTS. The focus on IELTS was not counterbalanced by her university in China, because it was simply understood that authentic discourse competence development would happen once immersed in the Australian context.

In her first year of study in Australia, Xiao Xiao encountered language shock in almost every aspect of academic discourse. Confusion was experienced in lectures, and there were intense struggles to keep up with reading requirements. Academic writing was a significant issue across her first year of study. Xiao Xiao recognised that the focus on IELTS had meant that many aspects of English academic writing were problematised; in particular, issues around avoiding plagiarism and writing extended 'logical' texts. Beyond the stress, Xiao Xiao's inadequate academic literacy meant that to survive her assessment, it became necessary to implement certain strategies, which had the effect of facilitating discourse competence development on hand, while complicating the extent to which she could engage with the content of her studies.

Eve: 'Hitting the ground running'

Eve's data told the story of a high achieving Chinese student, who needed to succeed on the IELTS so as to gain access to study in Australia. In contrast to many of the participants interviewed, Eve's subsequent experiences of language shock were minimal as the consequences of focusing on IELTS had been successfully counterbalanced through adequate EAP study at her university in China.

Eve was enrolled in a 2+2 program at a top-tier university in South-Western China. Having always been interested in studying abroad, Eve was excited when the opportunity arose to travel to Australia. Eve's motivation for studying abroad was not so much linked to an inherent interest in communicating in English, as the pragmatic benefits of developing her English. In other words, learning English was a career move for Eve. In order to meet the requirements of the partnership agreement, Eve needed to score adequately on the IELTS, as well as complete two full semesters of EAP study. The former requirement was supported by her university through the provision of a specific IELTS training course for 2+2 students. Interestingly, Eve also chose to enrol in another IELTS training course, outside of her university programme. The choice to do this highlights the significance of IELTS in relation to her plans to study abroad. The latter aspect of her language training involved one semester in an integrated skills EAP programme, while the second course focused entirely on English academic writing.

Eve's experience of IELTS was successful, despite the fact that she took the exam three times before 'passing'. Her difficulty was situated in the written component of the exam, which was the tendency across the cases. Eve reported studying very hard and attending her IELTS classes. She also worked with an IELTS textbook titled '10 days to conquer IELTS', reportedly using this book to writing and memorising forty model answers for different IELTS topics.

The critical aspect to Eve's story was the fact that beyond her focus on IELTS, Eve had opportunities to develop English academic discourse in more authentic ways and across a longer period of time. Eve's academic writing developed significantly through her process-oriented (scaffolded) experiences in the writing course, resulting in the production of an extended academic text. Through embedded feedback processes, Eve was able to experience researching, planning, and writing a tertiary level assignment. This course compensated the IELTS focus by developing students' understanding around avoiding plagiarism and the critical evaluation of sources of information, which are two crucial areas of academic writing that, to date, have not been incorporated into the IELTS.

Eve's experiences during her first year of study in Australia thus showcased a degree of confidence in her language skills. Throughout conversations with Eve, she repeatedly made reference to her perception that she had been adequately trained by her university, juxtaposing herself against other Chinese students who had not had the benefit of such support. Eve's data showed the importance of understanding the true-to-life limitations of high-stakes language tests like the IELTS, and counterbalancing those accordingly.

Discussion

Personal consequences

The impact of taking the IELTS test went beyond the academic aspects of language proficiency and academic literacy. A recurring theme in the interviews was the pivotal role that IELTS had assumed in these students' lives. Of those interviewees who were preparing to take the test, it seemed to dominate their thoughts and actions, so that their lives revolved around it. This preoccupation with IELTS did not end after they had sat for the test, with all of the participants taking the test multiple times. Planning the timing and budgeting the expense of the next test had to be carefully considered along with actual test preparation and study. Waiting for their results, they tried to plan for the future, hoping for a positive outcome while also envisaging worst-case scenarios and making contingency plans.

Unsurprisingly, participants appeared to be more preoccupied with the short-term goal of passing IELTS than the long-term one of completing a university degree. These considerations all took place while they juggled other aspects of their lives, such as their English classes, part-time jobs, and relationships. As a consequence, stress and anxiety were frequently mentioned, with participants feeling the pressure as time began to run out for them to achieve IELTS success. These insights indicate the emotional impact that taking a high stakes gatekeeper test may have on the test-taker.

Academic consequences

The intense focus on succeeding on the IELTS exam also resulted in academic consequences.

In their home countries, many of the participants were socialised in general English discourse through language study carried out in the schooling system, with the objective of performing on high stakes English language examinations. In many cases, there was very little socialisation in English academic discourse as a result. Thus, some positive washback from studying for the IELTS exam was reported.

Of the four macro-skills examined in the IELTS exam, meeting the requirements on the written component was often the most problematic, resulting in multiple attempts at taking the exam. As a result, intense test preparation familiarised the participants to fundamental aspects of English written discourse to which they had had very little exposure, such as the thesis-support-conclusion macrostructure of texts and experience using cohesive devices, such as conjunctive adverbs, to link ideas together in texts. Studying for IELTS generally involved working closely with writing samples, which were memorised along with lists of topic-specific vocabulary, referred to by some participants as 'high score' vocabulary.

Despite reports of positive washback, negative washback also manifested. Once in Australia, there was mutual agreement that a focus on IELTS without the counterbalancing effect of additional and more authentic academic literacy development, had resulted in language shock. Participants struggled to adapt to the daily pressures of listening and speaking in lecture and tutorial settings. Many needed to spend inordinate periods of time undertaking reading and researching tasks, which then negatively impacted on time available to carry out written assessment. Participants argued that learning to write a 250-word 'essay' based on personal opinion and experience did not provide the necessary socialisation in conceptualising, researching, outlining and writing 2000-word (or more) academic texts in a variety of genres. Another trade-off identified by many of the participants was that the IELTS exam did not incorporate assessment relating to the correct use and acknowledgement of sources in academic writing. The outcome of this was that the participants entered university in Australia with very little understanding in this area. A meta-awareness of this meant that many of the participants were concerned that their limited understanding might result in accusations of cheating or failure.

Implications to educational policy and practice

Institutional accountability

Language proficiency tests like IELTS are inarguably a useful tool in internationalising HE settings. Successfully hosting students who are shifting across linguistic borders requires that institutions define and enforce a minimum level of language proficiency appropriate to success in the new setting. To that end, language tests standardise assessment and minimise inconsistencies that may emerge from more individualised methods of ascertaining language proficiency (Bretag, 2007; Dunworth, 2010). The ethical determination of who has the adequate language proficiency to manage in the new setting and who does not, hinges on being able to minimise inconsistency (Ross, 2008). However, the stories presented here show that despite the benefits to implementing high stakes standardised tests like IELTS, there are problems. The personal and academic consequences on students in fact raise questions regarding institutional accountability in regards to applying tests in a way that promotes equity.

Problematising language entry requirements

Language proficiency requirements for students planning to study in Australia are determined by three factors. In neoliberal settings, a significant factor is that universities must consider the numbers of students that they need to remain sustainable (Feast, 2002). Financial sustainability can be negatively impacted if language proficiency entry requirements are too high. Institutions then make decisions on minimum levels of language proficiency by balancing this against what are considered to be the minimum skill levels required (Feast, 2002). However, this is problematised by the low levels of English language proficiency of students. Andrade (2010) has differentiated between the length of time required to develop different levels of language proficiency. According to Cummins (2008), Basic Interpersonal Communication Skills (BICS) takes approximately two years to develop, while Cognitive Academic Language Proficiency (CALP) takes between seven and ten years to develop. Thus, it is most likely the case that many students deciding to study abroad do not have the luxury of developing academic discourse competence for that length of time, resulting in relatively low levels of proficiency. This point is highlighted in the cross-cultural data presented on the IELTS website, which shows that the written component of the exam is the most challenging aspect for the average IELTS candidate (IELTS, 2014). It is also the case that many of the participants struggled to achieve the necessary score on the written component of the exam, resulting in multiple attempts. Thus, when many students in the target market have low levels of proficiency, this automatically places receiving institutions in the position of having to maintain sustainability by setting proficiency requirements that may be too low. This is supported by research that has shown faculty perceptions to be that universities do not set realistic language proficiency entry requirements where students can achieve positive outcomes without undue stress and anxiety (Andrade, 2010).

Language testing and performativity

This self-perpetuating cycle is further supported by the continuing focus on large scale standardised examinations in academic cultures such as those found in China and Japan. Using Judith Butler's concept of performativity, McNamara (2006) argues that test constructs in language testing are *performative achievements*, which means that it can be argued that students from certain cultures are more deeply socialised in taking exams and have a greater capacity in this regard. Furthermore, the notion of positive washback informs the focus on examinations as assessment in countries such as China. An example of this is the Chinese National Matriculation English Test (NMET), a high stakes exam for all Chinese high school students hoping to gain access to tertiary study. The NMET is administered with the specific intention of positively influencing the teaching and learning of English (Cheng & Qi, 2006). As IELTS is marketed as assessing the necessary English language proficiency for academic higher learning settings (IELTS, 2014), some students may feel that focusing on IELTS is adequate to support the development of the minimum language skills necessary.

Australian HE operates within a neoliberal framework, where hosting institutions must tread a fine line between ensuring sustainability and equitability. The data presented here complicates the idea of centring language proficiency entry requirements on the results of one test. Of the four cases presented, two students appeared to have a satisfactory outcome from their experiences with IELTS (Toshi and Eve). For Xiao Xiao and Pamela, focusing on IELTS proved to be problematic. Having been socialised in taking high stakes exams throughout her school years, Xiao Xiao was able to persist until meeting the necessary requirements. However, enrolled in her Australian university, her experiences of language shock suggest that Xiao Xiao did not have the necessary CALP to undertake her studies comfortably. Conversely,

Pamela was unable to gain access due to her anxiety and inability to perform on the test, despite her background, which had included co-authoring a paper in English.

Recommendations

University administrators must certainly consider academic qualifications and language proficiency when making decisions about the enrolment of international students, but how this should be done is a matter of some conjecture. In a case study of one Australian university, O'Loughlin (2008) found that administrators relied solely on IELTS scores to assess language proficiency. There was no flexibility from one individual applicant to the next. This system was seen to be fair by one set of stakeholders, the university administrators, for reasons mainly related to the perceived objectivity of the test.

If the practice of making judgements about people based on a single, high-stakes test lacks fairness, this leads to the question of what form of assessment might be a more suitable replacement for the traditional psychometric language test. The answer seems to lie in a more diverse range of assessment options, such as portfolios, observations, and projects, which cater to different learning styles and preferences and require different modes of performance. However, these forms of assessment can be impractical, unreliable and even biased if they are introduced without adequate training and support, leading to ethical concerns for those administering them (Hamp-Lyons, 1996). An alternative approach might be to base the decision on a wider range of criteria. In addition to a proficiency test score, this might include an interview by a trained member of the university staff. Whereas this procedure would be more time-consuming and would require more staff training in how to apply the criteria, it would certainly address the possibility of standard error of measurement and would mean that the decision was based on a variety of factors, rather than a one-off test. It would also be seen as fairer by another set of stakeholders, the students.

Conclusions

Large-scale language tests were presumably not designed with the intention of being the primary dynamic behind candidates' study of English academic discourse. They assess the fundamentals, nothing more. The inherent flaws in relying on these tests are the very characteristics allowing their convenient implementation as large scale standardised tests. This demands a critical approach by stakeholders (institutions) that rely on scores as gatekeeper mechanisms. Tertiary institutions need to understand the realities behind students' experiences of IELTS and adjust language proficiency entry requirements accordingly.

The stories outlined in this chapter show that hinging entry to universities on solely meeting language proficiency test requirements has the potential for unfavourable personal and academic consequences. It favours students who are au fait with this style of assessment, while potentially shutting out others. Testing is a part of life and there is a place for well-designed, valid and reliable standardised tests that institutions can use as part of the process of ascertaining whether a prospective entrant meets the minimum required standards that they need to cope in that setting. Large-scale, high profile English language tests such as IELTS and Test of English as a Foreign Language (TOEFL) will be used for gatekeeping purposes because of logistical considerations. However, more can and should be done to ensure that these tests are used ethically and appropriately.

References

Agosti, C., & Bernat, E. (2009). Teaching Direct Entry Programs effectively: Insights for ELICOS teachers and managers. *English Australia Journal, 25*(1), 27–41.

Ahern, S. (2009). 'Like cars or breakfast cereal': IELTS and the trade in education and immigration. *TESOL in Context, 19*(1), 39–51.

Andrade, M. S. (2010). Increasing accountability faculty perspectives on the English language competence of nonnative English Speakers. *Journal of Studies in International Education, 14*(3), 221–239.

Bachman, L., & Palmer, A. (2010). Language Assessment in Practice. Oxford, England: Oxford University Press.

Badger, R., & Yan, X. (2012). To what extent is communicative language teaching a feature of IELTS classes in China? *IELTS Research Reports, 13*, 1–44.

Brualdi, A. (1999). *Traditional and modern concepts of validity.* ERIC/AE Digest, 1–3.

Colman, J., & Everett, R. (2003). A critical analysis of selected IELTS preparation materials. *IELTS Research Reports, 5*, 1–84.

Fulcher, G. (2010). *Practical language testing.* London, England: Hodder Education.

Green, A. (2007). *IELTS washback in context: Preparation for academic writing in higher education.* Cambridge, England: Cambridge University Press.

Hamp-Lyons, L. (1996). Applying ethical standards to portfolio assessment of writing in English as a second language. In M. Milanovich & N. Saville (Eds.), *Performance testing, cognition and assessment.* Selected papers from the 15th Language Research Testing Colloquium, Cambridge and Arnhem (pp. 151–163).

Hawkey, R. (2006). *Impact theory and practice: Studies of the IELTS test and Progetto Lingue 2000*. Cambridge, England: Cambridge University Press.

Hughes, A. (1989). *Testing for language teachers*. Cambridge, England: Cambridge University Press.

IELTS. (2014). IELTS. Retrieved from http://www.ielts.org

Messick, S. (1996). Validity of performance assessment. In G. Philips, *Technical issues in large-scale performance assessment*. Washington, DC: National Center for Educational Statistics.

Mickan, P., & Motteram, J. (2009). The preparation practices of IELTS Candidates: Case studies. *IELTS Research Reports, 10*, 1–39.

Moore, S., Stroupe, R., & Mahony, P. (2012). Perceptions of IELTS in Cambodia: A case study of test impact in a small developing country. *IELTS Research Reports, 13*, 1–109.

O'Loughlin, K. (2008). The use of IELTS for university selection in Australia: A case study. (J. Osborne, Ed.) *IELTS Research Reports, 8*, 3–98.

Popham, W. J. (1997). Consequential validity: Right concern — wrong concept. *Educational Measurement, 16*(2), 9–13.

Ruch, G. (1924). *The improvement of the written examination*. Chicago, IL: Scott, Foreman & Company.

Shohamy, E. (2001). *The power of language tests: A critical perspective on the use of language tests*. Harlow, England: Pearson Education.

Taylor, L. (2012). Introduction. IELTS Research Reports , *13*, vii-xviii.

Woodrow, L. (2006). English in academic settings: A postgraduate course for students from non-English speaking backgrounds. In Snow & Kamhi-Stein (Eds.), *Developing a new course for adult learners* (pp. 197–218), Sydney, Australia: TESOL.

Chapter 11

Steps to Assuring EAL International Students' ELP at Exit: 'It's Not Rocket Science'

Sophie Arkoudis and Lachlan Doughney

Introduction

The English language proficiency (ELP) levels of graduates and entrants in Australian higher education have been an issue that has gained focus with Australian researchers and policymakers over the last decade. Some have raised doubt over whether students that graduate in the sector have appropriate levels of ELP for continued study and employment (Benzie, 2010; Birrell, 2006; Bretag, 2007). Birrell's seminal study was to provide the impetus for this emerging focus on the issue of graduating students' ELP, and was also to shape the discussion as something that particularly applies to international students who have English as an additional language (EAL; Birrell, 2006). He argued that the ELP of EAL international students does not necessarily improve after three years of study in an Australian university and that they graduate with low levels of ELP.

More recently, Foster's (2012) research questions the extent to which international students' work is soft marked in Australia. Foster (2012) studied 12,846 students in two Australian business faculties to analyse demographic, course and tutorial selection, as well as assessment grades. It was identified that EAL international students and students with non-English speaking backgrounds perform by and large worse than domestic students. It was also found that the greater the proportion of EAL international students within a given cohort the more their marks increased above the average. Foster interpreted this as a form of 'grading to the curve' that concealed international students' poor performance. For Foster, the reason for this was that academics were soft marking international students' work. In making these points Foster identified widespread low levels of ELP among EAL international students, and students who do not have English as a first language. She concluded that 'adjustment by the teacher to accommodate a larger fraction of lower-performing students is quite plausible' (p. 23). Her study questions whether EAL international students achieve the appropriate outcomes out of study in Australian higher education, and whether standards can be maintained in an environment where EAL international students have weak ELP.

Prior to Foster's study in 2012, in 2011 the Victorian Ombudsman's report into how universities deal with international students supported allegations of 'soft-marking' of international students with poor English language skills (Victorian Ombudsman, 2011). The Ombudsman focused on four Victorian universities and conducted interviews with staff, as well as experts in the field of English language teaching and assessment. He found that universities were not doing enough to ensure that international students have the necessary English language skills to study successfully. He also found that academics increasingly used group work, short answer questions and multiple-choice questions as tools for assessing students. This meant that English language ability of international students was not being adequately assessed. He argued for more rigorous assessment practices and suggested that concerns of soft-marking extend beyond international students to wider concerns over falling standards.

The increased accountability through the Tertiary Education and Quality Standards Agency (TEQSA) and the introduction of teaching and learning standards means that universities must become better at assessing, monitoring and evaluating English language learning outcomes of all their students. The Australian Government's Higher Education Standards Framework (DIISRTE, 2011) has stated that course design is appropriate and meets the qualifications standards where 'there are robust internal processes for design and approval of course of study, which ... provide for appropriate development of key graduate attributes in students including English language proficiency (p. 18).

The current higher education landscape is dominated by a paradigm in which the key imperative in providing quality assurance in teaching and learning is for institutions to demonstrate that their students have reached threshold standards at exit. In the past universities have relied on assessing the readiness of international students to undertake study where English is the medium of instruction, assuming that students will develop their ELP if they successfully complete their course of study. English language entry standards are important and a necessary part of a standards framework. But much more is required to assure ELP threshold standards upon graduation. More attention needs to be given to learning, teaching and assessment practices that ensure students graduate with the English language skills needed for employment or further study. While the answer is simply to integrate ELP

Chapter 11 Steps to Assuring EAL International Students' ELP at Exit: 'It's Not Rocket Science'

institutional quality assurance processes, this is difficult to achieve in universities. This chapter will draw on recently completed fellowship for the Office of Learning and Teaching (OLT) to present a blueprint of how institutions can effectively assure students' ELP standards upon exit.

Why English language entry pathways cannot be the sole ELP standard bearer

There are a plethora of pathways that EAL international students use to gain entry into higher education in Australia. Most publicised of these are English language tests taken by some EAL international students, like the International English Language Testing System (IELTS), and the Test of English as a Foreign Language (TOEFL). However, while these are the most well known pathways, as many as 80% of EAL international students do not use English language tests to enter into higher education in Australia, and instead use other pathways (Arkoudis, 2014). Figure 11.1, used by Arkoudis and Murray (2013), gives a broad insight into the kinds of entry pathways that can be taken by international students to enter into higher education in Australia.

The pathway types described in the figure comprise a diverse range of methods of entry into higher education themselves. For example, Vocational Education and Training (VET) courses and diplomas vary greatly. They range in their disciplinary content, from information systems to veterinary

Figure 11.1 Entry pathways that can be taken by international students to enter into higher education in Australia. Arkoudis and Murray (2013)

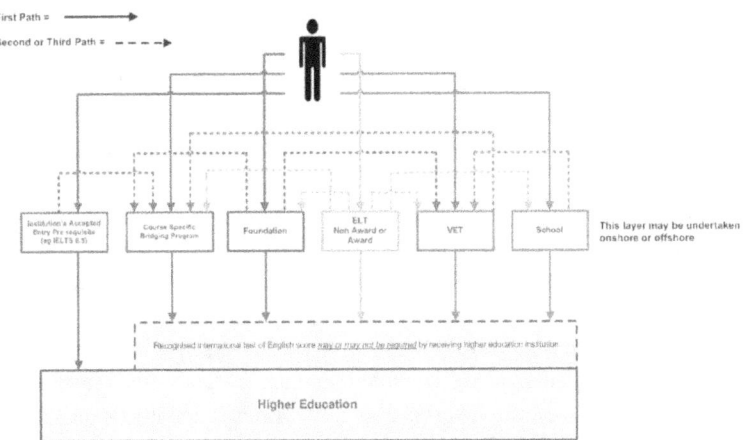

nursing, and they act as a pathway in to a course of study in different ways, with some providing entry in to the first year of bachelor degree, and others in to the second year. Also English Language Teaching (ELT) courses, both award and non-award, comprise a huge range of providers, whose standards for completion may differ substantially. In particular, English Language Intensive Courses for Overseas Students (ELICOS) make up a large number of the ELT courses in Australia, and these are provided by a myriad of Technical and Further Education (TAFE) providers and colleges. Even entry through the completion of high school is not a simple pathway, as the kind of entry involved will depend on the type of certificate of completion that the student receives from the state or territory out of which they graduate, and the kinds of subjects taken to achieve the certificate. In sum, the nature of existing pathways into higher education for international students is highly complex.

There is little clarity about the extent to which any given pathway into Australian higher education is comparable to another in the set of skills and capacities they provide for international students. This particularly applies to standards of ELP, as it is rarely assessed explicitly in many of the pathways out of which EAL international students arrive at Australian universities (see Arkoudis, 2013; O'Loughlin & Murray, 2007). Ultimately, in the current environment in higher education, it is difficult determine the level of ELP that students have coming from each pathway, and it is difficult to get an insight into the extent to which each pathway develops other skills that prepare EAL international students for study in Australian universities, like intercultural competence. The pathways are simply too diverse, and the kinds of evidence they use to determine international students competence are too varied, for any clear insight to be developed about their comparability in the preparedness to study that they provide EAL international students.

Adding further complexity to the issue has been the diversification of higher education in Australia, not only across domestic students, but also within the body of incoming international students. International students are arriving into Australian higher education from more diverse backgrounds than ever before, with different ELP development needs, and it is unclear how different pathways cater to these varied needs (i.e., for a distribution of the background of EAL international students in Australia see AEI, 2013). The range of pathways have evolved over a period of time and their main role has been to indicate students readiness to commence their higher education studies.

It is a plausible conclusion that pathways in to higher education for EAL international students have diversified in part because the international student body has become diverse. The global international market for EAL international students has become extensive. The Organisation for

Economic Co-operation and Development (OECD) data shows that there were around 4.3 million students enrolled in univerisities outside of their own country in 2011 (OECD, 2013). Of these, 83% were enrolled in G20 countries. In taking a slice of this large market, Australian univerities and pathway providers have had to provide an option that is attractive to EAL international students from widely varied cultural backgrounds. Moreover, they have had to do so while in direct competition with universities and pathway providers from other G20 nations. The raft of different options that have been developed over the past two decades for EAL international students could simply be seen as the result of Australian providers attempting to provide ever more attractive options for diverse EAL international students in a difficult and competitive market.

English language entry pathways have been argued in a variety of sources to be no guarantee of success within an Australian higher education environment, in particular in terms of assuring that students will have an adequate level of ELP at graduation (e.g., See Arkoudis, Baik, & Richardson, 2012). Instead, it has been reasoned that entry pathways are better understood as something that prepares students to commence study, and that to effectively approach assuring ELP and other skills at graduation, measures during the course of students' degree are required. In this light, a strict entry standard may not achieve the end of assuring that students have the requisite ELP to complete their studies. There would also be much contention over what that the preferred English language entry standards would be.

If Australian universities are to continue to attract a diverse range of EAL international students into higher education, the current range of pathways needs to be maintained, and perhaps broadened. Competitiveness in the global market demands it. It also provides a range of choices for international students, a range that can benefit both the market, and the students themselves. In sum, the pathway system now, while perhaps convoluted and imprecise, arguably has the capacity to provide the best option for Australian institutions, and for incoming EAL international students. However, as has been argued, this system cannot provide quality assurance that EAL international students will have the right ELP outcomes at the end of their degrees. Resources to achieve this end are best diverted elsewhere.

PELAs: Are they really worth the effort?

Post Entry Language Assessments (PELAs) have spread across the Australian higher education sector since diagnostic testing was recommended in guidelines for good practice principles for international students that were used a part of university audits (Australian Universities Quality Agency [AUQA], 2009). PELAs are diagnostic tools that assess students' ELP levels in order to identify students who require additional support to develop their ELP skills for university study. Universities have been keen to introduce PELAs. 27 out of 39 Australian universities currently use some form of PELA. These range in format, design, content, students targeted, feedback processes and follow-up (Dunworth, 2013). It makes sense for universities to test students and identify those who require extra support to develop their language skills in order to successfully complete their course of study. The reality is somewhat different.

There is currently much debate and mixed reports about the effectiveness of PELAs. While the intent is to raise students' awareness about developing their ELP and for academics to be aware of how they can assist students in this area, there is some evidence to suggest that this does not necessarily occur (Arkoudis, in press; Ransom, 2009). This is particularly the case concerning PELAs that are detached from disciplinary learning and teaching and that are targeted only at EAL international students. On the other hand, it appears that if PELAs are integrated within subjects then students undertake the test and academics use the results to inform their curriculum design (Arkoudis, 2014; Arkoudis, Baik, Bexley, & Doughney, 2014; Harris, 2013).

As was discussed in the previous section, EAL international students are entering Australian higher education with diverse ELP needs, and the entry pathways they enter through should not be expected to demonstrate that they have the ELP to complete their studies, but rather only to commence them. With this, there should be the expectation that EAL international students should be developing their ELP throughout their course of study, to achieve the highest ELP levels they can upon graduation. Moreover, domestic students are increasingly entering higher education with diverse backgrounds and needs, and the issue of ELP development is something that by no means only applies to EAL international students (See Arkoudis & Doughney, 2014; Briguglio, 2013, p. 12–14;). Perhaps then, resources might be better placed in developing ELP within disciplinary learning and teaching where they can target all students (i.e., see Arkoudis, 2014), rather than on administering PELAs when the outcomes of these efforts, in terms of international students ELP development, are not clear.

Is English language testing upon graduation a way of assuring ELP standards?

Exit testing has been raised as having advantages in assuring English language graduate outcomes for international students and to provide a clear data source regarding their ELP development. Australian universities do not have a history of exit testing. However, exit testing alone is perhaps not the magic bullet to assure EAL international students' ELP upon graduation.

Standardised English language tests were developed to measure student's readiness to enter university study. Little is known about how valid and reliable these tests are for assessing whether graduates have the necessary English language to enter the wide variety of professions available to graduates. A one-size-fits-all model of English language testing may not provide universities, graduates and employers with the occupational specific information required for assessing English for workplace readiness (Arkoudis et al., 2009). Studies that have been conducted to date have found that English language test results upon completion of university studies are variable, with students making no progress or limited progress between their entry and exit scores (Craven, 2012; O'Loughlin & Arkoudis, 2009). Furthermore, research into the relationship between English language tests and grade point average (GPA) has been inconclusive. For example, Craven found that students can gain a high result in an English language test, but only achieve modest results in their studies (p. 24). She concluded that 'a great many factors other than the level of English language proficiency as measured by the IELTS Test have an impact on GPA'. These studies highlight two important points. The first is that there is very little research in this area and secondly, what is available is small in scale and inconclusive.

If adopted in their current format, standardised English language tests may have significant limitations. However, there are moves to develop English language exit tests, and these could be useful in assessing the ELP levels of all graduates. New test development would need to be inclusive of all students, and not just for EAL international students. Tests would also need to be linked to English language standards required within professions. In addition, it could be implemented as part of a multi-pronged strategy, where evidence-based measures are first developed and implemented within the curriculum to ensure that English language is developed incrementally throughout the course of study, so that students can comfortably approach exit tests (For a similar point see Humphreys & Gribble, 2013).

A blueprint for integrating ELP into disciplinary curricula

Universities have relied primarily on English language entry standards but far less attention has been given to understanding and assuring ELP exit standards. As James (2014, p. 2) has pointed out that universities have not been 'swift to demonstrate how their pedagogies and assessment systems can protect minimum standards on graduation'. This is true with regards to ELP standards. However the challenge for ELP is that is has largely been situated outside of mainstream teaching and learning practices (Dunworth, 2012; Arkoudis, Baik, & Richardson, 2012), and it needs to become core business for universities and integrated within quality assurance processes for teaching and learning.

Part of the reason why ELP has not been core business within Australian universities is that it has been positioned as an international student issue, and therefore not central to mainstream teaching and learning. What is needed is genuine penetration of ELP within disciplinary curricula, and there is general acceptance of this within Australian universities (Arkoudis, 2014). This requires rethinking options and strategies within a higher education system that requires pedagogic shifts where ELP is repositioned as

- relevant to all students
- integrated within disciplinary teaching, learning and assessment practices
- incorporated into institutional quality assurance processes.

Ways institutions can approach the issue have been recently addressed in detail the recent OLT fellowship by Sophie Arkoudis (Arkoudis, in press). This fellowship addresses how responsibility is best distributed among key figures and groups at institutions to approach the issue of ELP, and the kinds of questions that should be asked of them in light of their responsibilities. Course coordinators are identified as the cornerstone of strategies for identifying how the assessment of ELP can be mapped across specific courses, in ways that assure that students exit their course of study having attained threshold levels of these skills. The way in which they can approach the issue will now be elaborated upon.

In order to develop a whole of university approach to ELP development, and assure ELP is assessed, it is suggested that deputy vice-chancellors (or their equivalent) at institutions across the country should be able to ask and have answers to the following two questions from each course coordinator:

1. What is an appropriate level of ELP at graduation for a student in this course?
2. Where and how are students assessed on ELP over their course?

To answer these questions course coordinators should consider what ELP should be defined as in their courses, and how they are going to assess it, perhaps through key subjects at both foundational and capstone level, ELP assessment scaffolded through the course, and/or Work Integrated Learning. There are five key aspects to the approach course coordinators should take:

1. Definitions about what ELP is within particular courses, and in light of these what students will be required to demonstrate, at minimum, to pass their courses.
2. Earmarking of subjects at different levels within courses where ELP is to be assessed and taught.

3. Pairing Academic Language and Learning (ALL) advisors with disciplinary academics in ELP focused subjects, in order to develop resources linked to the LMS that develop the types of ELP identified in subject learning outcomes.
4. Explicit incorporation of ELP components into marking rubrics, perhaps under the title of 'communication skills'.
5. Increasing student understanding of their responsibility to increase their ELP in order to be successful in their studies.

Placing the responsibility to define the nature of ELP for a specific course allows for a nuanced approach to the assessment of ELP to be developed. In each course there will be different kinds of ELP outcomes required at exit. For example, in their professional careers following graduation many students in veterinary science degrees will need to understand how to use different anatomical terminology, often with sensitivity to clients about the nature of the issues that their pets have. However, these are not the same ELP requirements of a student graduating from a business course, who may need to communicate effectively with a range of professional stakeholders in high pressure corporate environments.

So once coordinators have made the main decisions, what can academics reasonably do to integrate ELP learning outcomes within their teaching and learning contexts? There are easy to implement ideas that can make a difference in integrating ELP and disciplinary teaching. For academics this means emphasising to students the importance of developing their ELP for success in their studies, making the assessment of ELP more visible in teaching and assessment, and seeking support from ALL advisors who can design resources to enhance students' ELP development relevant to the assessment tasks. The following strategies are some provided from Arkoudis (2014) that can be used by academics.

For teaching and learning tasks:
1. Emphasise expectations to students in relation to the ELP levels required to complete assessment tasks.
    - Include ELP learning outcomes in information about the unit
    - Link learning outcomes to overall graduate outcomes of the course of study, and ELP in particular
    - Include ELP in the assessment criteria.
2. Ask ALL advisors to develop resources that will assist students to develop the ELP skills relevant to the assessment task/s.
    - Invite the ALL advisor to lectures to discuss the resources that are available to assist students with developing their oral and written language and literacy skills

- Seek advice from ALL advisors about online materials that could assist students in developing their ELP for the assessment tasks
- Emphasise resources available on the Learning Management System to support students' ELP development.

3. Model examples of good writing or oral presentations for students to see what quality work looks like (disciplinary knowledge will also be included in the discussion):
    - Place on the Learning Management System models for good work and annotate the strengths and weaknesses and ways it could be improved, including communication skills (this can be done by ALL advisor)
    - Ask students to prepare short pieces of writing for tutorials that reflect the assessment task, and incorporate advice about their academic writing that they have accessed from the LMS
    - Discuss effective techniques for oral presentations.

For assessment tasks:

1. Include an early assessment task (returned to students by week 4) as formative assessment
    - Highlight communication skills in order to provide students with feedback
    - Identify students in need of extra support
    - Offer feedback to the class as a whole on the assignment, and include comments on ELP
    - Highlight again the resources available on the Learning management System and support available from ALL advisors
2. Incorporate peer review of students work into assessment tasks
    - Use peer review to develop opportunities for students to discuss their work and identify how it can be improved
    - Focus more on what students learn about their own work from reviewing other students' work
    - One example of organising peer review is PRAZE (see example via Melbourne University web site: http://lms.unimelb.edu.au/teaching/assessment/praze/)
3. Use students self-assessment to encourage self-regulated development of communication skills
    - Ask students to refer to the assessment criteria and reflect on their learning and justify the grade they should receive. Their reflection should include their appraisal of their ELP development and identify areas that they seek to improve.

As seen, ALL advisors can be drawn upon by academics and course coordinators to assist in creating resources for ELP development that are linked to disciplinary learning. Since the 1960s ALL advisors have provided a variety of forms of ELP learning support to students in Australia (Chanock, 2011, A-60). Traditionally, the primary form of support that they have provided is

English language development advice to students, in either one-to-one sessions or workshops under a model that operates largely outside of disciplinary curricula. A common theme from ALL advisors is frustration in being unable to get traction to work with academics to improve students' learning outcomes within disciplinary curricula (Chanock, 2007; Harper, 2013). This strategy can give them sustainable access to students in the curriculum, with the resources they develop for the university LMS or in direct teaching support provided in ELP-focused subjects. The benefit this has over existing practice is that it is a top-down strategy provides continued involvement by ALL advisors within the curriculum. While existing efforts to incorporate ALL advisors in disciplinary teaching and learning have had some success, they are based upon the individual efforts of academics and ALL advisors, and there is some doubt over whether this kind of bottom-up approach is sustainable (Arkoudis & Doughney, 2014).

Research shows that assessment drives student learning (Arkoudis, Baik, & Richardson, 2012; Boud, 1999), and incorporating ELP assessment across the course of study will highlight importance of students developing their ELP during their studies. Importantly, students should be able to demonstrate that they have attained at least minimum levels of ELP in order for them to graduate form their course of study. This is a strategy that targets all students, as EAL international students are not the only group whose ELP at exit needs to be addressed. ELP development is an issue that concerns all students, and measures to address it need not to focus on one group at the expense of others. As such, this kind of approach can avoid polarising international students in ways that existing strategies which target them exclusively have the capacity to.

Conclusion

The focus in Australian higher education has shifted to assuring that students meet threshold standards at exit. In light of this shift, the issue of EAL international students' ELP must now concern ELP attainment at graduation. The model to approach this issue advocated here has at its core the strategic assessment of all students' ELP across their course of study. Under this model, it is the responsibility of course coordinators to determine where and how ELP should be assessed within course of study, and what type of ELP is relevant to the discipline area in question. This is one way to make sure that the issue of EAL international students', and indeed all students' ELP standards at exit is resolved, as through such a strategy students will not be able to pass through their course of study without a level of ELP appropriate to their discipline area.

This kind of strategy has a wide range of advantages over other possible methods. It does not polarise international students, and focuses on ELP in the way it should be approached — as something that is an issue for all students. It is a model that does not assume that EAL international students should be equipped to have the ELP to graduate when they arrive. Rather it is based on evidence that ELP needs to be addressed within the curriculum to address the needs of an ever more diverse student body. Moreover, it is flexible to the needs of different courses with different types of ELP requirements, given that it places responsibility in the hands of people in the know — course coordinators — to determine where and how it should be assessed. Finally, it is something that disciplinary academics can approach as part of their current practices without the stress of significant additional training or time expended, and it can incorporate the work of ALL advisors within the teaching context. If progress is to be made on this issue, this model is an effective way forward.

Acknowledgement

Support for the fellowship on which this material is based was provided by the Office of Learning and Teaching (OLT), an initiative of the Australian Government. The views expressed in this material do not necessarily reflect the views of OLT or the Australian Government.

References

Arkoudis, S. (2014). *Integrating English language communication skills into disciplinary curricula: Options and strategies.* Sydney: Office of Learning and Teaching.

Arkoudis, S. (2013). English language standards and claims of soft marking. In S. Marginson (Ed.), *Tertiary education policy in Australia.* Melbourne, Australia: Centre for the Study of Higher Education.

Arkoudis, S., Baik, C., Bexley, E., & Doughney, L. (2014). *English Language Proficiency and Employability Framework: For Australian higher education institutions.* Melbourne: Centre for the Study of Higher Education

Arkoudis, S., Baik, C., & Richardson, S. (2012*). English language standards in higher education.* Melbourne: Australian Council for Eduational Research.

Arkoudis, S., & Doughney, L. (2014). *Good practice report: English Language proficiency.* Canberra, Australia: Office for Learning and Teaching.

Arkoudis, S., Hawthorne, L., Baik, C., O'Loughlin, K., Hawthorne, G., Leach, D., & Bexley, E. (2009). *The impact of English language proficiency and workplace readiness on the employment outcomes of tertiary international students.* Canberra, Australia: Canberra, Australia: Department of Education, Employment and Workplace Relations.

Australian Education International. (2013). International student data 2013. Retrieved from https://aei.gov.au/research/International-Student Data/Pages/InternationalStudentData2013.aspx

AUQA. (2009). Good practice principles of for English language proficiency for international students in Australian universities. Canberra, Australia: Department of Education, Employment and Workplace Relations.

Benzie, H. J. (2010). Graduating as a 'native speaker': International students and English language proficiency in higher education. *Higher Education Research and Development, 29*(4), 447–459.

Birrell, B.(2006). Implications of low English standards among overseas students at Australian universities. *People and Place, 14*(4), 53–64.

Boud, D. (1999). Peer learning and assessment. *Assessment & Evaluation in Higher Education, 24*(4), 413–427.

Bretag, T. (2007). The emperor's new clothes: Yes there is a link between English language competence and academic standards. *People and Place, 15*(1), 13–21.

Briguglio, C. (2013). *Working in the third space: promoting interdisciplinary collaboration to embed English language development into the disciplines.* Sydney, Australia: Office for Learning and Teaching.

Craven, E. (2012). The quest for IELTS Band 7.0: Investigating English language proficiency development of international students at an Australian university. *IELTS Research Reports, Vol. 13.* Retrieved from http://www.ielts.org/PDF/vol13_Report2.pdf

Chanock, K. (2011). A historical literature review of Australian publications in the field of Academic Language and Learning in the 1980s: Themes, Schemes, and Schisms: Part Two. *Journal of Academic Language and Learning, 4*(1), A59A87.

Chanock, K. (2007). What academic language and learning advisors bring to the scholarship of teaching and learning: Problems and possibilities for dialogue with the disciplines. *Higher Education Research and Development, 26*(3), 269–280.

Department of Industry Innovation Science Research and Tertiary Education, DIISRTE (2011). Higher Education Standards Framework. Canberra, Australia: Commonwealth of Australia. Retrieved from http://www.comlaw.gov.au/Details/F2012L00003/Download

Dunworth, K. (2013). *Degrees of proficiency: Building a strategic approach to university students' English language assessment and development (Final Report).* Sydney, Australia: Office for Learning and Teaching.

Foster, G. (2012). The impact of international students on measured learning and standards in Australian higher education. *Ecomonics of Education Review, 31*(5), 587–600.

Harper, R. (2013). From principles to practice: Implementing an English language proficiency model at UniSA. *Journal of Academic Language and Learning, 7*(2), A150–A164.

Harris, A. (2013). Identifying students requiring English language support: What role can a PELA play? *Journal of Academic Language and Learning, 7*(2), A62–A78.

Humphreys, P., & Gribble, C. (2013). Discussion paper 3: Outcomes: English language and transition to work or further study. In *Five years on: English language competence of international students – Outcomes Report*. Retrieved from http://www.ieaa.org.au/documents/item/54

Humphreys, P., & Mousavi, A. (2010). Exit testing: A whole of university approach. *Language Education in Asia, 1*(1), 8–22.

Kemp, D. & Norton, A. (2014). *Review of the demand driven funding system*. Retrieved from http://www.education.gov.au/report-review-demand-driven funding-system.

James, R (2014). The Australian test: Uncapped student numbers. *Times Higher Education*. Retrieved from http://www.timeshighereducation.co.uk/features/the-australian-test-uncapped-student-numbers/2010630.article

Marginson, S. (2013). Labour's failure to ground public funding. In S. Marginson (Ed.), *Tertiary education policy in Australia*. Melbourne, Australia: CSHE. Retrieved from http://www.cshe.unimelb.edu.au/research/policy_dev/docs/Tert_Edu_Policy_Aus.pdf

OECD. (2013). *Education at a glance 2013: Highlights*. OECD.

Oliver, B, Souter K. (2013). Imagining the future of assessment: for evidence, for credit and for payment. In H. Carter, M. Gosper, & J. Hedberg (Eds.), *Electric Dreams*. Proceedings. Sydney, Australia.

O'Loughlin, K., & Arkoudis, S. (2009). Investigating IELTS score gains in higher education. *IELTS Research Reports, Volume 10*, 95–180.

O'Loughlin, K., & Murray, D. (2007). *Pathways — Preparation and Selection*. Canberra, Austrlaia: Australian Education International.

Victorian Ombudsman. (2011). *Investigation into how universities deal with international students*. Retrieved from http://www.ombudsman.vic.gov.au/resources/documents/Investigation_into_how_universities_deal_with_international_students.pdf

Chapter 12

'But Isn't IELTS the Most Trustworthy?': English Language Assessment for Entry into Higher Education

Kieran O'Loughlin

Background

In establishing the minimum acceptable English language entry requirements for local and international students, Australian universities have recognised a plethora of evidence over the last twenty years. Using data from a survey completed by 37 Australian tertiary institutions in 1995, Coley (1999) reported that there were as many as 61 different types of evidence accepted across them as proof of the English language proficiency of both international and local EAL students. These forms of evidence were extremely diverse and included various international and Australian tests of English as a foreign/second language, final year secondary qualifications including English subjects, university foundation studies, other post-secondary English qualifications, membership/registration with professional bodies, previous English medium instruction, scholastic aptitude tests, years of residence in Australia, and interviews. Fourteen universities indicated that they also accepted other unspecified evidence.

The most widely accepted forms of evidence reported in Coley's (1999) study were (in order): international and Australian English proficiency tests (mainly the International English Language Testing System [IELTS], and the Test of English as a Foreign Language [TOEFL]), Australian and other senior secondary English subjects and examinations, previous instruction through the medium of English, English pathway or bridging programs and university foundation programs. Of these, Coley, quite rightly, was most sceptical of previous instruction through the medium of English since it provides the least direct evidence of English language competence; that is, being taught in a language does not necessarily lead to a student to acquire a sufficient proficiency to be able to successfully use the language for the full range of required academic purposes. She indicated that some universities permitted this previous instruction to have occurred in secondary education or vocational programs in which the level of English required to successfully complete them is substantially lower than in the university course they are applying to enter.

In December 2010 an analysis of the English language requirements of all of Australia's 39 universities was undertaken by the author of this chapter as a follow up to Coley's (1999) study. This analysis was conducted by locating the English entry requirements of these universities on their websites. It was found that 48 different types of evidence of English language competence were used across all universities, thirteen less than in the earlier study. From a quality perspective, it was reassuring to find that results from old tests designed in the 1970s and 1980s were no longer accepted and that more informal forms of in-house testing were no longer used. Moreover, only five universities, compared to fourteen in Coley's (1999) study, indicated that they also accepted other unspecified (and therefore untrustworthy) evidence.

The main forms of evidence used in 2010 were very similar to those reported by Coley (1999). These were (in order of university popularity): international (but no longer Australian) English proficiency tests (mainly the IELTS but also the TOEFL and the Pearson Test of English [PTE] Academic), Australian and other senior secondary English subjects and examinations, English pathway or bridging programs, previous instruction through the medium of English (although accepted by fewer universities than in Coley's study) and university foundation programs.

As in Coley's (1999) survey, the IELTS remained the only form of evidence accepted by all Australian universities. The main reason for this is because, since the early 1990s, this test has been favoured by the Australian Government which has had a close relationship with IDP Education, a co-owner of the IELTS together with Cambridge English Language Assessment and the British Council. IDP Education was established in 1969 and is now jointly owned by 38 Australian universities in partnership with SEEK Limited, Australia's leading online employment and training company. IDP Education has played a key role in attracting and recruiting international students to Australian universities and colleges, especially over the last two decades. Thus, the relationship between the IELTS and Australian universities has been and continues to be a very close one, from both commercial and educational perspectives.

Finally, despite it widespread acceptance, the IELTS was not necessarily the most widely presented form of evidence by university EAL applicants in the 2010 review. They often presented other main types of acceptable evidence (also noted by Coley [1999]). Local EAL applicants tended to rely on Australian senior secondary qualifications, foundation studies qualifications or previous instruction in the medium of English. International EAL applicants who had been in the country for some time also used these forms of evidence as well as successful completion of English pathway and other bridging programs.

Proficiency versus achievement assessments

An important distinction in assessing English language competence is between proficiency and achievement tests. Proficiency tests (such as the IELTS, TOEFL and PTE Academic) are based on a theory of overall language competence and are not related to a specific syllabus or curriculum. They provide a measure of this competence at a given point in present time but are also future-oriented in the sense that they try to make predictions about how well an individual will cope in a target environment. Academic proficiency tests therefore attempt to predict how ready a student is to commence higher education study in the medium of English.

Standardised proficiency tests are often perceived by the general public and many staff within universities to be inherently more valid (truthful) and reliable (consistent) than achievement tests because of their independent, global and standardised nature. This perception also derives from the knowledge that they are produced by language testing experts working in well established testing agencies in the United Kingdom (UK) and United States (US). Their assumed higher reliability is especially emphasised by their non-language specialist supporters: these people believe that the results on the test will be the same whenever and wherever in the world a student sits for the test. However, no test scores are completely stable, especially when they include human ('subjective') ratings of test taker performance such as in the IELTS speaking and writing sub-tests. In addition, students may obtain different results on different occasions and in various locations depending on a range of factors which cannot be controlled or anticipated. These include, for example, the student's health or state of mind on the day of the test and the conditions under which the test is administered. The degree of a test's imprecision is summarised by the standard error of measurement (SEM) which is discussed further in relation to the IELTS in the next section of this chapter.

Some university staff who encounter or work with EAL students, such as selection officers, academic staff or academic advisors in support units believe that proficiency test scores do not accurately reflect whether a student's academic English competence is adequate for him or her to succeed in their studies. However, such a view represents a misunderstanding of the nature, purpose and limitations of proficiency tests. Tests like the IELTS, TOEFL and PTE - Academic only aim to elicit a sample of the student's English language on the basis of which to make predictions about whether their English competence is sufficient to study in a higher education setting where English is the medium of instruction. Because the tests are done in a relatively short time they cannot possibly sample every kind of academic language use that may be required for successful completion of a higher education program. Furthermore, proficiency test scores only indicate the extent to which a student is ready to *begin* studying in the medium of English: further language development, preferably discipline-specific, will most likely be needed. They also indicate nothing about how much aptitude the student has for further developing their language skills. This may be an even more important language consideration than proficiency in the context of university selection (Clapham, 2000).

Achievement tests, on the other hand, are based on a particular syllabus or curriculum. They are past-oriented in the sense that they measure how well students have learnt the content of a syllabus. Thus, final exams for senior secondary English and ESL subjects, English for Academic Purposes (EAP) subjects in foundation programs, and 'stand alone' English language bridging or pathway programs are achievement tests. The final result (the summative assessment) often also takes into account continuous assessment completed during the course as well as any final tests or examinations. Where they are designed locally by teachers, achievement tests have traditionally suffered from a lack of credibility in terms of their 'objectivity'. There is a public perception that teachers cannot accurately assess their own students because (a) a lack of skill in designing assessment tools, and (b) inevitable bias either towards or against different individuals they have taught over a period of time in their scoring of their test performances. However, such criticisms are not necessarily well founded.

The IELTS versus English pathway programs

This section will compare the trustworthiness of the information provided by IELTS scores with the assessments made on English pathway programs (as examples of proficiency and achievement assessments respectively) in determining the readiness of EAL international students for English-medium higher education.

The IELTS

The IELTS test has established itself as the most powerful high-stakes English language testing instrument in Australia for both studying and obtaining permanent residency. It is designed by Cambridge English Language Assessment in the UK. IELTS is available in two test formats: Academic or General Training. Applicants for higher education study must take the Academic module. There are four test components: Listening, Speaking, Reading and

Writing, and the whole test is of two hours and 45 minutes duration. All candidates take the same Listening and Speaking tests but both the Reading and Writing tests are different for the Academic and General Training modules. The Listening, Reading and Writing tests must be completed on the same day. Depending on the test centre, the Speaking test may be offered either on the same day or up to a week before or after the other tests.

Test takers receive a report form which provides separate 'individual band' scores for each of the four sections and an unweighted, rounded average as the 'overall band' score. The overall and each of the four individual band scores are reported on a scale from 0 to 9 with 0.5 increments. Labels and descriptors are provided for overall band scores in whole numbers from 0 to 9 but not for each 0.5 increment. Thus a score of 6.0 is representative of a 'Competent User' who 'has generally effective command of the language, despite some inaccuracies, inappropriacies and misunderstandings in some situations. Can use and understand fairly complex language, particularly in familiar situations'. This compares with a score of 7.0 which is indicative of a 'Good User' who 'has operational command of the language, though with occasional inaccuracies, inappropriacies and misunderstandings in some situations. Generally handles complex language well and understands detailed reasoning' (IELTS, 2013).

As Spolsky (1997) suggests, in the interests of fairness, it is extremely important for universities to set minimum entry cut-off scores which do not rely on differences smaller than the SEM of the test. Given that the SEM of the overall IELTS band score is less than 0.5, a minimum required score of 6.5 would clearly indicate that test takers who achieve this score do fall within the range of Band 6; that is, their score is well into the width of this band and doesn't risk being borderline (Taylor, 2009).

Universities set their own minimum entry standards on the IELTS. In establishing minimum entry levels they are advised by the IELTS partners that an overall score of 7.5 to 9.0 is 'acceptable', 7.0 is 'probably acceptable', and that 5.5 to 6.5 indicates 'English study needed' for 'linguistically demanding academic courses' such as Medicine, Law, and Journalism. An overall score of 7.0 to 9.0 is suggested to be 'acceptable', 6.5 'probably acceptable, and 5.5 to 6.0 'English study needed' for 'linguistically less demanding academic courses' such as Agriculture, Pure Mathematics and Technology, (IELTS, 2010). The minimum entry requirements to most Australian higher education courses, are still generally the same as Coley (1999) noted in her study: an overall band score of 6.0 or 6.5. This suggests that 'linguistically demanding courses' have entry scores which are too low since a score of 6.5 is considered only probably acceptable and a score of 6.0 indicates that English study is needed. Where English study is deemed necessary, no recommendation is made about whether it should be undertaken before or after the commencement of the higher education course. This ambiguity has caused some confusion when institutions set their entry levels and has even resulted in some universities only requiring students to reach the usual entry scores by the end of their course.

The IELTS test offers all the advantages of a standardised, internationally recognised proficiency test. In providing an overall score as well as scores in listening, speaking, reading and writing, the test provides institutions with clear evidence about the English proficiency of applicants for their programs. An important issue is how well IELTS test scores predict academic outcomes. While the IELTS aims to indicate how ready test takers are to commence university study in the medium of English, it does not claim to be able to predict how well they will perform academically on the basis of their test scores. As David Ingram, the Australian representative on IELTS development project at the University of Lancaster 1987 to 1988 and IELTS Chief Examiner in Australia from 1988 to1998, suggests:

> IELTS is no more than what it claims to be — a test of English language proficiency. Students' abilities to perform in academic and other contexts depends not only on their language competence but on many other factors, not least their understanding of the education culture in which they are studying. The different culture will affect many aspects of their performance such as how they relate to their lecturers, how they participate in a seminar, how they organise their writing to present a logical argument, and so on. IELTS cannot and does not try to measure these vitally important factors that contribute to students' success at university — and nor do any other language (proficiency) tests. (Ingram, 2005, p. 4)

Nevertheless, its predictive power has been widely researched in Australia by correlating test scores with academic results, often the grade point average (GPA; e.g., Elder [1993], Broadstock [1994], Cotton and Conrow [1998], Kerstjens & Nery [2000], Dooey & Oliver [2002], Feast [2002] and Woodrow [2006]). The findings in these studies generally show that IELTS test has only weak to moderate predictive power with reading scores more significant than the other scores. Dooey and Oliver (2002), for example, found that achieving the institution's minimum overall IELTS score (in this case 6.0) was only a partial predictor of academic success. They also found that some students who did not achieve this minimum level but were still admitted for other reasons were successful in the first year of their studies. Woodrow (2006) found that students admitted with the minimum required overall band score of 6.5 had very similar GPAs to those who had achieved an overall score of 7.0 on the IELTS test.

The common conclusion in all of these studies is that language is only one of many important factors contributing to academic grades. Such factors include, among many others, academic ability, discipline knowledge student motivation, financial support, adequate study skills and the use of English outside the classroom. Hirsch (2007, p. 198), for instance, suggests 'high academic grades can be linked to a high degree of existing specialisation in subject areas' (such as is sometimes the case at postgraduate level) and this may not be well reflected in IELTS (or TOEFL) scores. Other factors external to the individual student such as the types of assessment conducted in their university course as well as the degree to which language is considered in the assessment also influence academic grades. However, the research literature does suggest that an overall IELTS score of less than 6.0 at the point of entry into a tertiary course does makes a difference to academic outcomes.

Research examining the interpretation and use of the IELTS within higher education in the Australian context has only recently begun (see, e.g., O'Loughlin, 2011). It is vitally important that university staff who set entry scores and provide advice to students about the test have adequate levels of knowledge about proficiency testing in general and the IELTS in particular to ensure the test is used ethically and responsibly: after all, their advice and decisions may have far-reaching consequences for the lives of their prospective students (O'Loughlin, 2013).

English pathway programs

English (or EAP) pathway programs are typically conducted as intensive courses of about 20 hours duration over 5 to 10 weeks in a language centre which either belongs to or is associated with a particular Australian higher education institution. They aim to improve students' knowledge and use of academic English, study skills and their understanding of Australian academic culture. Through the completion of these programs, students are expected to have learnt the language and study skills which will provide a sufficiently strong foundation for them to commence learning in a specific academic discipline. When undertaken in Australia EAP pathway programs enable students who successfully complete them to satisfy the English entry requirements of their intended institution that approves them for this purpose. It should be noted, however, that preparatory EAP programs are not only delivered in Australia. Increasingly, universities are working with overseas partner institutions to develop suitable programs. Sawir (2005, p. 579) suggests that such preparatory programs (as distinguished from more narrowly focused IELTS preparation ones) that are conducted in students' countries of origin provide a 'broad based preparation for coping with language issues in the Australian academic situation'. However, students who have successfully completed such a program in another country do not satisfy the Australian Government's English requirements for obtaining a visa unless they also obtain the requisite minimum scores on an internationally recognised proficiency test.

English pathway programs therefore aim to prepare EAL international students for university study. An unresolved question, however, is the extent to which they should focus on improving students' English competence and/or developing their more broadly based academic and social skills. A number of studies that have been conducted over the last twenty years suggest that such programs are fulfilling both roles (Agosti, 2004; Banfield, 2006; Cargill, 1996; Cruickshank & Chen, 2005; Dooey, 2010; Felix & Lawson, 1994; O'Loughlin & Bailey, 2006; Terraschke & Wahid, 2011). These studies indicate that English pathway programs are extremely valuable to students as preparation for university study. A key ongoing research challenge is to identify the best balance in developing students' English competence and the broader academic skills that will enable to them to make a successful transition into university study.

Quality assurance has become an increasingly important issue for pathway programs. While they are accredited by the National ELT Accreditation Scheme (NEAS) as EAP programs, it is individual universities which approve them for entry purposes. The result is that there are no national standards for these programs in relation to the design, delivery and assessment of students. Leask, Ciccarelli, and Benzie (2003) proposed a framework for assessing the suitability of English pathway programs at their own university which could form the basis for a more co-ordinated national approach. It incorporates six different aspects: (1) aims, objectives and content; (2) teaching methodology; (3) assessment; (4) teaching and learning resources; (5) course structure and delivery; and (6) accreditation and benchmarking. They argue that this kind of framework is needed to ensure that these programs provide students with the academic and social language as well as cultural skills they will need to succeed in their university studies and live in Australia. In 2008, the peak national association of the English language industry, English Australia, developed a best practice guide for pathway programs exclusively for its member English language providers. However, there still remains no common set of standards to which these programs must adhere for the purpose of preparing students for university entry. This means that individual universities need to carefully monitor and evaluate these programs. A further issue, raised by O'Loughlin (2003), is the specific expertise that teachers need to work effectively on pathway programs. They certainly need to base their teaching on specialised, postgraduate EAP training and their own broader experiences of university study. Agosti and Bernat (2009) address this question, highlighting the importance of English teachers acquiring specialist EAP skills through postgraduate programs or professional development training.

Assessments on pathway programs

Assessments of student achievement on pathway programs normally cover students' English competence and associated academic skills. They are likely to focus on the four language macro-skills of listening, speaking, reading and writing. Normally students need to demonstrate they can apply specific academic language knowledge (in areas such as discourse, genre, syntax and vocabulary) across these macro-skills. There may also be non-linguistic as well as linguistic skills involved here. For instance, the assessment of speaking might include a student's competence to speak clearly and fluently, ask questions and provide clear explanations, prepare and conduct a seminar, negotiate procedures and outcomes in small groups, and produce and present an effective individual presentation. It is worth noting that, while the main focus is on speaking, the other three macro-skills are involved in these tasks. Assessment in English pathway programs thus often strives to integrate the four macro-skills and associated academic skills in ways similar to authentic academic language use. The construct of academic language competence underlying these assessments is therefore broader and more integrated than proficiency tests such as the IELTS which measure competence in each of the four macro-skills separately.

A student's final result is sometimes composed entirely of continuous assessment undertaken during the pathway program or else is a combination of continuous assessment and a final examination. Examples of continuous assessment tasks are research-based assignments and oral presentations. Examples of final examination tasks are essays on topics studied in the program or based on listening and reading inputs during the examination itself.

University staff and other stakeholders who have less faith in proficiency tests are more likely to trust the results obtained on an English preparation program as they will indicate a student's competence to master relevant academic language skills over the entire period of the course which generally run for period of between five and ten weeks. Such courses often have greater educational appeal than proficiency tests precisely because the assessment is integrated with the goals of a curriculum and therefore is likely to have a positive relationship with teaching and learning. While such assessments might appear to be more comprehensive than standardised proficiency tests, the reliability of teacher-based assessments for this kind of high-stakes purposes is an important concern and its significance should not be underestimated. Unless rigorous, ongoing moderation of these assessments takes place, they are unlikely to be regarded as sufficiently trustworthy by the higher education community. It is also desirable that they include some assessment of students' proficiency as well as their mastery of the specific skills covered in the English pathway program so that their final assessments can be meaningfully compared to standardised proficiency test scores

Assessments which include achievement tests often hold particular appeal for teachers of English preparation programs. As McNamara (2000, p. 7) notes, achievement tests 'are more easily able to be innovative and reflect progressive aspects of the curriculum'. However, in terms of their comparability with proficiency tests, the abilities these tests assess may be more than overall competence in the language because they may include skills which are not directly language-based such as knowledge of the topics or content covered in the course.

There is little research which has been conducted on assessment in pathway programs. This is surprising given that important decisions about whether students have met university English entry requirements are based on them. One key issue is the relationship between proficiency test scores and achievement assessments made on pathway programs. This question was addressed in O'Loughlin and Bailey's (2006) study where 23 students who successfully completed the pathway program also undertook an IELTS test at the end of the program. They found that only 14 of the 23 students achieved the minimum overall score of 7.0 set for entry to the graduate courses they were all entering in a faculty of education. This was surprising given that they had been required to have already achieved an overall score of 6.5 in order to be admitted to the pathway program which was of 250 hours duration. Of the remaining nine students only seven again achieved an overall score of 6.5 and two regressed to a score of 6.0 overall. This suggested that students did not necessarily need to improve their overall proficiency to pass their English pathway program. Nevertheless, the subsequent first year university results of the 23 students were very good, with all of them achieving an average grade of at least a pass level. Many of them achieved credits and distinctions in their subjects. On the basis of these results O'Loughlin and Bailey (2006) concluded that the probability of academic success at university was high when students have reached slightly below the minimum required overall proficiency test score and successfully completed a pathway program. This may be true irrespective of whether their English proficiency has improved over the duration of the pathway program. This finding confirms that students may develop other academic skills on these programs apart from their competence in English. Indeed, for a minority of students these academic skills may compensate for the lack of improvement in English competence, enabling them to perform successfully at university.

A related issue is whether achievement assessments made in pathway programs can be benchmarked against proficiency test scores. O'Loughlin (2009) undertook a study which attempted to benchmark the written examination of a university English pathway program against the writing component of IELTS academic module. Initially, this appeared to be very difficult to achieve because the tasks on the pathway program examination were of a highly integrative nature (involving listening and reading as well as writing skills) whereas the IELTS test involved only a minimal amount of reading in order to complete the two written tasks. The results, however, indicated that with some adjustments to the examination tasks and scoring criteria the pathway program examination could be successfully benchmarked against the IELTS writing test without compromising the integrative nature of the pathway program examination. This kind of research is not straightforward given the different nature of proficiency and achievement assessments but it may become increasingly important to raise the credibility and trustworthiness of pathway programs.

Another important advantage of pathway programs is that the continuous assessment, which normally forms part of them, has the potential to feed back into the teaching and learning cycle to improve student learning outcomes. This is known as the formative function of assessment. Cross and O'Loughlin (2013) explored this issue. They reported that the program they studied was overly dominated by summative assessments which contributed to students' final results. Furthermore, the opportunities for formative assessment were limited to practice assessment tasks which simply mirrored the summative assessment tasks with teacher feedback (where it was provided) having little to do with subsequent teaching/learning activities. The researcher suggested that the number of assessments should be reduced so that there was a better balance between teaching, learning and assessment. These improvements were subsequently made to the program. There is a real danger that pathway programs may incorporate excessive summative assessment requirements to shore up their credibility.

Finally, the reporting of student achievement on pathway programs has hardly been examined at all. There are much richer ways of doing this other than simply reporting a final score. In the UK context, Banarjee and Wall (2006) provide a very interesting model involving a comprehensive assessment checklist to be completed by teachers at the end of a pathway program. Much more research is needed into this and other aspects of assessments on Engliah pathway programs in the Australian context, including their validity and reliability.

Notwithstanding these assessment challenges, the available research cited previously in this chapter suggests that English pathway programs serve as a highly valuable introduction to university study in Australia. Ideally, all students should complete such a preparatory English program, if not in Australia, then in their country of origin before they arrive given the range of linguistic and academic skills such programs can help students to develop before they commence their university studies. From this angle, demonstrating acceptable results on a proficiency test may be insufficient evidence that students can apply their English language competence successfully to their academic and social participation in a university setting. It is recommended that all Australian universities should require new international EAL students in particular to successfully complete a dedicated preparatory English course immediately before or after they arrive in Australia, even if they have already satisfied one or more of their institution's other minimum English requirements. However, the benefits of these pathway programs still need to be better articulated and researched than they have to date if they are to gain greater acceptance by higher education institutions and the public more broadly.

References

Agosti, C., & Bernat, E. (2009). Teaching direct entry programs effectively: insights for ELICOS teachers and managers. *English Australia Journal*, 25(1), 27–41.

Agosti, C. (2004). *Six direct entry courses at Macquarie: meeting students' various needs*. Paper presented at the 17th EA Conference. Retrieved from www.englishaustralia.com.au

Banarjee, J., & Wall, D. (2006). Assessing and reporting peroframances on pre-sessional EAP courses: developing a final assessment checklist and investigating its validity. *Journal of English for Academic Purposes*, 5, 50–69.

Banfield, J. (2006). *From EAP to university; a case study of Chinese students in Melbourne*. Unpublished Masters, the University of Melbourne.

Broadstock, H. (1994). *The predictive validity of the IELTS and TOEFL: a comparison*. The University of Melbourne, Australia.

Cargill, M. (1996). An integrated bridging program for international postgraduate students. *Higher Education Research and Development*, 15(5), 177–188.

Clapham, C. (2000). Assessment for academic purposes: where next? *System*, 28, 511–521.

Coley, M. (1999). The English language entry requirements of Australian universities for students of non-English speaking background. *Higher Education Research and Development*, 18(1), 7–18.

Cotton, F., & Conrow, F. (1998). An investigation of the predictive validity of IELTS amongst a group of international students studying at the University of Tasmania. *IELTS Research Reports*, 1, 72–115.

Cross, R., & O'Loughlin, K. (2013). Continuous assessment frameworks within university English Pathway Programs: Realising formative assessment within high-stakes contexts. *Studies in Higher Education*, 38(4), 584–594.

Cruickshank, K., & Chen, H. (2005). *Preparation and proficiency: co-requisites or opposing goals?* A study of IELTS and internal EAP pathways to tertiary study in Australia. Paper presented at the 30th annual ALAA conference.

Dooey, P., & Oliver, R. (2002). An investigation into the predictive validity of the IELTS test as an indicator of future academic success. *Prospect, 17*(1), 36–54.

Dooey, P. (2010). Students' perspectives of an EAP pathway program. *Journal of English for Academic Purposes, 9*, 184–197.

Elder, C. (1993). Language proficiency as a predictor of performance in teacher education. *Melbourne Papers in Language Testing, 2*(1), 72–95.

Feast, V. (2002). The impact of IELTS score on performance at university. *International Education Journal, 3*(4), 70–85.

Felix, U., & Lawson, M. (1994). Evaluation of an integrated bridging course on academic writing for overseas postgraduate students. *Higher Education Research and Development, 13*(1), 59–69.

Hirsch, D. (2007). English language, academic support and academic outcomes: a discussion paper. *University of Sydney Papers in TESOL, 2*(2), 193–211.

IELTS (2013) IELTS Guide for educational institutions, governments, professional bodies and commercial organizations. http://www.ielts.org/PDF/Guide_Edu-%20Inst_Gov_2013.pdf

IELTS. (2014). IELTS Band Scores. Retrieved from http://www.ielts.org/institutions/test_format_and_results/ielts_band_scores.aspx

Ingram, D. (2005). English language testing: A pass for proficiency is not necessarily the answer. *UniNews, 14*, 4–5.

Kerstjens, M., & Nery, C. (2000). Predictive validity in the IELTS test: A study of the relationship between IELTS scores and students' subsequent academic performance. *IELTS Research Reports, 3*, 85–108.

Leask, B., Ciccarelli, A., & Benzie, H. (2003). Pathways to tertiary learning: a framework for evaluating English language programs for undergraduate study. *English Australia Journal, 21*(1), 17–29.

McNamara, T. (2000). *Language testing.* Oxford, England: Oxford University Press.

O'Loughlin, K. (2003). English for academic purposes: Where are we now? *English Australia Journal, 20*(2), 17–24.

O'Loughlin, K. (2009). 'Does it measure up?' Benchmarking the written examination of a university english pathway program. *Melbourne Papers in Language Testing, 14*(1), 32–54.

O'Loughlin, K. (2011). The interpretation and use of proficiency test scores for university admissions: how valid and ethical are they? *Language Assessment Quarterly, 8*(2), 146–160.

O'Loughlin, K. (2013). Developing the assessment literacy of university proficiency test users. *Language Testing, 30*(3), 363–380.

O'Loughlin, K., & A. Bailey (2006). *An evaluation of an intensive English language preparation program for postgraduate study in education.* Unpublished report.

Sawir, E. (2005). Language difficulties of international students in Australia: the effects of prior learning experience. *International Education Journal,* 6(5), 567–580.

Spolsky, B. (1997). The ethics of gatekeepinng: what have we learned in a hundred years? *Language Testing, 14,* 242–247.

Taylor, L. (2009). Introduction. *IELTS Research Reports, Volume 10,* 1–9.

Teeraschke, A., & Wahid, R. (2011). The impact of EAP study on the academic experiences of international postgraduate students in Australia. *Journal of English for Academic Purposes, 10,* 173–182.

Woodrow, L. (2006). Academic success of international postgraduate Education students and the role of English proficiency. *University of Sydney Papers in TESOL, 1,* 51–70.

Chapter 13

An Investigation into the Knowledge, Education and Attitudes of Chinese, Arab (Gulf Region) and Indian Candidates to IELTS: The Case of Australia

Abe W. Ata

Although it is widely debated that students' attitudes towards a certain language proficiency test may affect their performance on that test, research on attitudes of these groups towards the International English Language Testing System (IELTS) is still absent. And crucially, how such attitudes might affect their overall band score in a standardised test such as IELTS is lacking. The purpose of this study is to investigate the relationship between Chinese, Indian and Arab IELTS candidates' knowledge, education and attitudes and their performance on IELTS and address significant gaps in this area of research study.

Much has been written about the IELTS methods of operations; validity of assessing the candidates readiness to move to higher education, and its contribution to the learning process in university environments (Coleman, Starfield, & Hagaen, 2003). The current study extends the research further to focus on the benefits and drawbacks as perceived by three national groups: Chinese, Indian and Arab (Gulf region) candidates.

Chinese and Gulf Arab learners are now the fastest growing group of international students in Australia (Marginson, 2011). Huge population, rapid economic growth and strong aspiration of studying have all contributed to such an upsurge in studying IELTS in preparation for enrolments at accredited universities in both countries. Other reasons such as flexibility, affordability, reputation and accessibility to courses clearly play additional roles in attracting them to Australia (Lo Bianco, 2005; Marginson, 2011).

Holmes (1992) states that if people feel positive toward those who use the language, they would be more successful and also more highly motivated toward learning it. Van Lier (1996) claims that working with interesting and meaningful manifestations of language enhances motivation and positive attitudes to language and language learning

Subsequently, one could assume that if second language learners initiate their language learning while they have negative attitudes towards the target language and the people using that language, they are not expected to make considerable progress in their process of language learning. This assumption was held as far back as 1995 when Truitt (1995) hypothesised that students' beliefs and attitudes about language learning may vary based on cultural background and previous experiences. Thus, it can be argued that positive or negative attitudes do not develop accidentally but have some reasons for their emergence. Malallaha (2000) investigated the attitudes of Arab learners towards English and discovered that they have positive attitudes toward the English language and their proficiency in tests was positively related to their positive attitude to English. Hence, it can be argued that having positive or negative attitudes towards a certain language can exert considerable effect on the learners' performance on a language test.

Other studies on the relationships of causality summarised below are equally crucial. One of these focuses on the relationship between IELTS preparation programs and candidates' performance on the actual IELTS test. Read and Hayes (2003) for instance, investigated the impact of IELTS preparation programs on international students' academic performance on tertiary study in New Zealand. Their study revealed that there were a number of substantial differences between the performance of the group which had undergone preparation programs and the group which had not. In 2007 Lewthwaite found among United Arab Emirates (UAE) IELTS candidates that the nature and type of activities used to prepare for their test was a major determinant of the balance of positive and negative attitudes. Others, like Elder and O'Loughlin (2003) investigated the relationship between intensive English language study and band score gain on IELTS. The results of their study revealed that students made variable progress in English during the three month period with an average gain of about half a band overall.

Attitudes that have been explored in relation to language learning range from anxiety about the language and the learning situation, through to attitudes to speakers of the second language the country in which it is spoken, the classroom, the teacher, other learners, the nature of language learning, particular elements in the learning activities, tests and beliefs about learning in general (Johnson and Johnson, 1998).

According to Brown (2000), second language learners of English benefit from positive attitudes; negative attitudes may lead to decreased motivation. Nevertheless, he believes negative attitudes can be changed, often by exposure to reality — for example, by encounters with actual persons from other cultures.

Unlike the findings during the 1970s and the 1980s showing a positive relationship between attitude and linguistic abilities, Rasti (2009) found that candidates who have positive attitude towards IELTS, do not differ from other groups in their performance on the test. Rasti concludes that merely having a high attitude towards this test does not guarantee gaining a good score and no formal study has shown this either. She notes that candidates should go through learning effective strategies to approach the test and attending IELTS preparation programs can be a good and effective step.

While students saw the benefits of having a speaking component to the exam, both felt high anxiety. This finding contrasted with those of Read and Hayes (2003) who report overall 'positive attitudes about IELTS amongst teachers and strong motivation amongst learners'.

Merrylees (2003) conducted a study to investigate two IELTS user groups: candidates who sit the test for immigration purposes, and candidates who sit the test for secondary education purposes. He believed that with the increase in candidature of both user groups, there is an increasing need to investigate and analyse how each group is performing on the test in terms of nationality, age, gender and other factors, instead of making broad comparative analysis.

It is equally essential that consideration is directed at the broader issue of the role of the publications in preparing students for the IELTS and in the development of language skills in general, with particular reference to preparation for further study. Ata (2010), for example, found that poor lexical or specific cultural knowledge of English by Arab-speaking students can cause several negative interferences. His study produces a significant recommendation — one which implies that IELTS preparation materials should include more texts and tasks that would contribute to the social and academic acculturation of students.

And finally, Morgan Terry (2003) claims that the strong motivation and serious purposes of IELTS candidates is taken for granted. However, he believes that publishers need to respond more to the growing market for IELTS preparation and to start investing in colourful, attractive, motivating publications that can help promote learning for IELTS candidates in the way they have for students preparing for other exams.

Rationale and significance of this research

The main premise underlying the literature reviewed earlier is this: students at large have positive or negative attitudes towards the language they want to learn and the people who speak it. Having positive attitudes towards tests is also claimed to be one of the reasons which make students perform better on the tests (Malallaha 2000). Studies which have investigated the relationships between attitudes and proficiency in the language clearly show that attitudes and other affective variables are as important as aptitude for language achievement. (see for example, Bayliss and Ingram, 2006; Malallaha 2000 & Coleman et al., 2003).

It is widely accepted amongst IELTS researchers that, because the IELTS exam is now taken by candidates from over 170 countries, the rubric should be as culture-free and as international as possible; and that where possible, culturally nuanced 'situated' contexts should be adapted to many IELTS rubrics. At a recent IELTS conference a participant noted that Task 1 in the academic writing test often reflects an Anglo-centricity because graphs often reflect aspects of North American or European life, and as such students would not have the necessary socio-cultural experience to argue for, for instance, the freedom of the press. Hence, it is likely that candidates from China and the UAE would not be ready for such a question, or others such as: what are the characteristics of good or inferior journalism?

Lethwaite (2007), for example, found a strong overlap between what the IELTS writing tasks required and what UAE students and staff thought was needed in a writing course and that those who are really motivated and interested will read more widely. It might not be that the exam 'encourages' such reading, he stressed, but it might mediate it or at least facilitate it. As regards the nature of the questions inviting personal opinion, some personal reflection on and prior assessment of various issues inevitably precede formulating a good written response.

This project will present relevant evidence to support or refute these premises and fill in much needed gaps in the overall discussion about students' attitudes to IELTS. One of these premises for example is that IELTS developers engage in a research agenda that explores a range of international English language issues such as specific lexical or cultural knowledge that might disadvantage test takers. Another premise is that IELTS is not only a proficiency test to evaluate linguistic competence but it is also a comprehensive test which measures other components such as communicative competence.

Implications from conducting this research can be drawn to benefit all the stakeholders including candidates intending to sit the test, centers running IELTS preparation programs, teachers wishing to teach such programs and IELTS test administrators.

Objectives

The aims of this study are: to seek access to viewpoints of Chinese, Indian and Arab (Gulf) students in critically evaluating their attitudes, perception and knowledge of IELTS; and to reveal the effects of positive attitudes, or their lack of, on the overall test results. In examining whether a meaningful relationship exists between sex, age, nationality, educational background and

IELTS scores one is able then to identify differences and similarities amongst the three national groups and make appropriate recommendations to both teachers and policy makers.

The joint-funded IELTS research program in 2011 states that one of the areas of interest for IELTS external research purposes is *to* investigate the attitudes and perceptions towards IELTS among users of test scores (test takers). The aims of this study squarely and fully reflect this objective.

This survey was not administered to IELTS educators as Coleman (2003) did years earlier. In his study Coleman (2003) then found that IELTS students in their sample were generally more knowledgeable than staff about the form and function of the IELTS and the meaning of test scores.

Methodological procedure

The survey unit was pre test and post test IELTS candidates. A structured questionnaire was administered to 200 Chinese, Arab and Indian students at Monash University, and Deakin University language centres. (Access to these universities provides a compelling advantage as the researcher is an IELTS' examiner at these 3 language centres.) He has also held Research Honorary Fellowship positions at these universities including an Emeritus Professorship currently active at Deakin University).

A structured questionnaire was designed in a manner that would determine the differences and association between a wide range of variables, and to gauge the reliability of the candidates' response. It was devised primarily to collect data underpinning the following themes:

- appropriateness of taking the test
- demographic attributes of respondents
- areas of knowledge
- comparative effectiveness of IELTS versus other English tests
- attitudes to IELTS purpose and value
- perceptions of test demands and outcome.

The format of the questionnaire was largely, though not exclusively, adapted to Likert scale, as the candidates will be asked to indicate their attitudes by choosing one of the three alternatives: Agree, Undecided, Disagree.

A number of statistical methods were be adopted in making simultaneous comparisons of significance between two or more means; in measuring internal consistency; and, in determining whether a significant relationship exists between selected variables. These methods included factor analysis with Vairmax rotation, Anova: analysis of variance, t test, cross tabulation and Pearson's correlation.

Table 13.1 Demographic characteristics

Demographic Characteristics	
Sex	
Male	134
Female	106
Religion	
Muslim	82
Hindu	4
Sikh	4
Buddhist	36
Christian	12
Other	74
N/A	28
Birth place	
Gulf/Middle East	76
China	88
Other	70
N/A	6
Have you lived/studied in an English speaking country?	
Yes	88
No	140
N/A	12
Which country have you studied/lived in?	
Home	22
English speaking country	70
N/A	148
Language spoken at home	
Arabic	56
Chinese	92
Other	80
N/A	12
Language spoken with friends at language Centre	
Arabic	4
Chinese	14
English	136
Arabic and English	22
Chinese and English	32
Other	12
N/A	20

Findings and discussion

It is widely proposed in social debate that international students in Australia and beyond bring a very different cultural, social and intellectual experience from that which awaits them. The suggestion being that attitudes to knowledge, to styles of learning, and to study focus can lead to a shock for both students and educators alike.

A number of questions were presented to find out how the three national/regional candidates comprising Arab, Chinese and Indian students differ in the way they perceive of the IELTS tests at large (see Figure 13.1).

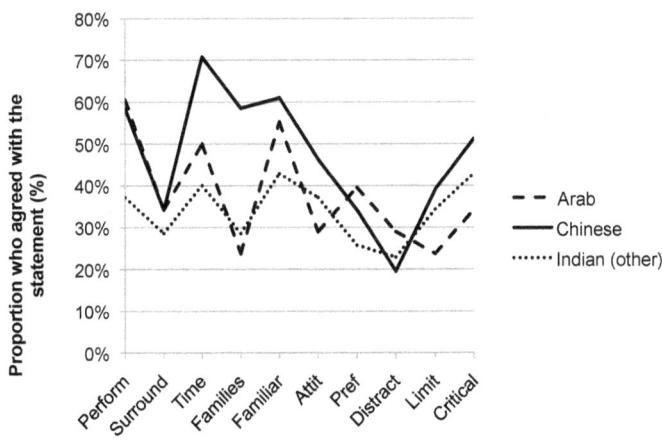

Figure 13.1 General attitudes to IELTS.

General attitudes to IELTS: statements and significance (computation includes Non response adjustment)
perform = Fear of taking the IELTS test affected my performance
X2(9,N = 240)=19.15,p= .024
Surround = The surroundings such as lighting, temperature, floor, desks affected my performance
X2(9,N = 240)=19.15,p=.443
time = The time of taking the IELTS test affected my performance
X2(9,N = 240)=19.15,p=.013
Families = Being familiar with the place where I took the IELTS test helped my performance
X2(9,N = 240)=19.15,p=.00
familiar= Being familiar with the design, structure and format of the test helped my performance
X2(9,N = 240)=19.15,p=.005
Attit = My attitude to IELTS test is largely positive
X2(9,N = 240)=19.15,p=.004
Pref = I prefer IELTS to other English Language tests
X2(9,N = 240)=19.15,p=.042
Distract = I found the announcements and administration of the text itself distracting
X2(9,N = 240)=19.15,p=.026
Limit = In my country our socio-cultural experience such as the freedom of the press, limits my ability in performing well in the IELTS tests.
X2(9,N = 240)=19.15,p=.018
Critical = In my country students are not encouraged to develop critical thinking as in Australia.
X2(9,N = 240)=19.15,p=.016

Overall, the findings show that with the exception of the variable 'the surroundings such as lighting, temperature, floor, desks that affected my performance' variation in the response by the three cohorts is highly significant. It is also shown that Chinese students exhibit the strongest expression on all the variables, except the following two for which Arabs students from the Gulf Region took the lead:

- I prefer IELTS to other English Language tests
- I found the announcements and administration of the text itself distracting.

It would appear that being familiar with the design and structure and venue of gave the Chinese cohort a positive feel in performing well. In the same instance they registered the highest response in not being encouraged to develop critical thinking in Australia, and their ability to perform well is hampered by the socio-cultural experience in their own country. These responses have a wider implication and interpretation which are communicated in the concluding section of this chapter.

Of the three groups the lowest response directed at the following items was communicated by Arab students:

- My attitude to IELTS test is largely positive
- Being familiar with the place where I took the IELTS test helped my performance
- In my country our socio-cultural experience such as the freedom of the press, limits my ability in performing well in the IELTS tests.
- In my country students are not encouraged to develop critical thinking as in Australia.

Of the three groups the Indian cohort participants indicated the lowest dislike on several items including the following:

- Fear of taking the IELTS test affected my performance.
- The surroundings such as lighting, temperature, floor, desks affected my performance.
- The time of taking the IELTS test affected my performance.
- Being familiar with the design, structure and format of the test helped my performance.
- I prefer IELTS to other English Language tests.
- In my country our socio-cultural experience such as the freedom of the press, limits my ability in performing well in the IELTS tests.
- In my country students are not encouraged to develop critical thinking as in Australia.

The latter two attitudinal statements listed from the Indian cohort participants arguably indicate an awareness, perhaps a subdued criticism of the reality that students in their country of origin were 'not encouraged to develop critical thinking as in Australia'. Psycholinguists including Yeh and Inose (2003) found that social connectedness, liberal thinking, freedom of movement and social support satisfaction in Western countries are major factors behind it. The negative link between gender and the response to these two statements was not significant. The suggestion being that both male and female international students are equally impacted in terms of showing a better performance.

Listening Section

Findings in Figure 13.2 present responses to what they disliked about the Listening section of IELTS with the Chinese group ranking highest on the following statements:

- Tempo or speed (60%)
- Responding at the same time whilst listening (44%)
- Performance deteriorated as the test moved forward (54%)
- Not enough time for the answers to be transferred to the answer sheet from the question booklet (47%)
- Test does not really evaluate listening comprehension (45%)
- But showing the lowest ranking towards 'the test being not useful for their future studies'(11%).

It is not possible to make a conclusive statement explaining this variation. One may reason that being socialised in a traditional society may have contributed to being more restrained in mixing with genders of other nationalities — English speaking or otherwise. Frequenting movies and other Australian cultural–social events, eateries and the like, particularly in evening hours provide a wider exposure and accessibility to spoken English. Another factor is related to international students from the same background to live together in preference to renting in family households where they are less likely to communicate in English.

Reading section

Students showed a mixed feelings recognising that their reading section pushed them hard but it was not accurate in mirroring their study of being relevant to their study needs in the future (see Figure 13.3). The statement the 'Test is not useful for my future studies' drew the lowest response from the three cohort groups combined, with Chinese students scoring the lowest response at 11%, followed by the Arab group at 28% and Indians at 35%.

Whereas a higher percentage at 50% for the Chinese and Arab speaking and 70% 'Other' did not see any benefits in 'reading a lot of English texts

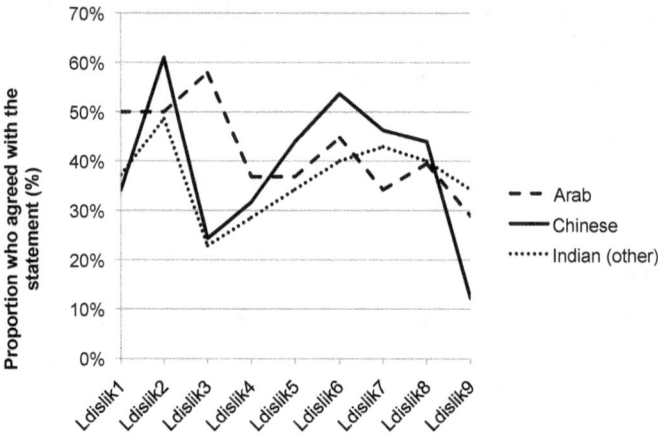

Figure 13.2 Attitudes to the Listening Section
Attitudes to the Listening Section: Statements and significance (computation includes Non-response adjustment)

Ldislike1 = Non-familiarity Australian accent X2(9,N = 240)=19.15,p=.070
Ldislike2 = tempo or speed X2(9,N = 240)=19.15,p=.038
Ldislike3 = lack of opportunity to wear headphones X2(9,N = 240)=19.15,p=.000
Ldislike4 = poor quality of the voice X2(9,N = 240)=19.15,p=.0379
Ldislike5 = Responding at the same time whilst listening. X2(9,N = 240)=19.15,p=.726
Ldislike6 = Performance deteriorated as the test moved forward X2(9,N = 240)=19.15,p=.357
Ldislike7 = Not enough time for the answers to be transferred to the answer sheet from the question booklet X2(9,N = 240)=19.15,p=.226
Ldislike8 = Test does not really evaluate listening comprehension X2(9,N = 240)=19.15,p=.640
Ldislike9 = Test is not useful for my future studies X2(9,N = 240)=19.15,p=.003

before the exam'. These largely mixed negative feelings arising from working hard but not accurate mirroring their study needs was also cited by Spratt (2005).

Writing Section

Several variables were introduced to assess the reasons and degree behind disliking the Writing Section (see Figure 13.4). The two main groups who recorded the highest dislike to the first 4 variables are the Chinese and Arabic speaking. The limitation or lack of knowledge of the world or information related to a given topic (variable Dislike4) clearly shows that different dimensions of assessment of literacy may need to be prioritised (a) for different disciplines, such as language testing, where knowledge of what it means to know and use a language is surely essential; (b) within particular academic and professional domains, where language requirements may vary; and (c) with particular users such as students, parents, school administra-

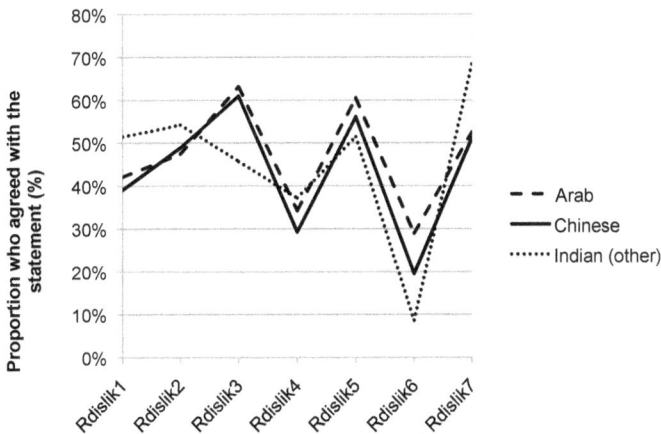

Figure 13.3 Attitudes to the Reading Section

Attitudes to the Reading Section: Statements and significance (computation includes Non response adjustment)

Rdislike1 = Reading is immediately after listening
$X2(9,N=240)=19.15, p=.0.111$
Rdislike2 = Disliked the variety of question types
$X2(9,N=240)=19.15, p=.0.258$
Rdislike3 = Lengthy passages
$X2(9,N=240)=19.15, p=.0.084$
Rdislike4 = Test is not useful for my future studies
$X2(9,N=240)=19.15, p=.0.214$
Rdislike5 = Texts became more difficult towards the end of the reading section
$X2(9,N=240)=19.15, p=.0.367$
Rdislike6 = Knowledge of vocabulary and grammar is not important
$X2(9,N=240)=19.15, p=.0.016$
Rdislike7 = Reading a lot of English texts before the exam
$X2(9,N=240)=19.15, p=.0.001$

tors, teachers, or test developers whose needs for and uses of information are highly diverse depending the nature and the level of their involvement in the assessment process (Taylor 2009).

None of the variables in this section were significant with the exception of Wdislike5 = being given more than one task (sig, .0013).

This greater focus on assessment brings with it the need for *assessment literacy*, defined variously as having the skills needed for test development and validation, the knowledge required to make informed an principled score-based decision-making, and the ability to read and make sense of assessment-related research data (Newfields, 2006).

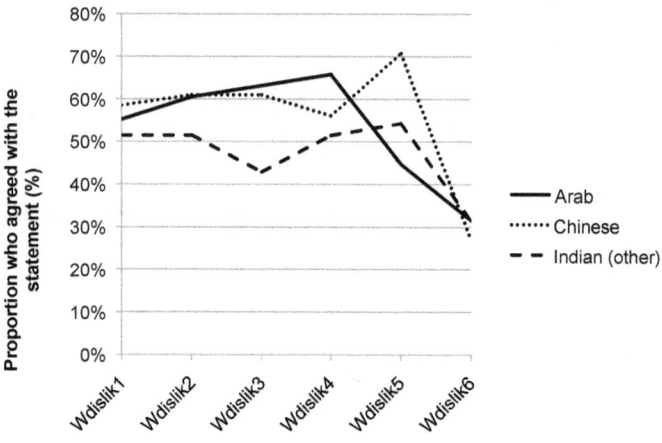

Figure 13.4 Attitudes to the Writing Section

Attitudes to the Writing Section: Statements and significance (computation includes Non response adjustment)

Wdislike1 = Tired in this section because of their performance on the first two sections
$X2(9, N = 240) = 19.15, p=. 0.362$
Wdislike2 = lengthy topics cause difficulty in concentration
$X2(9, N = 240) = 19.15, p=. 0.281$
Wdislike3 = knowledge of vocabulary and grammar is crucial in this section
$X2(9, N = 240) = 19.15, p=.0.077$
Wdislike4 = not enough knowledge of the world or information related to the given topic
$X2(9, N = 240) = 19.15, p= 0.056$
Wdislike5 = being given more than one task
$X2(9, N = 240) = 19.15, p=.0.013$
Wdislike6 = test is not useful for my future studies
$X2(9, N = 240) = 19.15, p.=.288$

Other language educators like Lewthwaite believe that the writing task is 'non-academic' in the sense that a personal opinion was asked for and respondents are not able to, and not expected to, draw on empirical evidence, statistical data or the academic expertise of published material. (2007, p. 8).This would explain why Arabic speaking candidates in particular scored highest (65%) on the variable 'Wdislike4' that there was 'not enough knowledge of the world or information related to the given topic' — a common observation made about school curriculum and rote learning styles in schools in the Middle Eastern countries.

As an IELTS examiner and academic the writer has found that IELTS tasks required more use of prior knowledge than did university tasks. As Lewthwaite's (2007) experience in teaching IELTS to UAE students shows:

> IELTS tests had more limited rhetorical functions (an emphasis on hortatory at the expense of other functions such as explanation, comparison, summarisation) and focused much more on 'real world' contexts compared with the greater emphasis on abstract ideas in university tasks.

Although written in 1999, an article by Moore and Morton suggested that Task 2 'may be more akin to public non-academic genres (newspapers, magazines) than characteristic of university assignments' (see also Lewthwaite, 2007).

Several students mentioned the unrealistic time limit of (recommended) 20 minutes for the exam task cause difficulty on concentrating on lengthy topics (Figure 13.4, variable Wdislike2). This reaction was corroborated by 60% of Arabic speaking and Chinese candidates and 50% 'Other'. The response of these groups to being given more than one task in a short time was almost the same (Figure 13.4, Wdislike5).

While it might reflect one type of university writing — writing exams under time constraints – it was unclear whether this was helpful to another major form of university writing, that of research activity.

Speaking Section

The direction of the results for the Speaking Section (see Figure 13.5) is more pronounced than the Writing part. That is, feedback about difficulties experience in the Speaking section was stronger, varied and more pronounced than the Writing Section. The Chinese cohort in particular ranked highest on the following three statements:

- (Sdislike4) Having stress or lacking confidence at the time of interview (75%)
- (Sdislike5) Being asked too many questions in rather a short time (48%)
- (Sdislike3) Interviewer's accent (67%).

The Indian group ranked lower and the Arab candidates ranked the lowest on these statements.

Another difference that affected performance amongst the 3 groups relates to the gender of the examiner with 50% Arabs, 48% Chinese and 29% Indians indicating agreement that the examiner's gender affected their performance. Such a relatively high response in an exam environment is not easy to explain notwithstanding calculation for a level of significance. One linguist surmised that the teacher, male and female alike 'is placed in the driver's seat — a position of primary influence in terms of the teacher beliefs, attitudes, educational level and experience, and personalities' (Spratt, 2005, pp. 17–23).

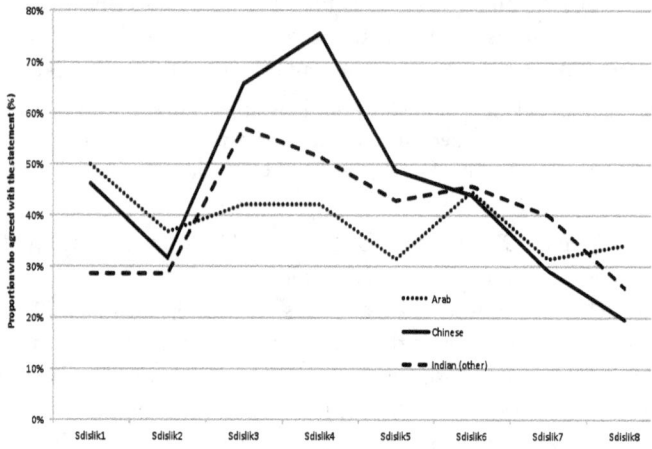

Figure 13.5 Attitudes to the Speaking Section

Attitudes to the Speaking Section: Statements and significance (computation includes Non response adjustment)

Sdislike1 = The examiner's gender affected their performance
$X2(9, N = 240)=19.15,= p0.056.$
Sdislike2 = Test examines one's listening ability, not one's speaking ability
$X2(9, N = 240)=19.15, p=.0.268$
Sdislike3 = Interviewer's accent
$X2(9, N = 240)=19.15, p=.0.005$
Sdislike4 = Having stress or lacking confidence at the time of interview
$X2(9, N = 240)=19.15, p=. 0.000$
Sdislike5 = Being asked too many questions in rather a short time
$X2(9, N = 240)=19.15, p=. 0.064$
Sdislike6 = Being recorded would add to their test anxiety
$X2(9, N = 240)=19.15, p= 0.228$
Sdislike7 = The questions in this section were not related to each other
$X2(9, N = 240)=19.15, p= 0.061$
Sdislike8 = The test is not useful for my future studies
$X2(9, N = 240)=19.15, p=.0.080$

Other factors that may contribute to this finding are lack of motivation, so if the learners do not want to interact, they will not; and insufficient language, so if the learners do not have enough English language, it will be difficult for them to interact (Howarth, 2006).

Summary and conclusions

While the above findings are preliminary, based as they are on a small sample of respondents drawn from a single institution, they suggest some lessons that might be learned about the assessment literacy of test users in the higher education context (which may also be applicable to other language use domains). The fact that test users, savvy as they appear to be, are neither particularly knowledgeable nor interested in learning about language tests like the TOEFL, suggests that information provided to them by test developers should be both carefully targeted, limited in scope and accessible when needed.

There appears to be two broad attitudes underpinning these findings: the first is widespread acceptance of the quality of the language tests used for selection as well as satisfaction with and trust in the information provided.

Also, if we were to rank order the unfavourable attitudes for both sexes relating to the four IELTS sections the following primary patterns emerge:

Several variables were introduced to assess the reasons and degree behind disliking the Writing Section. The two main groups who recorded the highest dislike to the first 4 variables are the Chinese and Arabic speaking. The limitation or lack of knowledge of the world or information related to a given topic (variable Dislike4) clearly shows that different dimensions of assessment of literacy may need to be prioritised (a) for different disciplines, such as language testing, where knowledge of what it means to know and use a language is surely essential; (b) within particular academic and professional domains, where language requirements may vary; and (c) with particular users such as students, parents, school administrators, teachers

It has been proposed that Learning contexts and familiarity information and issues lead to a greater fluency and accuracy in performing English Language tests (Mehnert,1998). If that premise holds true then writings task related to women's issues, questioning parental attitudes, organ donation, freedom of thinking and rote memory learning at school and the like would disadvantage students from traditional cultures. The constrains of how the spontaneity of addressing these task mirror task requirements later on in tertiary institutions requires further investigation.

The direction of the results for the Speaking part is more pronounced than the Writing part. That is, feedback about difficulties experience in the Speaking section was stronger, varied and more pronounced than the Writing part.

Students showed a mixed feelings recognising that their Reading section pushed them hard but it was not accurate in mirroring their study of being relevant to their study needs in the future. The statement, 'Test is not useful for my future studies', drew the lowest response from the three cohort groups combined, with Chinese students scoring the lowest response at 11%, followed by the Arab group at 28% and Indian at 35%.

As regards the unfavourable attitudes to the Listening section, one may reason that being socialised in a traditional society may have contributed to being more restrained in mixing with genders of other nationalities —

English speaking or otherwise. Frequenting movies and other Australian cultural-social events, eateries and the like particularly in evening hours provide a wider exposure and accessibility to spoken English. Another factor is related to international students from the same background to live together in preference to renting in family households where they are less likely to communicate in English.

This survey has raised a number of questions aimed at areas that require further probing. Of significance are the following: Is there a principled basis for the setting of minimum entry standards and whether the current cut off scores are appropriate? Is there a need to address the lack of systematic data collection to evaluate their [entry standards] appropriateness and, by extension the rationale of determining that language test scores are the basis for selection decisions? Why do IELTS stakeholder continue to make little reference to other relevant factors which might have a bearing on students' chances of academic success? And, does achieving the specified minimum IELTS score imply that students' English proficiency is sufficient to successfully complete rather than commence their courses?

On the basis of the overall response for this section, one could safely surmise that the relative acceptance and trust in what benefits students will gain as a consequence are not to be underestimated. This however does not translate into a general understanding of or interest in language proficiency test content, scoring procedures, cut off scores and cross test equivalences or associated validity evidence, as perceived by the respondents to meet their needs.

The broader response to several questions relating to core issues surrounding IELTS remains inconclusive. Questions relating to bilingual and English language learning by international students have been raised by numerous researcher including Dooey (2010) and Lasagabasete (2008).

There is a deep division, for example, in the view as to whether current cut off scores are appropriate. Others raise questions behind the principled basis for the setting of minimum entry standards; and why is there an overemphasis on language test scores as the basis for selection decisions based on language test scores without reference to other relevant factors which might have a bearing on students' chances of academic success! And lastly — does achieving the specified minimum IELTS score imply that students' English proficiency is sufficient to successfully complete rather than commence their courses!

These conclusions are largely subject to a number of caveats. The findings, for example, apply to particular cohort groups in a particular learning social context – one where to extent of its applicability to other groups in other contexts is unknown. Another obvious limitation shows that self reporting almost always becomes embedded in the analysis of the data itself. It also seems important to test for the degree to which the developers of language tests may communicate complacency about their own levels of expertise and understanding about the qualities of tests, the meaning of test scores and the informational needs in these contexts.

In order to test for a high predictive validity of the nature of IELTS test score in relation to university requirements of acceptable language proficiency, this study needs to be extended further to include perception of teachers themselves. How the two group, educators and students differ in their attitudes would accurately indicate the relationship between the language skills reflected in IELTS scores and abilities required by the universities to succeed.

The chasm as to how staff and students differed in their perception of predictive nature of IELTS test scores in determining the languages abilities at tertiary institutions was widely demonstrated in one of the IELTS Research Reports by Coleman and others (2003).

Acknowledgement

This research was supported by Deakin University and William Angliss Charitable Fund (Victoria).

References

Ata, A. W. (2010). Grammatical interference from Arabic to English can pose big challenges for students. *EL Gazette (Britain)*, 4, 22–23.

Bayliss, A., & Ingram , A.(2006). IELTS as a Predictor of Academic Language Performance. *Australian International Education Conference*, 1–12.

Coleman, D., & Strafield, S., & Hagan, A. (2003). The attitudes of IELTS stakeholders: student and staff apperception of IELTS in Australian, UK, and Chinese tertiary institutions. *IELTS Australia Research*, 5, 20–34.

Dooey, P. (2010). Students' perspectives of an EAP pathway program. *Journal of English for Academic Purposes*, 9(4),184–197.

Elder, C., & O'Loughlin, K. (2003). Investigating the relationship between intensive English language study and band score gain on IELTS. *IELTS Australia Research*, 4, 82–-93.

Holmes, J. (1992). An introduction to sociolinguistics. London: Longman.

Howarth, P. (2006). Increasing student interaction. Retrieved from www.teachingenglish.org.uk/think/speak/interaction.shtml

Lewthwaite, M. (2007)). Teacher and Student Attitudes to IELTS writing tasks: Positive or negative washback?. Action Research Report. *UGRU Journal*, 5, 1–23.

Lo Bianco, J. (2005). Asian Languages in Australian Schools: Policy Options, Melbourne. *Asia Policy Papers*, 7, University of Melbourne, Australia.

Malallaha, S. (2000). English in an Arabic environment: current attitudes to English among Kuwait University students. *International Journal of Bilingual Education and Bilingualism, 3*, 19-43.

Marginson, S., (2011). Global Position and Position Taking: *The Case of Australia. Education Dynamics, 36*, 375–392.

Merrylees, B. (2003). An impact study of two IELTS user groups: Candidates who sit for the immigration purposes and candidates who sit for secondary education purposes. *IELTS Australia Research, 4*, 27–39.

Moore, T., & Morton, J. (1999). Authenticity in the IELTS Academic Module Writing Test: A comparative study of task 2 items and university assignments. *IELTS Review, 2*.

Rasti, I. (2009). Iranian Candidates' Attitudes towards IELTS. *Asian EFT Journal, 11*(3), 5.

Read, J., & Hayes, B. (2003). The impact of IELTS on preparation for academic study in New Zealand. In R. Tulloh (Ed.), *IELTS Research Reports 2003, 4*, 153–205.

Spratt, M. (2005). Washback and the classroom: the implications for teaching and learning of studies of washback from exams. *Language Teaching Research, 9*(1), 5–29.

Taylor, L. (2009). Developing assessment literacy. *Annual Review of Applied Linguistics, 29*, 21–26.

Terry, M. (2003). IELTS Preparation Materials. *ELT Journal, 57*(1), 66–76.

Truitt, H. (1995). Beliefs about language learning: A study of Korean University students learning English. *Texas Papers in Foreign Language Education, 2*, 12–28.

Van Lier, L. (1996). *Interaction in the language curriculum: Awareness: Autonomy and authenticity.* London, England: Longman.

Yeh, C., & Inose, M. (2003). International students reported English fluency, social support satisfaction, and social connectedness as predictors of acculturative stress. *Counselling Psychology Quarterly, 16*(1),15–28.

Yao, L. (2004, September 15–17). *The Chinese overseas students: An overview of the flows change.* Paper presented at 12 Biennial Conference , The Australian National University Australian Population Association, Australian National University, Canberra, Australia.

Chapter 13 Knowledge, Education and Attitudes of Chinese, Arab and Indian Candidates to IELTS

Chapter 14

Globalisation and Internationalisation: The Influence of Race, Ethnicity and Gender on Education Policy Reforms

Joseph Zajda

Globalisation and its impact on education

Globalisation, marketisation and quality/efficiency driven reforms around the world since the 1980s have resulted in structural and qualitative changes in education and policy, including an increasing focus on the 'lifelong learning for all', or a 'cradle-to-grave' vision of learning and the 'knowledge economy' in the global culture. Governments, in their quest for excellence, quality and accountability in education, increasingly turn to international and comparative education data analysis. All agree that the major goal of education is to enhance the individual's social and economic prospects. This can only be achieved by providing quality education for all. Students' academic achievement is now regularly monitored and measured within the 'internationally agreed framework' of the Organisation for Economic Co-operation and Development's (OECD) Programme for International Student Assessment (PISA). This was done in response to the growing demand for international comparisons of educational outcomes (OECD, 2001, 2008, Education Policy Analysis, p. 8). To measure levels of academic performance in the global culture, the OECD, in cooperation with the United Nations Educational, Scientific and Cultural Organization (UNESCO), is using World Education Indicators (WEI) program, covering a broad range of comparative indicators, which report on the resource invested in education and their returns to individuals.

I would like to define 'globalisation', from a social and cultural transformation perspective, as a new dominant ideology of cultural convergence, which is accompanied by corresponding economic, political, social, technological and educational transformations (Zajda, 2014a; Zajda, 2014b). Such a process is characterised by increasing economic and political interdependence between nations, and which ultimately, transforms the ethnocentric core of nation-state and national economy. This was already exemplified by Wallerstein's (1979) world-system concept map model of social change, which is still relevant as a major theoretical perspective on explaining globalisation, where 'the world system' is a network of unequal economic and political relationships between the developed and less developed nations (Wallerstein, 1989; Wallerstein, 1998). His model of the world-system is also relevant to theories of social stratification and discourses of inequality. Social stratification is commonly defined as unequal distribution of socially valued commodities, such as power, status, occupation, education and wealth.

It needs to be stressed that one of central and unresolved problems in the process of globalisation within a post-structuralist context is the unresolved tension, and ambivalence 'between cultural *homogenisation* and cultural *heterogenisation*' (Appadurai, 1990, p. 295, emphasis added), or the on-going dialectic between globalism and localism, between faith and reason, between tradition and modernity, and between totalitarianism and democracy.

Apart from the multi-faceted nature of globalisation that invites contesting and competing ideological interpretations, numerous paradigms and theoretical models have been also used, ranging from modernity to postmodernity, to explain the phenomenon of globalisation.

Globalisation and the internationalisation of higher education

Global competiveness has become one of the most visible changes in the internationalisation of higher education. It is characterised by the neoliberal ideology of marketisation of performance, standards, and quality (Rust & Kim, 2015; Zajda, 2014b). In higher education policy rhetoric, both locally and globally, there is a tendency to argue, using a powerful tool of logic, that there is a need to increase global competitiveness, and to improve excellence and quality in higher education, training and skills.

Globally, neo-liberalism in higher education policy reforms has been characteristic of capitalist societies, including Australia, since the 1980s. It resulted in 'education and training, public debates regarding standards and changed funding regimes' (Davies & Bansel, 2007, p. 247). Hence, the politics of higher education reforms in Australia reflect this new emerging paradigm of accountability, 'globalisation and academic capitalism' (Delanty, 2001, p. 120), performance indicators and 'standards-driven policy change' (Zajda, 2010b, p. xv).

Globalisation, policy and the politics of the internationalisation of higher education reforms in Australia suggest new economic and political dimensions of neo-liberalism, and a new dimension of cultural imperialism. Globalisation, policy and higher education reforms in Australia suggest new economic and political dimensions of neo-liberalism, and a new dimension of cultural imperialism. Forces of globalisation, manifesting themselves as a neo-liberal and bourgeois hegemony, tended to legitimate an 'exploitative system' (McLaren & Farahmandpur, 2005), and have contributed to the ongoing neo-liberal globalisation of the higher education sector in Australia.

This is fuelled by a relentless global competitiveness, or what Val Rust (2015) calls 'the global competition phenomenon' (Rust &Kim, 2015), and a resultant drive towards global standards of excellence and quality, globalisation of academic assessment (OECD, PISA), global academic achievement syndrome (OECD, World Bank), global academic elitism and global league tables for the universities (Zajda, 2015b). The latter signifies both ascribed and achieved status, the positioning of distinction, privilege, excellence and exclusivity. In higher education policy documents in the OECD, the World Bank, and Australia, policy reforms appear to be presented as a given, and as 'a necessary response to economic globalisation and global competitiveness' (Zajda, 2014b).

One of the outcomes of higher education policy reforms globally and demands for accountability and transparency is world university rankings and university league tables. The first university league tables appeared nearly 20 years ago and have been subjected to ongoing criticism regarding research methodologies employed and the quality, validity and reliability of the data collection process. Current major and global university ranking models include the Shanghai Jiao Tong University's (2003) Academic Ranking of World Universities (ARWU), the Times Higher Education (THE) World University Rankings (powered by Thompson Reuters, 2010), QS World University Rankings (2010), and the European Commission's U-Multirank (2010). These four main global ranking schemes of universities use the 'databases provided by Thomson Reuters and Elsevier' (Robertson, 2012, p. 242). The US has its own rankings of universities and colleges, reported annually in US News and World Report. According to Rust and Kim, the US has 'long maintained rankings of its universities and colleges ... the most prominent current example is the annual rankings by US News and World Report' (Rust & Kim, 2012, p. 6). The ARWU and THE university rankings are the two most widely used models among 'more than 30 variably known ranking systems' (Robertson, 2012, p. 241). All of these models for ranking universities are different in design, scope and data collection methods. In Australia, higher education policymakers are very keen to contribute to 'the making of Australia's higher education system as a world-class standard' (Zajda, 2014b).

The internationalisation of higher education

There are at least four factors contributing to the internationalisation of higher education process globally: international students coming to a country, students going abroad, foreign languages taught at a university, and international content in courses taught (Rust &Kim, 2015). Rust and Kim argue that the 'most obvious indicator of internationalisation is whether a university actively and successfully recruits students from abroad'. The second indicator of internationalisation of higher education is study abroad, which involves short-term exchanges of students in immersion programs or travel study. The third indicator of internationalisation of higher education is foreign language instruction, and the fourth indicator of internationalisation of higher education is curriculum content and degrees:

> We might, for example, assess the level of information courses contain about other countries, people, events, and places. Of course, foreign languages, area studies, comparative government and comparative literature are inherently international in scope. However, some universities are designing international programs where the international content is traditionally not obvious (Rust &Kim, 2015, p. 176).

The most successful countries in attracting international students are United States (US), the United Kingdom (UK) and Australia. They have attracted over 40 percent of students studying outside their home country in 2007. Half of the world's international students were from the Asian region. China was the main source country, followed by India and South Korea (Murray, D. Hall, R. Leask, B. Marginson, S. & Ziguras, C. (2011). In 2014, international students accounted for 18 percent in the UK and 19 percent in Australia, according to OECD (Choudaha, 2014).

Australia is the third most popular destination for international students, attracting nearly 7% of the world's international students. Some 300,000 international students studied in Australia in 2014. The majority of international students were enrolled in the higher education sector. International students contribute to $16 billion industry, representing Australia's fourth largest export. The 'economic footprint' of international students has a significant impact on the Australian economy:

> The economic footprint of international students, however, is much larger than just the fees they pay. International students directly facilitate domestic participation in higher education. They generate significant spill over benefits including job creation and increased tourism and are a key source of migration that can help address skill shortages as well as contribute to Australia's long-term economic prosperity (Group of Eight Australia, 2014).

However, some critics question whether internationalisation of higher education is now an instrument of the less attractive side of globalisation:

> Recent national and worldwide surveys of university internationalisation priorities show that establishing an international profile or global standing is seen to be more important that reaching international standards of excellence or improving quality. Capacity building through international cooperation is

being replaced by status building projects to gain world class recognition. International student mobility is now big business ... More international academic projects and partnerships are becoming commercialised and profit driven as are international accreditation services ... And all of this is in the name of internationalisation? (Knight, 2011).

As Murray, Hall, Leask, Marginson, and Ziguras (2011) argue internationalisation in Australia, has focused, in the main, on the recruitment of 'fee paying overseas students so that levels of internationalisation have been equated with numbers of international students on campus, numbers of offshore programs, percentage of revenue earned through international activities'. According to them, these are the usual descriptors of internationalisation in Australian education (Murray et al., 2011, p. 32).

The latest Austrade data on international student enrolments in Australia, show that between September 2013 and September 2014, international students who began higher education courses increased by 14.7%. China accounted for 37.3% of those enrolments and India, 10%. Students starting postgraduate research rose 9.2% and postgraduate coursework students, 18.9% (Cervini, 2014).

As Rust and Kim (2015) argue globalisation, internationalisation, and global competitiveness have 'transformed higher education and are now central to university plans, mission statements, and programs', but at a cost, the emerging global model (EGM) of elitist and desirable, in terms of attracting both local and international students, research universities:

> However, a shadow side of internationalisation is the tendency to establish a single set of criteria that shapes institutions: 'all of this emphasis ... gravitates towards an ideal, a typical picture of a particular type of institution' (Huisman, 2008), what Kathryn Mohrman, Wanhua Ma & David Baker (2008) call the Emerging Global Model (EGM) of the top stratum of research universities ... The danger is that internationalisation could remove a university from its local context and purpose and demand conformity. (Rust & Kim, 2015)

Racial stratification and education

Race continues to be a significant dimension in higher education and academic achievement in the US and elsewhere. In the US, only one-quarter of community colleges can be considered racially integrated, where on average 37 percent of their students are from minority groups One recent study (see Goldrick-Rab & Kinsley as cited in Fain, 2013) reported that some 75% of the variation in 'racial composition in the two-year sector is directly attributable to the racial composition of their surrounding geographic locales':

> The problems of those communities resulting from neighbourhood segregation and the concentration of poverty are simply transferred up the educa-

tional pipeline. Segregated community colleges with large shares of needy students not only receive fewer monetary resources, but they likely produce less student learning. (Goldrick-Rab & Kinsley as cited in Fain, 2013)

Carnevale (2013) argues that US higher education is colour blind in theory, it 'in fact operates, at least in part, as a systematic barrier to opportunity for many African-Americans and Hispanics'. Carnevale (2013) demonstrates that since the mid-1990s, student enrolment in American higher education has grown increasingly stratified along racial lines with white students overwhelmingly populating the '468 most well-funded, selective four-year colleges and universities while African-American and Hispanic students are more and more concentrated in the 3,250 least well-funded, open-access, two- and four-year colleges' (Carnevale, 2013).

Hence a better and more meaningful understanding of race and racialisations in education are needed in order to see the real experiences of minority groups in educational systems, as they negotiate inequitable and discriminatory social and cultural conditions in increasingly stratified societies (see Rezai-Rashti & Solomon, 2008). Gosa and Alexander (2007) demonstrate how the dimension of race still matters in schooling and success. They argue that racial discrimination affects both working-class and middle-class African Americans. Well-off African-American children, in general, are not as successful in academic achievement as white American students:

> While the educational difficulties of poor black students are well-documented and have been discussed extensively, the academic performance of well-off African American children has received much less attention. However, despite economic and educational resources in the home, well-off African American youth are not succeeding in school at the levels of their white peers (Gosa & Alexander, 2007).

Freeman (2006) in attempting to explain under-achievement of black children argues that this is due to the process of cultural assimilation and the loss of social identity (p. 51). By examining the socialisation process in schools, assimilation, prejudice and stereotypes, one could argue that the schools' ethos and classroom environment contribute to black children's low self-esteem, low motivation and lack of desire and interest in maximising their educational and human potential. Furthermore, since African Americans lagged behind Whites in college attendance, they lacked 'access to many of the necessary skills that higher education provides' (Freeeman, 2006, p. 48). Gosa & Alexander (2007) suggest that cultural capital, education, income, and other SES indicators are insufficient to explain these differences in academic achievement. Instead, it may well be that the perception of race itself in the society is the real issue. Both whites and non-whites have constructed and internalised their racial identities:

[T]he race at issue is a social construction, imbued with meaning through its particularhistory and current place in the social fabric. The liabilities that prevent black parents from passing on advantages to their children are racial, in the sense that they follow from the contemporary and historic social ecology of race. Closing the black-white education gap, and keeping it closed, necessarily will involve strategies that acknowledge and address the continuing significance of race ... differences in school quality, segregative patterns within schools, and teacher relationships intersect to hinder the academic development of better off black youth. Consequently, the family background advantages that middle-class whites enjoy in positive schooling outcomes are not realised to the same extent by middle-class blacks. (Gosa & Alexander, 2007)

Court (2008; Bar-Ilan University) in her recent study critically examines the school culture of an Israeli elementary school, which has a large cohort of the children of Ethiopian immigrants, and the associated socialisation processes in the building of Israeli cultural identity (Court, 2008). She discusses various dimensions of identity —religious, cultural and national — and suggests that in the case of Ethiopian Israeli children, skin colour is an additional attribute. According to her, being a black Israeli would be a different experience to being a Russian Israeli child. Thus, the notion of race contributes to the formation of group identity in Israel and elsewhere (see also Freeeman, 2006; Zajda & Freeman, 2009).

Similarly, Troyna (1987) and his co-authors discuss in the 1980s various strategies for combating racial inequality in education. They were able to depict the extent and manner in which racism and its associated practices have become embedded in the institutional, social and political structures of the UK. Ogbu (1994) continues the analysis of race and inequality of educational opportunities in the US. He discusses the persistence of inequality between blacks and whites, noting why a gap persists in the school performances of the two groups. He considers social stratification and racial stratification — in the light of civil rights and social change. Ng et al. (2007) also examine research highlighting Asian American students' voices, identities and choices. Their findings reveal complicated realities that involve a variety of factors beyond simply dimensions of ethnicity or race. However, they stress that racism does exist in the US, and Asian Americans, as other minority groups, had to negotiate and challenge racially constraining representations:

> New educational research takes primarily an intersectional approaches; introducing other sectors of identity. ... These intersectional approaches assert the multiplicity and hybridity of the Asian American experience. ... However, we cannot deny that racism exists and that Asian Americans must negotiate and challenge racially constraining representations. This reality is evident by the fact that even high-achieving Asian American groups such as

East Asians and South Asians, who may appear to be the model minority, remain either not fully integrated or seen as White (Ng et al., 2007).

More recently, Rezai-Rashti & Solomon (2008) have examined racial identity models and the notion of racial identity in social settings. Their findings indicate that 'people of colour' have 'different orientations, understandings and experience of race, racism and race privilege' in institutional settings (p. 184).

International students, ethnicity and academic achievement

According to Rientjes, Beausaert, Grohnert, Niemantsverdriet, and Kommers (2012) more than 3 million students study outside their home country, primarily at a Western university. They argue that a 'common belief among educators is that international students are insufficiently adjusted to higher education in their host country, both academically and socially:

> Several researchers argue that studies on adaptation of international students should widen its focus to the underlying mechanisms that leads towards this 'misalignment' … International students with a (mixed) Western ethnic background perform well on both academic and social integration, and also attained higher study-performance in comparison to domestic students. In contrast, international students with a non-Western background are less integrated compared to other international students. Nevertheless, they have a similar study-performance. Finally, academic adjustment is the main predictor of study-performance for Dutch, Western and Mixed-Western students. Social adjustment was negatively related to study-performance. The lack of fit for predicting long-term study success of non-Western students indicates that their academic and social integration processes are more complex and non-linear. (Rientjes et al., 2012)

The relationship between ethnicity and academic achievement has been examined by numerous scholars during the last four decades, and more recently by Baker, Keller-Wolff, & Wolf-Wendel (2000), Rabiner, Murray, Schmid, & Malone (2004), Juhong & Maloney (2006), Freeman (2006), and Zajda, Biraimah, & Gaudelli, 2008. Baker et al. (2000) note that the 'heterogeneity of academic performance in reading and math' was demonstrated between Hispanic and Asian/Pacific Island students, using the National Educational Longitudinal Study of 1988:

> In the case of both the Hispanic and Asian/Pacific Island aggregate groups there are substantial, though not always statistically significant, academic performance differences among ethnic subgroups (Baker et al., 2000).

Furthemore, Rabiner et al. (2004) note that although students from different ethnic backgrounds make up a significant and increasing percentage of the American public school population, accounting for almost 40% of the national enrolment in the fall of 2000, for the past 30 years, significantly fewer minority students have been considered proficient in reading, and minority students score lower on standardised tests compared to Caucasian students. Research dealing with minority students and academic performance, especially students from disadvantaged ethnic groups — black Americans in the US — demonstrates that such students have poorer academic records in secondary and higher education sectors (see Freeman, 2006; Zajda, Biraimah, & Gaudelli., 2008; Zajda, Davies, & Majhanovich, 2008). Juhong & Maloney (2006) report that similar results depicting the gap between ethnicity and academic achievement have been found in New Zealand, where poorer average educational achievements in secondary school were often reported for Maori and Pacific Islanders:

> Among students with the same gender, measured ability and socioeconomic levels, Maori students generally received lower School Certificate marks than European students in mathematics, science, and English exams. Average science and mathematics scores in the tests from the Third International Mathematics and Science Study for Maori students are lower than those of non-Maori students…The poorer academic achievements of Maori and Pacific Island students have been linked to their lower participation rates in tertiary education and lower lifetime income levels (Juhong & Maloney, 2006).

Gender inequality

Gender inequality in education globally, is another enduring dimension of social stratification and division of power. It reflects the existing patriarchy. Using population-adjusted cross-national data, as well as social indicators covering economic, political, and educational and health domains, current research conducted in the US documents persistent trends in global gender inequality. Dorius (2006) when evaluating global trends in gender inequality from 1970 to 2000, and using indicators covering economic, political, and educational and health domains, argues that absolute gender inequality increased among paid adult workers, surviving adults, literate adults, as well as total years of school attainment and life expectancy. Gender inequality is also tied to issues of ethnicity, race, power, status and class. Women are encouraged to develop skills that are useful in low-paying jobs, such as clerical work, which leads to lower income and status. The inability of many women to work fulltime and overtime due to heavy family responsibilities prevents them from keeping and advancing in their jobs (as most cannot find affordable childcare).

Gender disparities in education continue to remain in 40% of the countries with data. Of these, disparity is at the expense of girls in more than 80% of cases. South and West Asia is home to four of the ten countries with the highest gender disparities globally (EFA Global Monitoring Report, 2014, p. 5). Gender disparity in education has to be addressed in Brazil, China, India, and South Africa. India (like other BRICS countries) suffers from substantial inequities in education. India is one of the countries with the highest adult illiteracy rate, according to the Education for All (EFA) Global Monitoring Report (2014). Furthermore, the gender disparity in India in access to education is providing a hindrance in achieving complete literacy, as per The Millennium Development Goals Report (2013). According to 2011 census the overall male literacy in India was 81%, whereas women literacy rate was around 65% (Dervin & Zajda, 2015, p. 25).

While gender inequality in education exists in developing countries, this is not the case in recent higher education enrolment patterns. Vincent-Lancrin, (2008) examined gender inequalities in participation in higher education and degree awards in OECD member countries. He concluded that there exists a reversal of gender inequality, which is a new pattern in higher education enrolments:

> This reversal of the gender inequalities in higher education stems from various demographic, economic, sociological and educational factors. None of the factors which help to understand it appear likely to disappear or reverse in the next few decades. On the contrary, some of them point to more rapid growth in the level of women's education compared with men (which nevertheless continues to rise). Educational inequalities disadvantaging men are very likely to persist and increase. Generation replacement means that the female population will in any case continue to be better educated than the malepopulation (Vincent-Lancrin, 2008, p. 293).

Cross-cultural perspectives on race, ethnicity and gender in education

In my recent work I have argued that there is a need to reassert the relevance of intercultural dialogue in an increasingly interdependent world of globalisation and social change (Zajda, 2009). Discussions surrounding race, ethnicity and gender in education need to reflect a cross-cultural perspective. Discourses surrounding other cultures, nation-building and identity politics can often lead us to identify and question beliefs and assumptions that are taken for granted, by making the familiar strange and the strange familiar, and questioning the 'universality' of our beliefs and assumptions. It is not sufficient to depict cultural differences in intercultural research, and there is now a need to rediscover to what degree such cultural differences can be 'generalised' across cultures. In particular, the issues to be addressed in future research should include: What kinds of roles do our perceptions concerning identity (in this case perceptions of race, ethnicity and gender) and the nation state play in intercultural dialogue and conflict analysis, and the relationship between globalisation, social change and emerging cultural values.

Globalisation and academic achievement

Since the 1980s, globalisation, marketisation and quality/efficiency driven reforms around the world have resulted in structural, ideological and qualitative changes in education and policy (Zajda, 2014a). These changes include an increasing focus on the UNESCO's concepts of knowledge society, the lifelong learning for all (a 'cradle-to-grave' vision of learning) representing the lifelong learning paradigm and the 'knowledge economy' and the global culture. In their quest for excellence, quality and accountability in education, governments increasingly turn to international and comparative education data analysis. All agree that the major goal of education is to enhance the individual's social and economic prospects. This can only be achieved by providing quality education for all. Students' academic achievement is now regularly monitored and measured within the 'internationally agreed framework' of the OECD's Programme for International Student Assessment (PISA). This was done in response to the growing demand for international comparisons of educational outcomes (see Zajda, 2014b). To measure levels of academic performance in the global culture, the OECD, in cooperation with UNESCO, is using World Education Indicators (WEI) programme, covering a broad range of comparative indicators, which report on the resource invested in education and their returns to individuals.

The 2011OECD report addresses the importance of achieving equality of outcomes through ensuring equity — defined as a 'fair allocation of resources', giving importance to school inputs. This has become a dominant ideology in educational standards (Zajda, 2014a). The report refers to factors which affect educational outcomes, including 'attending a school with positive student-teacher relations, certified teachers, and a strong infrastructure' (OECD, 2011, p. 454). Furthermore, the significance of inclusive school systems — those that support diversity among all learners - is highlighted in the Education at a Glance (2011), which states that: 'school systems with greater levels of inclusion have better overall outcomes and less inequality' (p. 455). Schools systems tend to be inclusive when experienced teachers and material resources are evenly distributed among schools:

> In some school systems, inequality is entrenched through the mechanisms in which students are allocated to schools, including tracks that channel students into different schools based on their prior achievement or ability, private schools and special programmes in the public sector' (OEDC, 2011, p.455).

The 2011 and 2013 OECD's reports on income inequality, Divided We Stand (2011), Inequality rising faster than ever (2013a), and Crisis squeezes income and puts pressure on inequality and poverty (2013b) documented that the gap between rich and poor in OECD countries had widened continuously over the last three decades to 2008, reaching an all-time high in 2007. According to the OECD (2013a) report, economic inequality has increased by more 'over the past three years to the end of 2010 than in previous twelve'. The report also notes that inequality in America today 'exceeds the records last reached in the 1920s. The US has the fourth-highest level of inequality in the developed world' (OECD, 2013b). The widening economic and social inequalities in education are due to market-oriented economies, governance and schooling. Social inequalities, based on economic and cultural capital, and socio-economic status (SES) and exclusion, are more than real (Zajda, 2011a; Zajda, 2011b; Zajda 2014a). Access and equity continue to be 'enduring concerns' in education (OECD, 2001, p. 26; OECD, 2013a).

Comparative view of academic achievement

The OECD's PISA international survey presents an encyclopaedic view of the comparative review of education systems in OECD member countries and in other countries. PISA 2012 was the programme's 5th survey. It assessed the competencies of 15-year-olds in reading, mathematics and science (with a focus on mathematics) in 65 countries and economies (covering almost two-thirds of the world). At least half of the indicators relate to the output and outcomes of education, and one-third focus on equity issues (gender differences, special education needs, inequalities in literacy skills and income). The major focus of the OECD survey was on quality of learning outcomes and the policies that shape these outcomes. It also contained the OECD's Programme for International Student Assessment (PISA), the performance indicators which examined equity issues and outcomes — with reference to gender, SES and other variables. The performance indicators were grouped according to educational outcomes for individual countries.

Many countries are influenced by these OECD performance indicators, and by adopting them, set up their own systems of quality control based on the measurement of academic achievement. The focus on standards-driven reforms, and the current outcomes-based quality debate, which is driven by assessment and examinations results, may be one-dimensional in essence. We need to include a whole range of other indicators, which describe individual, social, cultural, economic, and political dimensions impacting in the on-going education quality debate. Unless we do this, our present quality education debate, with its ubiquitous focus on norm-referenced testing, which refers to standardised tests that are designed to compare and rank students against one another, will remain linear and one-dimensional, which is at odds with diversity and pluralism in societies (Zajda, 2014c).

Psacharopoulos (1995) was one of the first researchers to question the validity and reliability of international comparisons of education policies, standards and academic achievement. In examining the changing nature of comparative education he offers a more pragmatic educational evaluation of policy, which is based on deconstructing international comparisons. He comments on the controversy surrounding the validity of international achievement comparisons (IEA and IAEP studies on achievement in different countries), unmasks an erroneous use of the achievement indicators (including the use of gross enrolment ratios, which neglect the age dimension of those attending school, rather than net enrolment ratios). Psacharopoulos (1995) suggests various new approaches to comparative data analysis:

> Comparative education research has changed a great deal since Sadler's times. The questions then might have been at what age should one teach Greek and Latin? Or how English schools could learn from the teaching nature in Philadelphia schools? Today's questions are:
> - What are the welfare effects of different educational policies?
> - What are determinants of educational outputs?

This critique of globalisation, policy and education suggests new economic and cognitive forms of cultural imperialism. Such hegemonic shifts in ideology and policy may have significant economic and cultural implications on national education systems and policy implementations. For instance, in view of GATS constrains, and the continuing domination of multinational educational corporations and organisations in a global marketplace, the "basis of a national policy for knowledge production may be eroded in a free-market context of a knowledge-driven economy" (Robertson, Bonal & Dale, 2002, p. 494). This erosion signifies the corresponding weakening of the traditional role of the university, being the pursuit of knowledge for its own sake (intrinsic):

> the heart of the academic dogma is the pursuit of knowledge for its own sake. Knowledge and the processes of coming to know are good in themselves, and the university, above all institutions, is — or used to be — devoted to them. To investigate, to find out, to organise and contemplate knowledge, these are what the university is about (Nisbet, 1971, p. vi).

It can be said that globalisation may have an adverse impact on the higher education sector, and education in general. One of the effects of globalisation is that the university is compelled to embrace the corporate ethos of the efficiency and profit-driven managerialism. As such, the new entrepreneurial university in the global culture succumbs to the economic gains offered by the neo-liberal ideology (Zajda, 2014b). From the macro-social perspective it can be argued that in the domains of language, policy, education and national identity, nation-states are increasingly influenced by a new form of cultural domination, and a knowledge-driven social stratification.

Conclusion

The above demonstrates that global competiveness has become one of the most dramatic changes in the internationalisation of higher education. It is fuelled by the neo-liberal ideology of marketisation of performance, and global university league tables. The above analysis indicates that we need to re-examine, with reference to international students, issues of race, ethnicity and gender in the regional and global cultures in the higher education sector. We also need to focus more on the unresolved tensions between religion, politics and values education, and the implications for equity, access and democracy. We also need to critique the overall interplay between intercultural dialogue, education and the state, and how it affects race and ethnicity debate and education policies. This can be accomplished by drawing upon recent major and significant studies in the areas of education, intercultural dialogue and transformational and global pedagogies, which specifically address multicultural education, race, ethnicity and gender. By referring to Bourdieu's call for critical policy analysts to engage in a 'critical sociology' of their own contexts of practice, and post-structuralist pedagogy, we need to understand how central discourses surrounding the debate concerning race, ethnicity and gender are formed and defined politically, economically and socially. This critique has to be performed in the contexts of dominant ideology, power, and culturally and historically derived perceptions and practices, which consolidate the status quo of stratified societies, tradition and cultural identity, despite rapid economic, political and social changes in the global culture, and the higher education sector. Finally, we need to focus, with reference to international students in particular, on the competing discourses of globalisation and internationalisation surrounding global dimensions of race, ethnicity and gender in education and their consequences for life chances for billions of individuals affected.

References

Appadurai, A. (1990). Disjuncture and difference in the global cultural economy. *Theory Culture and Society, 7*, 295–310.

Baker, B., Keller-Wolff, C. & Wolf-Wendel, L. (2000). Two steps forward, one step back: Race/ethnicity and student achievement in education policy research. *Educational Policy, 14*(4), 511–529.

Carnevale, A. (2013). U.S. higher education deeply stratified along racial lines, study says. Retrieved from http://diverseeducation.com/article/54956/

Cervini, E. (2014, December 8). Challenges and competition in attracting international students. *The Age*, National, Education [online].

Choudaha, R. (2014, 17 November). Attracting international students: Can American higher education maintain its leadership? Retrieved from http://www.huffingtonpost.com/rahul-choudaha-phd/can-us-higher-education-m_b_6161588.html

Court, D. (2008). A lot of ropes, but no lion: School culture and Ethiopian Israeli students' struggle for identity. *World Studies in Education, 9*(2), 73–92.

Davies, B., & Bansel, P. (2007). Neoliberalism and education. *International Journal of Qualitative Studies in Education, 20*(3), 247–259.

Delanty, G. (2001). The university in the knowledge society. Organization, 8(2), 149–153. doi: 10.1177/1350508401082002

Dervin, F. & Zajda, J. (2015). Governance in education: Diversity and effectiveness. Paris, France: UNESCO.

Dorius, S. (2006). *Rates, shares, gaps and ginis: are women catching up with men worldwide.* Draft report. Pennsylvania State University.

Fain, P. (2013, May 28). Race and inequity. Retrieved from https://www.insidehighered.com/news/2013/05/28/consequences-racial-and-economic-stratification-community-colleges/

Freeman, K. (2006). 'If only my eyes were different': The loss of identity and the underutilization of black children's educational potential — rethinking assimilation and social justice. In J. Zajda, S. Majhanovich, & V. Rust (Eds.), *Education and Social Justice* (pp. 39–55). Dordrecht, the Netherlands: Springer.

Gosa, T. & Alexander, C. (2007). Family (dis)advantage and the educational prospects of better off African American youth: How race still matters. *Teachers College Record 109*(2), 285–321. Retrieved from http://www.tcrecord.org

Group of Eight Australia. (2014, March). *Policy Note: International students in higher education and their role in the Australian economy.* Retrieved from https://go8.edu.au/publication/international-students-higher-education-and-their-role-australian-economy

Harman, G., & Harman, K. (2008). Strategic mergers of strong institutions to enhance competitive advantage. *Higher Education Policy, 21*, 99–121.

Juhong, B. & Maloney, T. (2006). Ethnicity and academic success at university. New Zealand Economic Papers. Retrieved from www.accessmylibrary.com/coms2/summary_0286-34487926_ITM - 31k –

Klein, S., Richardson, B., Grayson D. A., Fox, L. H., Kramarae, C., Pollard, D. S., & Dwyer, C. A. (Eds.) (2007). Handbook for achieving gender equity through education. New York, NY: Routledge.

Knight, J. (2011). Has internationalization lost its way? Perspectives on the Future. *Borderless 2011*, 10. Retrieved from www.obhe.org

Mohrman, K., & Wang, Y. (2010). China's drive for world class universities. In V. D. Rust, L. M. Portnoi & S. S. Bagley (Eds.), *Higher Education, Policy, and the Global Competition Phenomenon*. New York, NY: Palgrave Macmillan.

Murray, D., Hall, R. Leask, B., Marginson, S., & Ziguras, C. (2011). Background paper: State of current research in international education. Retrieved from http://www.lhmartininstitute.edu.au/documents/publications/murraystatepaper.pdf

McLaren, P., & Farahmandpur, R. (2005). *Teaching against global capitalism and the new imperialism*. Lanham: Rowman & Littlefield.

Ng, J. Lee, S. & Pak, Y. (2007). Contesting the model minority and perpetual foreigner stereotypes: a critical review of literature on asian americans in education. *Review of Research in Education 31*(1), 95–130.

Ogbu, J. (1994). Racial stratification and education in the United States: Why Inequality Persists. *Teachers College Record 96*(2), 264–298.

OECD (2002). Education policy analysis. Paris, France: Author.

OECD (2006). Education policy analysis. Focus on higher education 2005–2006. Paris, France: Author.

OECD (2011). Education at a glance. *OECD Indicators*. Paris, France: Author.

OECD (2012). Education at a glance. *OECD Indicators*. Paris, France: Author.

OECD (2013). Education at a glance. *OECD Indicators*. Paris, France: Author.

OECD (2013a). Inequality rising faster than ever. Retrieved from http://inequality.org/oecd-report-inequality- rising-faster. Paris, France: Author.

OECD (2013b). Crisis squeezes income and puts pressure on inequality and poverty. Retrieved from http://www.oecd.org/els/soc/OECD2013-Inequality-and-Poverty-8p.pdf. Paris, France: Author.

OECD (2014). Education at a glance. *OECD Indicators*. Paris, France: Author.

Rabiner, D. L., Murray, D. W., Schmid, L., & Malone, P.S. (2004). An exploration of the relationship between ethnicity, attention problems, and academic achievement. *School Psychology Review, 33*(4).

Rientjes, B., Beausaert, S., Grohnert, T., Niemantsverdriet, S., & Kommers, P.A.M. (2012) Understanding academic performance of international students: the role of ethnicity, academic and social integration. *Higher Education, 63*(6), 685–700.

Rezai-Rashti, G. & Solomon, P. (2008). Teacher candidates' racial identity formation and the possibilities of antiracism. In J. Zajda, K. Biraimah & W. Gaudelli (Eds.), *Education and social inequality in the global culture* (pp. 167–187). Dordrecht, the Netherlands: Springer.

Robertson, S. (2012). World-class higher education (for whom?). *Prospects, 42*(3), 237–245.

Rust, V., & Kim, S. (2015). Globalisation and global university rankings. In J. Zajda, *Second international handbook of globalisation, education and policy research* (pp.167–180). Dordrecht, the Netherlands: Springer.

Stacki, S. (2008). Moving gender boundaries. In J. Zajda (Ed.). *Education and Society* (pp. 201–219). Melbourne, Australia: James Nicholas Publishers.

Stromquist, N. (2000). Women's literacy and empowerment in Latin America. In J. Zajda (Ed.), *Education and Society* (pp. 119–134). Melbourne, Australia: James Nicholas Publishers.

Stromquist, N. (2006). *Feminist organizations and social transformation in Latin America.* Boulder, CO: Paradigm Publishers.

Talbani, A. (2008). Women's education in India and Pakistan. In J. Zajda (Ed.), *Education and Society* (pp. 133–150). Melbourne, Australia: James Nicholas Publishers.

Troyna, B. (Ed.) (1987). *Racial inequality in education.* New York, NY: Routledge/Chapman & Hall.

United Nations Development Programme. (2008). Human development report 2007/2008. Retrieved from http://hdrstats.undp.org/countries/country_fact_sheets/cty_fs_CUB.html

UNFPA State of World Population (2005). Gender equality fact sheet. Retrieved from http://www.unfpa.org/ swp/2005/presskit/factsheets/facts_gender.htm.

Vincent-Lancrin, S. (2008). The reversal of gender inequalities in higher education: An on-going trend. Retrieved from http://www.oecd.org/edu/ceri/41939699.pdf

Wallerstein, I. (1979). *The capitalist world-economy.* Cambridge, England: Cambridge University Press.

Wallerstein, I. (1989). *The modern world-system III: The second great expansion of the capitalist world-economy.* New York, NY: Academic Press.

Wallerstein, I. (1998). The rise and future demise of world-systems analysis. *Review, 21,* 103–112.

Zajda, J. (2005) *The international handbook of globalisation, education and policy research.* Dordrecht, the Netherlands: Springer.

Zajda, J. (Ed.). (2010). *Global pedagogies.* Dordrecht, the Netherlands: Springer.

Zajda, J. (2010b). Globalisation, ideology and education policy reforms. In J. Zajda (Ed.), *Globalisation, ideology and education policy reforms* (pp. xiii–xxii). Dordrecht, the Netherlands: Springer.

Zajda, J. (2011a). Globalisation and schooling: equity and access issues. *Cultural Studies of Science Education, 6*(1), 143–152.

Zajda, J. (2011b). Globalisation and the impact of social change and economic transformation in lifelong learning in Russia. In London, M. (Ed.), *The Oxford handbook of lifelong learning.* Oxford, England: Oxford University Press.

Zajda, J. (2014a). Ideology. In D. Phillips (Ed.), *Encyclopedia of educational theory and philosophy*. Thousand Oaks, CA: Sage.

Zajda, J. (2014b).Globalisation and neo-liberalism as educational policy in Australia. In H. Yolcu & D. Turner (Eds.), *Neoliberal education reforms: A global analysis*. New York, NY: Taylor & Francis/Routledge.

Zajda, J. (2015). Understanding the quality debate in education. *Educational Practice and Theory* (under review).

Zajda, J., Biraimah, B., & Gaudelli, W. (2008). (Eds.). *Education and social inequality in the global culture*. Dordrecht, the Netherlands: Springer.

Zajda, J., Daun, H., & Saha, L. (2009). *Nation-building, identity and citizenship education: Cross-cultural perspectives*. Dordrecht, the Netherlands: Springer.

Zajda, J., Davies, L., & Majhanovich, S. (2008b). (Eds.). *Comparative and global pedagogies: Equity, access and democracy in education*. Dordrecht, the Netherlands: Springer.

Zajda, J., & Freeman, K. (2009). *Race, ethnicity and gender in education: Cross-cultural understandings*. Dordrecht, the Netherlands: Springer.

Index

A
Academic achievement,, 11, 37, 215, 217, 219, 220, 222, 223, 225-227, 230
Academic literacies, 81, 83-87, 89
Accounting, 7, 18, 59-61, 64, 65, 68, 69, 71, 75, 103, 222
Achievement tests,, 183, 184, 190
Affiliation, 103
Arabic language, 8, 121, 123, 125, 127, 129-131
Asia-relevant capabilities, 105
Assessment, 5, 9, 26, 56, 75, 77, 78, 80, 82-85, 89, 90, 103, 141, 143, 151, 152, 156, 158, 160-165, 167, 168, 173-177, 179-182, 184, 187-193, 198, 204-206, 209, 212, 215, 217, 225, 226
Ata, A, 211
Autostereotyping, 20

B
Blended learning, 45, 53, 55
Bourdieu, 61-63, 73-76, 228

C
Case study, 26, 56, 66, 67, 89, 90, 152, 163, 165, 192
Chinese students, 6, 13-25, 27, 137, 146, 159, 192, 202, 203, 209
Class, 5, 19, 45-49, 51, 63, 95, 127, 154, 176, 219, 223, 230
Communication skills, 7, 60, 68, 71, 161, 175, 176, 178
Communicative theory of identity 93, 94
Content analysis, 92-94, 103
Conversation analysis, 93, 94, 103
Cosmopolitanism, 29, 30, 33, 34, 37, 40
Cultural differences, 6, 37, 40, 43, 44, 47, 50, 51, 66, 133, 137, 224
Cultural factor,138
Cultural sensitivity, 46, 48, 52, 53
Cultural translation, 6, 29, 30, 33, 35, 38, 39, 41
Culture shock, 4, 25, 46-48, 52, 69

D

Difference, 8, 17, 30, 32, 33, 40, 52, 87, 106-108, 113-116, 118, 130, 136, 138, 140, 175, 187, 207, 228

Discipline-tailored English language tests, 81

E

Education policy, 7, 10, 11, 26, 56, 76, 178, 180, 215-217, 227-231

Educational factor, 139, 224

Employability, 59, 60, 64, 178

English as an additional language (EAL), 167

English language, 4, 5, 7-10, 14, 19, 23, 26, 29, 51, 55, 59, 64, 71, 72, 74, 77-86, 88-92, 94, 95, 99-103, 122, 123, 131, 132, 134, 135, 138-140, 142, 147, 149, 150, 152, 155-157, 160-162, 164, 167-173, 177-184, 186, 188, 192-196, 198, 201, 208-211

English language assessment, 89, 90, 179, 181, 182, 184

English language entry pathways, 9, 169, 171

English language proficiency (ELP), 9, 167

essentialised representations, 115, 118

Ethics, 25, 38-41, 109, 119, 194

Ethnicity, 5, 10, 11, 17, 56, 215, 217, 219, 221-225, 227-232

Ethnographic studies, 6, 44

Everyday life of international students, 14, 15, 17

Exit standards, 172, 173

Exit testing, 172, 180

Experiential thirding, 105, 107, 115, 117, 118

F

Focus group, 64, 93, 97, 99-101

G

Gatekeeper tests, 160

Gender, 5, 10, 11, 17, 18, 29, 63, 76, 152, 197, 203, 207, 208, 215, 217, 219, 221, 223-229, 231, 232

Globalisation,, 2, 10, 15, 29, 41, 215-219, 224, 225, 227, 228, 231, 232

Good Practice Principles, 78, 82, 89, 102, 103, 171, 179

H

High-stakes testing, 9, 163

Higher education, 1-7, 10, 11, 13-16, 24-27, 30, 55-57, 61, 64, 71, 77, 78, 83, 84, 88-91, 101-103, 105, 133, 142, 145-147, 149, 164, 167-172, 174, 177-181, 183-187, 189, 191-193, 195, 209, 216-220, 222-224, 227-231
Higher education, Australia, 217
Hybridity, 24, 114, 221

I

Identity, 4-6, 13, 15, 16, 18, 20, 21, 23, 25-27, 29, 38, 43, 53, 57, 63, 70, 72-74, 90, 93-97, 102, 108, 110-112, 114-119, 154, 220-222, 224, 228-230, 232
IELTS, 5, 9, 10, 59, 65, 66, 68-70, 72, 74, 80, 89, 90, 101, 103, 123, 149-165, 169, 173, 179-187, 189-199, 201-203, 207, 209-212
IELTS, validity, 80, 81, 149-151
IELTS, attitudes, 153-159
In-country experience, 110, 117
Institutional identity, 6, 13, 16, 18, 21, 53, 221, 228
Intercultural becoming, 11, 109
Intercultural competence, 11, 87, 88, 170
International education, 1-7, 10, 11, 13, 15, 24, 26, 43, 91, 101, 131, 145-147, 164, 179, 180, 193, 194, 211, 229, 230
International English Language Testing System (IELTS), 5, 74, 80, 123, 149, 169, 181, 195
International student, 7, 11, 16, 29, 32, 39, 40, 47, 50, 54, 59, 63, 77, 93, 94, 97, 99, 101, 102, 170, 174, 179, 215, 219, 225, 226
International students, 1-10, 13-18, 20, 23, 24, 26, 27, 35, 40, 43, 44, 46-50, 52-57, 59, 64-66, 68, 74, 78, 79, 82, 83, 87, 89, 91-97, 99-103, 105, 121, 130, 132-147, 149-152, 154-156, 163, 167-173, 177-182, 184, 188, 192, 194-196, 200, 203, 210, 212, 217-219, 222, 228-230
Internationalisation,, 1-4, 13-15, 55, 57, 84, 102, 147, 215-219, 228
Ironic distance, 30

K

Kostogriz, A, 25, 119

L

Language acquisition, 5, 8, 31, 121, 122, 131, 132
Language interference, 123, 127, 130, 131
Language proficiency, 5, 9, 55, 74, 78, 83-86, 89, 99, 101-103, 135, 140, 149-153, 155, 156, 159, 161-164, 167, 168, 173, 178, 179, 181, 186, 193, 195, 210, 211
Language testing, 4, 5, 9, 74, 80, 89, 123, 149, 150, 162, 164, 169, 172, 173, 181, 183, 184, 193-195, 204, 206, 209
Linguistic factors, 135

M
Multicultural learning environment, 3, 44
Murray, D., 180, 218, 230

N
Narrative inquiry, 152
NESBs, 83, 133-136, 138
New identity, 114

O
Other-representation, 20
Othering, 4, 108

P
Partial cosmopolitans, 37
Participant-observer methodology, 17
Pathway programs, 10, 184, 187-192
Post Entry Language Assessments (PELAs), 171
Post-enrolment language assessment, 82
Pre-enrolment assessment, 80
Proficiency tests, 150, 156, 161, 181-183, 186, 189, 190

R
Race, 5, 10, 11, 72, 118, 215, 219-224, 228, 229, 232
Race,, 5, 10, 11, 72, 118, 215, 219-224, 228, 229, 232
Rhetorical factor,136

S
Social mobility, 77
Social relationality, 16
Stance, 93, 94, 97, 99, 100, 111, 113, 114
Strategic assessment, 177
Students' attitudes, 43, 44, 51, 90, 195, 198
Students' perceptions of learning, 139

E
The English language question, 7, 77, 78

T
Third-space pedagogy, 116

U
University entry, 188

V
Validity, 5, 81, 89, 149-151, 153, 164, 165, 191-193, 195, 210, 211, 217, 227
Void, 30, 32, 33, 35, 38, 41

W
Wallerstein, I.,, 231
Washback, 149-151, 160, 162, 164, 211, 212
World-mindedness., 106, 118

Z
Zajda, J., 229-232

www.ingramcontent.com/pod-product-compliance
Lightning Source LLC
Chambersburg PA
CBHW072144290426
44111CB00012B/1968